A Journey Behind Prison Walls

Lanette Escobar

A Journey Behind Prison Walls
RiverHouse Publishing, LLC
5100 Poplar Avenue
Suite 2700
Memphis, TN 38117

Copyright © 2011 by Lanette Escobar

All rights reserved. No part of this book may be reproduced, stored in a retrieval system or transmitted in any form or by any means without written permission of the Publisher, excepting brief quotes used in reviews.

All **RiverHouse, LLC** Titles, Imprints and Distributed Lines are available at special quantity discounts for bulk purchases for sales promotions, premiums, fund-raising and educational or institutional use.

First RiverHouse, LLC Trade Paperback Printing: 11/15/2012

ISBN: **978-0-9839819-8-5**
ISBN: **0-9839819-8-5**

Printed in the United States of America

This book is printed on acid-free paper.

www.riverhousepublishingllc.com
www.Godstrials.com

Acknowledgments

There were many that blessed me on my Journey Behind Prison Walls, that are not mentioned within this book. I want them to know that they were not forgotten. There is not enough paper for me to write everything that I learned, and mention all that helped me on my journey. I would like to take this time to say thank-you, to each and every one of you that helped me through a difficult time in my life. I pray a blessing over you and your family that you will receive ten times what you showed to me, be blessed and receive the blessings and favor of God.

There are so many that I would like to thank, for helping me in the writing of A Journey Behind Prison Walls. First and for most, I want to give thanks to my Lord and Savior Jesus Christ. I know with all my heart that God guided me and helped me put into words all that He taught me on my journey behind prison walls. But without the prayers of my friends and family this book would have never been written.

The three small groups that I belong to, Gordon's, Sue Renard, and Rosemarie Pinto; I wish to say thank-you. Your support and prayers were so much needed and received. Eileen Duffy for all her prayers and standing with me in the preparation of the finale draft, you have been a true blessing to me. June Greenbaum, and Jean Staropoli, my two spiritual mothers who were there for me throughout my journey, before, during and after. Bill and Judi Pettitt for being there for me and writing everyday while I was in prison. I want to say thank you to Thaiseke Smith for all his help before, during and after, including the creations of the web site.

My family went through a lot, before, during and after. I want to say thank-you for standing beside me and praying for me when it was hard for me to pray for myself. You have all stood beside me and believed in me throughout. The story told in the book, A Journey Behind Prison Walls is not only a testimony to what I endured, by you all also, I would like to say to you all; job well done. I thank you for your continual support before, during and after; I love you all and want to say, thank-you.

To my dear husband, Narciso Escobar, I want to thank you for your prayers, support and encouragement. You were there for me during the long days and nights of writing, and the emotions that I had to endure, during the writing of A Journey Behind Prison Walls. You are a true blessing to me, I am thankful to God for you, and all that you do for me.

Introduction

Have you ever been in a place that you thought your whole world was crashing in on you? Everything you thought you had learned up to this point seemed to go right out the window. Before this period of time in your life you may have thought that everything looked to be going as you thought it should be. Job and family are all in place, or at least they seem to be. Yes we know that we are not perfect, but we do try to keep it all under control to a point. You could say we try to have a plan of action. But maybe that is what we are about to learn - our ways are not God's ways, and things are not always what they seem.

God is always trying to teach us and bring us to a place with Him that is better than the day before, if we would only let Him. Yes, we have our ups and downs, but for the most part life can be good if we would only let God show us His will for our lives. You may even be living the American dream, as you may call it. But then a storm blows in that you did not see coming, no warning but it hits just the same. Now you find yourself in a place that is so unfamiliar that you have to ask yourself, what am I going to do? This is exactly what happened to me.

I was taken completely by surprise when a storm rolled in on my life that I did not see coming. I did not understand at the time that God had been preparing me for a time such as this; I would learn this much later during my journey through the storm. I had been seeking God and asking Him to show me His will for my life and that was exactly what God was doing. At this time in my life, I had my own ideas to what God's will was for me, I think we all do this at one time or other. Then when God starts showing us His will, and it's completely different from what we had planned, we are then faced with the decision of surrendering to God's will or our own. When we choose to surrender to our Father in heaven and His will, most of us truly do not understand the sacrifice it may ask of us. But God knows what is in us. He knows us better than we know ourselves. As we walk through many storms in our lives, most of the time we believe nothing good can come out of them. This is when we have to ask God to show us the storm through His eyes, not our own.

As with the disciples in;

Matthew 14:25-27 *And in the fourth watch of the night He came to them, walking on the sea. 26) When the disciples saw Him walking on the sea, they were terrified, and said." It is a ghost!" And they cried out in fear. 27) But immediately Jesus spoke to them, saying, "take courage, it is I, do not be afraid."* (NASB)

In reading this scripture we see that the disciples could not see anything good coming out of the storm. We do the same thing when we are in a storm or going into one. We look into our storm and see nothing good coming out of it, for ourselves or anyone else. The key here is to look at the storm with the eyes of God. What is God trying to use the storm for in our life? That is when key verses you have studied will come to mind. God's promise is to finish the good work in you and me.

Philippians 1:6 *For I am confident of this very thing, that He who began a good work in you will perfect it until the day of Christ Jesus. (NASB)*

Even in the midst of the storm when things look bad, God's will for us is still good; even when bad is what it looks like. God can see into our situation and the good that the storm will bring, something we are normally unable to see; God's ways are not our ways. He can see beyond the current storm and what it will bring out of us if we would only let God have His way.

I would like to invite you on a journey with me; A Journey behind Prison Walls; and watch how God blessed me, and many others that I came in contact with. The journey we are about to take together is one that can change your life for the better and change your outlook on the storms that come and go in your life, if you let it; it changed mine. My prayer for you is that God shows you and touches you in the areas of your life that need to be healed or brought in line with God's will for your life. This is exactly what God did for me, and my prayer is that you allow God to do the same for you.

Chapter 1

Frightened and Confused

As I looked out the window and watch all the cars as they passed me by, I could not stop myself from thinking about all the people that were in the cars, and where they were going; homes, jobs and a life full of adventure. Here I sat in a van with shackles on my feet and hand cuffs on my hands. Everyone I could see outside the van had so much ahead of them. They had families and jobs to go home to, a future with both. They had their whole lives ahead of them, able to dream and get up and try to put steps in place for their dreams to come true. But here I sat in a van, and it looked to me that all my dreams were gone. I can't even dream Lord, has that too been taken from me in this storm Lord, the ability to dream?

I knew God's Word and what it said about how God would never put any more on us than we can bear, but this one I couldn't see my way through. In the van I looked around and I could see so many others that were on their way to Miami Federal Detention Center along with me, men and women we were all there together. I couldn't stop the tears from flowing no matter how hard I tried. I cried to the Lord, what is ahead of me Lord, I am so afraid. Over the years I had read the Word of God often and I knew what God's Word said in reference to God wanting good for us and that He loved me. I did not question that even as I sat in the van, but I was still afraid.

With the tears running down my face all I could do was call on the Lord, I wanted to hear His voice of comfort so badly, but I could not hear it. I asked, are you there Lord? I knew He was, but God seemed so far from me at the time. I asked God to please remove me from this place; this it too much for me to bear I cried, I need to hear your voice my Lord I cried, I pleaded to God to not keep Himself from me; I was so frightened. But even as I bowed my head and prayed for this all to be a bad dream that I was going to wake up from any moment, I opened my eyes and lifted my head - I was still in the van. I had experienced dreams in the past that felt so real to me while I was dreaming them, that I would cry out in the midst of the dream to wake up and I would, but this was not a dream; this was real. At this time, I did remember a dream that had frightened me so badly back in the year 2000 that I screamed in the midst of it to wake up and I did. I now believe as I remember this dream that there was more to that dream than I had realized at the time when I dreamed it.

Back then I had a dream one night that frightened me so badly that I woke up in a panic screaming out to the Lord. In the dream I was on the top bunk of a set of bunk beds. I was looking up at the ceiling and I was in a prison cell. All the emotions that I felt that night when I woke up from the dream yelling out to the Lord I was now feeling them again; I was scared and overwhelmed. I felt then, like I felt now. "It was not a dream, was it Lord?" I asked. "It was you showing me what was ahead."

But now I thought to myself, what was the dream really all about, Lord were you trying to encourage me and prepare me for a time such as this. Is there anything that could prepare someone for a storm like this? I did believe with all my heart that God had prepared me for a time such as this, but I surely do not feel like it; and I was still frightened. All I felt at the time was fear and off balance. How I felt was causing me to lean more on my Jesus than I had ever done in the past. Maybe that was what this was all about, learning how to lean and trust God and not on the things of this world? I thought back as I sat in the van to what had happened and how I had come to be where I was. I looked up to God and said, Lord I did not think this storm would come to this. But do we ever think a storm will take the turns that is does?

A Storm I Did Not See Coming

In leaving the courtroom, I could hear my daughters cry out in the background. Being a mother, I wanted to comfort them and assure them we would all get through this, but I was not allowed to have any contact or communication with anyone once the sentence was read and the bailiff was told to remove me from the courtroom. I have to be honest I was not feeling like everything was going to be okay at the time myself.

When the judge said forty-six month and told me I would also have three years of probation along with helping pay the restitution of $82,000 that my ex-boss Mike had already been assessed; I was overwhelmed to say the least. I could not even make sense of it all at the time, or the impact it would all have on me and my family in the years to come. I knew it was only the Lord that helped me stand to my feet to hear all that was being said to me by the judge. Inside I felt like I wanted to fall to the floor and find a hole to crawl in. I can only give credit to the Lord for the strength that was within me as I stood before the judge.

As I was asked by the bailiff to stand I was then instructed to remove all of my jewelry and put it all on the table in front of me. I was so frightened, but so much was going through my mind at the same time. The courtroom was in an uproar with my family and friends in shock, including my own lawyer; he himself was crying and could not even console me in anyway due to his own emotions. I was instructed that I was not allowed to turn around for any reason, even to say good bye to my family and friends. Once I had taken off all my jewelry and the hand cuffs and shackles were placed on me, the bailiff led me out of the courtroom. I had no idea what was ahead of me and I was terrified. As I left the courtroom I did not cry, but it took everything in me to stop the tears. I did not want my family to see me crying. I was concerned to how this was going to affect my two daughters; we were real close and we three had never been separated; this was going to be hard on us all.

As I was led past the judge and out of the courtroom, the bailiff then led me down a long hallway. I could not stop the tears any longer, I was now crying uncontrollably, with a hurt that was so deep inside of me I can't even put it into words exactly how I felt. I felt like I had died, but I was still walking this earth without any direction or hope. I don't know what stopped me from crying in the courtroom, other than the Lord. I thanked the Lord for helping me to hold it together for my family and friends. But now I was in a place of despair.

The hurt and pain that I felt at the time, I did not understand. I was in a place that was so unfamiliar to me. I had been told by my lawyer I would not go to jail – yes, there was a chance, but since I didn't have a criminal history, I should only get probation. My lawyer had told me if I was given any prison time at all it would be short, and I would not be taken into custody that same day, giving us time to appeal the judge's sentencing. None of this was true and here I was unprepared and frightened, at least from my point of view, but God knew me better than I knew myself.

I was led down a long hallway by the bailiff to a cell. I was now crying uncontrollably and was not paying too much attention to where we were going. When we reached the cell that I was going to be placed in, the officer open the cell door and motioned for me to enter; in looking around the cell I noticed there were about eight to ten women already sitting inside the cell. I walked in and had a seat at the end of one of the benches. I did not pay too much attention to all of the women sitting around me at the time when I sat down due to how overwhelmed I was; but I did notice that I was in the same cell that I had been in before when I was first arrested and arraigned. Now the memories of that day started to flood my mind in what God had done through me in this exact cell; it all started in this cell, my journey behind prison walls had begun right here about one year before; and here I was back to where it all started.

Chapter 2

Where it all started, 2002

"Early one morning in December of 2002 I was sound asleep and there was a knock at the door. It was about 5:30 AM. My husband got out of the bed and went to the door to see who could be at our door at such an hour of the morning. I remember being frightened to who it could be, since our youngest daughter was pregnant with her second child at the time.

It was not common for us to have anyone at our door at such an hour of the morning. We did have a young man living with us at the time; he had been a close friend with both of our daughters and with my husband and me when we lived in NC. We lived in Fayetteville NC for about five years while my husband, Anthony, was still in the Army and this was where we had befriended Shuron.

This young man had gone to school with both of our daughters, and he spent a lot of time with us all, he was like a son to us. Even during that time, he was having a hard time in school and was not making good choices. Once we moved to Florida, we kept in touch with him and his mother and found out that he had gotten himself into some trouble again. This was when we brought him to Florida with the hope and prayer that we would be able to help him find his way. But since he had been in Florida he had gotten himself in with the wrong crowd a few times, and I was not sure if the person at the door knocking had something to do with Shuron; I definitely had a lot of things going through my mind.

When my husband didn't come back to the room and he had not called out to me to explain the company that was at our door, I got out of the bed to go and see for myself. I was wearing some white silk pajamas, so I grabbed my robe and opened my bedroom door. Once I had my door open I found several US marshals with guns drawn all yelling at me to freeze. From what I can remember there were about four to five men standing on my loft. All were shinning a flash light in my face making it very difficult for me to see them clearly. I was then asked by one of them, was my name Lanette Black? I answered yes and who are you, and why are you in my house?

My questions went unanswered, I was only told to stand still that they needed to search me. I then asked for a woman officer, and this was when I was informed that there was not a woman officer available and I needed to let them search me. The men officers proceeded to tell me I could have a gun hidden on my person, and they had to search me for their own safety. I was humiliated as the officer moved his hands over my body and felt in places only my husband would have been allowed to touch. I started to cry in fear of what was going on and all my questions continued to go unanswered. They only told me that I would find out everything later.

I was told to go into my room and find some clothing to change into, because I would be going with them downtown. I was only allowed to put in my contacts and brush my teeth. The officer would not leave the room at any time, even for me to get dressed; I had to dress with two officers in the room with me at all times, watching my every move. I was told that I may have a weapon hidden in the room and if I was left alone, I would then

A Journey Behind Prison Walls 11

have an opportunity to retrieve it and put them in harm's way. Again I was totally humiliated, I felt like a piece of meat, one with no value.

No matter what I asked, my questions would go unanswered. I was only told that they had a warrant for my arrest and it was given to my husband downstairs to read. My husband was not allowed to come upstairs at any time. Once I was dressed I was then led downstairs.

My husband and the young man, Shuron, which was staying with us, were both standing at the bottom of the stairs waiting for me with a very sad, almost crying, look on both of their faces. When the officer began to tell my husband where I was going to be taken so he could come and bond me out, this is when Anthony told the officer that I had asthma, and I needed my inhaler and could he get it for me so I could take it with me.

They allowed Anthony to get the inhaler and bring it to me. The young man staying with us was in tears by now and was lost for words, other than saying, "I will be praying for you, Mom." He was also asking the officers questions while they were taking me away, but his questions went unanswered also.

As I was led into the car outside, all I could do was call on the Lord. My husband was standing in front of the police car, telling me not to worry; Anthony said he would be right behind me in order to post my bond. I instructed Anthony to not call our daughters that we would tell them later once I was back home on bond. I did not want to worry my girls; but God had a different plan.

Anthony did call Falcasha our youngest daughter, and God used her to find a lawyer very early in the morning before I was arraigned. If this had not happened I would have had to stay in jail over the weekend and wait for a new arraignment hearing.

Faleasha got on the phone at 6AM and called a family member who was in law school. She gave Faleasha her professor's home phone number, who in turn gave her a home phone number of a lawyer he had for a student and recommended him highly. In calling William, my daughter found out that on a normal day she would not have been able to reach him at home.

Normally he would have already had left the house in preparation to be in court. This was the first day in a long time that he was not required to be in court, and this was the only reason he was at home to receive my daughter's call. He met with my family and took the case and was in the courtroom when they called my name to be arraigned.

The check that my daughter gave the law office for a retainer was $5000. She wrote the check out of my bank account not knowing if the check would be good. There was not enough money in the bank at the time to cover the check when it was written; but my daughter did not know what the balance was, but God provided all the money by the time the check was deposited.

My daughter told my lawyer, William that she was not sure if the funds where available and to give her a few days to make sure the money would be there upon him depositing the check, and God provided everything we needed; my family and I were in amazement at how quickly all the money was made available when the check was deposited. God amazed us all often over the next four to five years as we journeyed through this storm together in how He always provided for our every need.

When my husband was standing in front of the police car he told me later what was going through his mind. He felt that he had failed as a man to protect his wife. Anthony could not get over how men had come into his house and took his wife and he could do nothing. He felt that he had failed as a man in protecting me. This hit Anthony hard being a military man for most of his life. He had put his life on the line to protect his country and now he could not even protect his own wife. I later learned this was something that Anthony never forgot or overcame. Every time he would see me or go through the system to visit me in prison, it would remind him of his failures. It was too much for him to bear and it caused him to leave our marriage and seek out comfort in others.

God showed me that this was his way of leaving the pain behind him and creating a new life that would not bring forth the pain anymore, at least this was what Anthony thought at the time. It was a trick of the enemy, because the pain was not gone - only subdued; God was the only one that could help Anthony with what he was feeling and give him victory in it. Anthony did not allow God to show him the good in his storm.

We are too concerned with our pain so much of the time. Instead of letting God take us inside the pain and show us the root of it to begin with. Now in this situation God had so much more to teach Anthony in this storm. But the devil as a thief and liar wrapped Anthony up in his lies and he bought it. Anthony was on the brink of greatness and a new level with God, but he missed it due to the enemy's lies.

We all are so close to this very thing happening to us in every storm. If we don't trust God in the midst of our storms, the devil will have his way with us. We have to realize we have only two options in the midst of a storm; to buy into the devil and his lies, or let God do what He does best; show us the hidden things in our life that a storm will bring out and let God put it all in order. Cleaning house is what needs to happen a lot of time in the midst of a storm. Now this is not the only thing that happens in a storm. It is all tailored to each of us and what we need. I was about to learn this on a whole new level.

At this time I was working in full time ministry as the President and founder of Financial Freedom Christian Counseling. I was at a place in my life that I was of the understanding that I was in God's will; I did not understand what was going on. Now all kinds of things were going through my mind. As I was led to the police car and put in the back seat, I bowed my head and prayed. I heard the Lord remind me of all who had gone to prison for charges they had not done in the Bible. Joseph and Paul came to mind. I was not sure what God was trying to show me, but calm came over me in a very strange way. I was still frightened and crying but felt God's presence. I was not consumed with my fear.

When I was in the back seat of the car there was a US Marshal who was sitting with me and he wanted me to sign a paper that he had. I could not read it because it was still dark outside. I told him I could not sign a paper I could not read. This was when the man that was driving the car spoke up and said it could wait until we arrived at intake.

The men kept asking me questions about the time when I was working for Mike and how the companies were run. This prompted me to ask again, why did you arrest me? Neither one of them would answer my question; they only told me that all would be explained to me by the prosecutor once we reached intake. I then informed them both that I would not answer any of their questions since they would not answer any of mine. I bowed my head and continued to pray and that was when both men left me alone. God showed up for me in that squad car as I prayed. This is what we all have to learn as we go into a storm, we must call on our Lord and He will give us peace in the midst of the storm, if we would only let Him.

God's Word says in;

James 4:7-8 *Submit therefore to God. Resist the devil, and he will flee from you. 8) Draw near to God, and He will draw near to you. Cleanse your hands, you sinners; and purify your hearts, you double minded.* (NASB)

Did you notice here what we are instructed to do first; God is showing us that we must first submit to Him. This is the only way that we are able to resist the devil; we can not do this by our own strength. By submitting ourselves to the Lord first; we are only then able to resist the devil with God's help.

While I was sitting in the back seat of the squad car all kinds of things were going through my mind and it was not all from God. The devil was trying to gain my attention and he was the author of my fear; but I continued to resist him. I knew the only one that could help me get through was God, and I was calling on Him all the way to intake. If I had not done this I would have been consumed with my fear, but I was submitting to God and this was the only reason I was able to resist the devil.

Now yes, I was still crying and fear had not been completely removed from me, but I was not consumed by it. In the book of James we read in verse eight, when we draw near to God, He will draw near to us. God was drawing near to me because I was drawing near to Him. God knew what was ahead of me, I did not. But because I was drawing to Him, he was going to not only help me get through the storm, but help others through me.

Once we arrived at the intake building I was again asked to sign the same papers that the officers had in the squad car. I now could read the papers and could see what they were asking me to sign; if I had signed the papers, I would have waived all my right to an attorney. I responded to the officers that I wanted a lawyer, and this was when everyone stopped talking to me and their demeanor changed toward me for the worse.

I was finger printed and processed and then was taken to the Federal building in Fort Lauderdale to be arraigned. I found out later, I was only taken to the intake building in order for me to talk to the prosecutor, but when I asked for a lawyer they were not allowed to talk to me without a lawyer present. This was something they had not planned on me doing, asking for a lawyer. The whole morning was about intimidating me to be so fearful that I would talk to them out of fear. My Lord helped me to not be intimidated by them, by me resting on Him. Now they had no choice, they had to take me directly to the Federal building for arraignment.

Once at the Federal building I was taken into a small cell. This cell had two metal benches and a small concrete wall that was as high as my waist. This was in place to give some privacy when using the restroom that was located behind it. Trust me, it was not much protection - you could still be seen.

As I was led into the cell, I was still crying, but I did notice a young woman who was already sitting on the opposite bench to me. She looked to be not much older than thirty and not younger than twenty-five. I was still crying, but I looked up at her and said to her, "I am not sure why I am here, but I am an evangelist for the Lord and my passion is to share the good news of Jesus Christ to all who will listen. I must be here for you, what is your story?"

She then looked at me and started to cry. She told me that she was a heroin addict and she was going to be leaving soon to go into an in-house treatment center. If she was not able to stay clean this time, she would be going away to prison for a long time. This was her last chance.

I looked at her with not a thought of where we were and asked her this question; "do you know Jesus Christ as your Savior?" She told me she used to, but she had been so messed up that even Jesus had given up on her. I said to her, "baby girl that is so far from the truth." The Word says that He will never leave you or forsake you. I told her that Jesus is right here with us right now in this cell. He wants you to know He loves you and you do not have to take this journey alone.

I asked her then, do you want me to pray with you? She answered me yes. There were some men in the other cells that kept yelling at her to talk to them. She yelled out to them to please be quiet, and she also told them that a woman of God was in her cell with her and she was going to pray for her and she wanted to hear what I had to say, again she asked them to please be quiet. I prayed and we both cried. God showed up and did what He does best, heal and bring all things to a place of peace.

When I left her, I could see a different look about her, she was not alone now. God had done such a great thing for her, brought her a light in a dark place. He had used me in the midst of this storm, but I had to be willing. God knew what was in me, but I had to allow God to show it to me. We do not always feel like shining for Jesus; but if we would only seek Jesus in the midst of whatever we are going through, He will shine through us even if we don't feel like it.

An officer came into our cell to take her outside to meet with her probation officer in order for her to be taken to the treatment center, and then the officers came to get me and take me to the courtroom to be arraigned. The officers put back on the shackles and hand cuffs and then led me into the courtroom and sat me down in a chair. When my name was called I was surprised to see I had a lawyer. I did not see my family yet, but they did come in while my lawyer was talking to the judge. I remember how embarrassed I was for my family to see me in shackles and hand cuffs. I was also concerned to how this would make them feel seeing their mom/wife this way.

The lawyer came over to me and told me he had worked it all out that I would be on bond - my house would be the collateral. William told me that he and my family would be right outside waiting for me once they took me to the back and signed me out. As I walked back to the holding area, I looked up at a woman who was at the front desk. She said this to me "I have to say I have never seen anyone come in and out of here as fast as you" I looked at her and said, "It is only God who works these things out like this." She smiled and directed me to the door on the left to exit. She said you should find your lawyer and family on the other side of that door. She removed the shackles and hand cuffs from my feet and hands and I then left out the door she had instructed me to leave by.

My lawyer and family were outside waiting for me as she had promised. But the young woman I had prayed for inside the cell was also outside with her probation officer. At this time God did a miracle. The probation officer gave me her business card with all of the young woman's info on the back. I would then be able to take her some things she would need later. I now knew the center she was going to be at and her full name. I found out she had only the clothes on her back. So I and some others in the ministry got together, and gathered some things she would need. I took them to the center along with a Bible and study material and left them for her at the front desk. I was not allowed to visit her at the center since I was not a close friend or family member. Over the next several months, myself and many others at the ministry prayed for her and her family.

Three months later I received a phone call from a woman out of town. When I answered the phone she asked me if I was Lanette Black. I told her I was; she then told me that she had received a call from her daughter who had met me in jail. I was excited because I knew exactly who she was talking about. I asked her how she was doing. She told me that the reason for her call was to share with me what her daughter had told her over the phone.

The woman told me that her daughter had shared with her this; "Mom I have been clean for three months and I am going to make it this time because I am doing this with Jesus. And it was all due to God sending me an angel in prison to pray for me." Her mom thanked me and I thanked her for calling me. I told her to give all the credit to God; all I did was let God use me. That is what we all are to do, we are only the vessel He uses; He is the one who get all the credit.

Now as I walk into this cell again, you would think as I remembered back to what God had done through me before in this exact cell, I would have been able to stop crying and look around and see what God had for me this time. But that is not what happened inside of me at all. I am so glad that God doesn't work through us in our way of thinking but shows up and does what He does best; be God. I was now sitting at the end of one of the benches and not paying too much attention to anyone around me. Then God started to work. A woman sitting across from me on the other bench asked me a question.

With us all being in jail for one reason or other the question she asked me seemed strange. I found out later her name was Diana; Diana looked at me and asked me, "what do you do for a living?" Now what ran through my mind first before I answered her was, we can't network or exchange business cards, why would she ask me such a question in jail? I looked up at her with tears running down my face and said, "I am an evangelist for the Lord with a passion to tell all who will listen about the goodness of Jesus Christ." Sound familiar; yes this is exactly what I told the young woman who was sitting in this exact cell on my first visit. Once I said this, Diana stood up and put her hands in the air and said "Praise the Lord. We have been praying for someone like you to come in here and teach us about Jesus Christ."

I was a bit taken back with her response and told her they must have been praying awful hard, because there were a lot of people praying for me that I would not come into prison. I continued to cry and they started to help me with what was ahead of me. I needed to use the restroom but the only place to go was right in the cell. I was not too happy with that. There was only a half of a wall hiding the toilet, and cameras were everywhere watching every move we made. Now remember men were watching over us as well as women. Even though we were all women, this did not mean that we would only have women officers oversee us. I learned that this was going to be the case most of the time everywhere I went. But when I mentioned that I needed to go to the restroom all of the women in the cell stood up and made a wall for me so I could have some privacy. I could not stop crying and the woman that I found myself with in this small cell was about to become good friends of mine. God was going to use them all to teach me, while He used me to teach them about His son Jesus Christ.

I had no idea of the Journey I was about to embark on. Diana and some of the other women started educating me in how I was expected to act and what was going to happen on the trip to Miami FDC; Federal Detention Center. I was told to not talk to the officers unless asked a question.

We were all then led into a hallway in order to wait to be taken outside to the van that we were all to be transported in. I was instructed by the women in the cell that we all had to face the wall and not look at the officers while we were waiting to be loaded into the van. I was also told if you do have any interaction with an officer for any reason to not look at them in the eye, but to look at the floor. I had so much to remember. I did not see how I was going to keep up with it all.

I did think that maybe some of the things that the women were telling me, to do and not do may be exaggerated, but I learned later as we were joined by the men in the other cells; what I had been told by them was true. The men that had joined us had gotten out of line a few times, I heard with my own ears as the officers instructed the men to do exactly what the women had told me to do. I was thankful for all of their instructions. Because of this I did not have to learn it as the men did, by being yelled at by the officers.

God was with me in so many ways, I thanked Him for all the things He was doing to help me in my storm and make my Journey more bearable, but we do have to make a choice to listen. Are you listening to God's instructions in the midst of your storm? Sometimes it is the little things that we take for granted that can make or break us. I learned to pay attention to every little detail. Things are not always what they seem, and the small things can be the exact thing that God is trying to use to help you weather your storm.

Have you ever been in a place that you did not know how you were going to make it through? I felt like I was lower than dirt. I had no purpose. It was like I had been removed from this planet and I did not exist. The body I was walking in seemed to not be mine anymore. I was numb. Walking down the hall with hand cuffs and shackles on my ankles was so hard; all I could do was cry. The women had told me to put my pants on the inside of the shackles so they would not bruise me so badly. It did help, but I was still bruised and the shackles did hurt. My hand cuffs were also too tight, but I could not get anyone to loosen them. My hands and ankles hurt and I felt lost and confused and on a journey that I had no idea of what was ahead of me.

I continued to call out to God to help me. I needed Him so much, more than I could understand; I knew Jesus was the only one that could get me through this storm, but I still could not hear Him or feel Him. The pain was so unbearable; I know now that Jesus was the one that carried me through that part of my journey, as God would many times to come in the days ahead. I was not capable of walking by my own strength; I was not even aware that God was carrying me due to my despair; it was all God who got me through. I could not feel God but He was with me. I am so thankful that our Lord is working on our behalf even when we don't know what to ask. Jesus understood my cries and He did what was needed to be done; He carried me and tended to me only like a Father could. God will do this for us all; we only have to let Him.

Chapter 3

Walking Into A World I Knew Nothing About

I had never been so scared in my life and trust me I have been through a lot, but this was different. I was living right, doing what I thought God wanted me to do. So what happened? We are not completely surprised when bad things happen to us when we are all wrapped up in self and the world. Now don't get me wrong I am not perfect and I was not then. But I was not in the world like I had been in the past. This was not what I had expected, even though I did not understand it at the time, I was on a journey with God and He was about to teach me more than I had ever thought was possible.

When we arrived at Miami it was impossible for me to step down out of the van without falling due to the high heels I was wearing. The steps were too steep for me to step down due to the shackles on my ankles. The officers told me I would not be able to step down without falling. I was then instructed by the officers to step down and they would catch me. I took a step and I fell right into an officer, who caught me. They all thought this was funny. I did not see the humor at all. I was embarrassed, and reminded again how much I was not in control of anything.

Now I had to go inside and be processed. I was not looking forward to this at all. We women were taken into a small cell to wait for the officers to come and process us in. I was new so it would take longer for them to get to me. But the women I was with had told me everything to expect. The rest of the women were taken first, they had come from Miami FDC. The women that were with me in the cell and in the van had came from Miami that morning to go to court at the Fort Lauderdale Federal Courthouse. Since they had gone through processing when they first arrived at Miami FDC, they did not have to go through the same process again as I did. They all only had to be searched and changed out of the traveling clothes they were wearing. This caused them to go up to the unit quickly.

I was taken out of the cell and had to fill out a lot of paper work. Since I was not allowed to bring my purse with me, it had to be left with my lawyer in the courtroom. All the information that was needed on the documents I had to fill out by memory. I am bad with phone numbers and I had gotten use to having a cell phone with everyone's phone numbers saved within it. This caused me to be more frustrated trying to remember everything I needed to put on the forms given to me.

I was so overwhelmed by everything else that was happening to me, it was hard for me to remember my own name much a less anything else. The paper work needed not only phone numbers, but addresses, social security numbers of everyone that would be coming to visit me and more. I did not have all that information with me, and I was not going to be able to remember it right then ether. It took me a long time to complete all I did remember; at least it seemed like it to me. It didn't help that the officers kept yelling at me, "are you done yet" and calling me a cry baby.

I could not recall everyone's information that I needed. I knew mine and my husband's and that was the information I would have to use. I had no idea that God was going to provide a way for me to get all the information I needed later that night. I did use my phone number as the number that my daughter could be contacted at, and it worked, because my daughter did decide to keep my phone with her at all times. The officers asked me if I wanted to donate my clothes to the inmate closet, the clothing in this closet was used for women who would be released but did not have any decent clothing to wear. I did not even want to think about doing anything like that at the time, I was going home soon in my mind, and I would need some clothes to go home in.

I didn't have any idea at the time that I would never wear the suit or shoes again that I was wearing. My appeal attorney had told me that he would get me out on an appeal bond if I was taken into custody, and not to worry, but I could not stop myself from worrying no matter how hard I tried. I was then given a box by one of the officers to mail my clothes home.

I was then taken all alone into a big room to be strip searched; this was a blessing to me because normally you are searched with a lot of other women. God knew it would have been too hard for me to go through the strip search with everyone watching me. The woman officer who took me into the room to be searched was kind to me and also did not make fun of me for crying.

All the other officers had given me a nick name, cry baby. I did not care; my whole world had fallen apart. I was given a large jumper that I was to put on after the search; it was two sizes too big and was difficult to walk in. In order for me to walk in the jumper I had to hold it up or I would have tripped; but it was the smallest one they had so I had to make do. Once I had the jumper on, I was told to put all of my clothing into the box that had been given to me earlier that day. The officer took the box from me and sealed it in front of me. I was then told that the box would be mailed to my family the next day.

All I could think about in watching the officer tape the box in preparation to be mailed, how hard it would be for my family to receive the box. In opening it, they would be receiving the clothing that they all last seen their mom/wife wearing when she was removed from them in the courtroom. As I watched, I prayed for my Lord to please be with my family when they open the box, please don't let them be overwhelmed with grief. God answered my prayer, when my family received the box; it did not cause them any pain from what they told me.

I was then taken down a long hallway and into a small cell; there were other women in the cell all ready that I had not seen before. When I went into this cell I had an overwhelming urge to find a closet and hideaway in it. When I was younger and even up into my late thirties I would hide in closets to feel safe. I found comfort in closets, whenever I felt afraid or unsure of anything that was going on in my life; I would find a closet and stay there until I felt safe.

With the help of Jesus I thought I had overcome the need of the closets in my life to feel safe when I was faced with hard times. God was showing me I had not. I went over to the corner of the room and put my hands up around my face to make an illusion of a closet. I was crying out to God, "Lord all I want is a closet to hide in." But, I had none; "Lord please, help me," I cried. I was crying uncontrollably when the Lord said to me "see this is still here, we will work on this together."

I was the last one to leave this small holding cell. I was taken into a room with an officer and was allowed to call my family. I called my cell phone, and I was right, my daughter had it with her. My family was all together trying to comfort one another, and trying to figure out what had happened and how to get me home. I told her I was okay, but she could tell I had been crying. I told them how they could come and see me and what I needed them to mail to me. I also had to have them mail me a money order so I could get a few things off commissary and have money for my phone account to call them. I had my daughter give me all the other phone numbers so I could add them to my approved phone list. I found out that I was only allowed to call people that were approved by the institution. This phone call was hard, I did not know at the time it would be four weeks before I would be able to see any of my family.

My daughters told me later that all the family came to the house that night and cooked fish and stayed with them all to help them through this process. I was told later by my daughter that it felt like they had lost a family member to death. It was like going to a funeral that never ends. I was not given enough time to talk to anyone but my one daughter, Faleasha, when the prison allowed me to call home.

I could hear in her voice fear and confusion, I would find out much later that I was correct in this when we were able to talk freely. The officer started to motion to me that my time was up and I needed to wrap up my phone call. I told her I loved her and to tell everyone to not stop praying for me and them. I told her that we will get through this with God's help and each other.

She told me she loved me and missed me already, and she would keep my phone with her as long as needed. She said, "we are all okay and don't worry about us we have each other; you are the one we are concerned about. Be

A Journey Behind Prison Walls 29

careful, mom. We love you." It was very hard for me to go back to the cell once off the phone. I wanted to be with them all so badly. But all I could do was lower my head and cry and ask God, "Please help me and my family get through this Lord."

All inmates had to see the doctor before they could go up to their assigned unit, and I was the last one seen due to all the medications that I was on. I had asthma, high blood pressure and had been diagnosed with heart disease only a few months prior to coming into prison. By the time I was done, it was about 10:30 PM. I had arrived at Miami FDC about 2:00 PM earlier that day. I had a lot of time to spend thinking and praying while I waited to be taken to my unit. My eyes were red and swollen from crying so much. I had not eaten much even though they had given me something to eat earlier that day, I didn't have much of an appetite. Now I was getting ready to walk into a world that I knew nothing about.

When I was told by the guard that it was time to go up stairs to the unit I was so unsure what that meant. I had no idea what was ahead of me. I was given some things that I was going to need once in the unit, two sheets, a small blanket and a pillow case but no pillow. I was also given a small tooth brush and tooth paste with a small comb and soap. Then it was time to go up stairs to the unit, I was led through the metal detector and then to an elevator. I was still crying and the officer that was escorting me was not full of joy at all.

As we walked down the hall, I noticed that all the walls were white and cold. So many doors to walk through and every door had to be unlocked before we could go through it, and then locked after we had gotten to the other side. I could hear the clang, clang of the doors locking. I had no idea that this was a sound that I would have to get used to; but I had not gotten used to it yet and the sound sent chills down my spine.

As we approached the unit that I had been assigned to my stomach was full of butterflies. The unit was quiet and I found out later that this was due to it being time for lock down, meaning everyone was in their cells for the night. The officer over the unit came and took charge of me and took me to my cell. He started by explaining some of the rules to me as we walked, but I did not understand or hear much of what he said due to the fact that I was still crying and very much afraid. I did hear him say that they did not have a pillow for me, but as soon as one was found, it would be given to me. I found out later that the unit was only given enough pillows for each inmate to have one, but when someone would leave the unit others would take the pillow and keep it. This would cause a shortage of pillows and then the officers would go cell to cell looking for who had the extra pillow. That was what the officer meant by when it was found it would be given to me.

As I walked across the unit there was a woman sitting at a table in what was called the common area. I found out later that orderlies were allowed out of their cells at night to clean. The woman sitting at the table was named Anita. She and I would become good friends. But as I walked by her, Anita said something to me that surprised me "Lanette, we have been waiting for you. Get some rest and we will help you in the morning"

When she said this to me I got chills all over my body. It was the Holy Spirit speaking to me and showing me something. Now I was not ready to hear it all right then, but I knew God was with me and speaking to me.

How did she know my name, and what did she mean when she said "they had been waiting for me."

Once we arrived at my cell, the officer opened the door and instructed me to enter. The door was then closed behind me and locked. The sound of the doors being locked behind me sent chills again down my spine, it was beginning to hit me that I was no longer a free women; life as I had known it had changed forever. I started to cry even more. I had a roommate but she was sleeping. I was assigned the top bunk and I tried to be as quiet as I could. The room had two floor foot lockers against one wall. Both were red and looked like an army foot lockers.

There was a small sink and toilet with a small counter. We also had two plastic chairs, one for each woman in the cell, and of course the metal bunk beds. I put a sheet on my bed but did not tuck it in. I climbed up into the bed by climbing on to the counter; I did not have a ladder to use to get into the bed; I used what looked to be my only option. I found out later that this was how everyone climbed into the top bunk. I stayed in my jumper and put the cover over my head and cried.

I kept telling God, I can't do this and why would you allow me to be here for something I did not do. I cried out "Lord Help me. I can't do this." That is when God spoke to me saying "Did you not say when I asked <u>whom shall I send</u> and you said send me." I answered and said yes Lord but, God answered me quickly saying "are you now going to tell me where, when and how to use you?" I felt small at this time; because I knew what God was saying to me and, of course, He was right. I answered "no I am not" and I cried and prayed myself to sleep.

I did fall off to sleep but I have no idea to how long it took me. I was woken up by the door being unlocked by the morning officers, and then I heard a woman call out my name from the other side of the door. I got out of bed and brushed my teeth and combed my hair the best I could. We had no mirrors and that was probably for the best. I am sure I looked a mess. I had been given two medicine cups for my contacts from the officer the night before; I did not have any contact solution so I used tap water and put my contacts back into my eyes. My roommate was still sleeping; it was a Saturday so she was not required to get up yet. When I stepped out of the cell I was surprised at what I saw.

There were about eight to ten women outside my door. One of the women standing in the back, yelled out over everyone with a question, was I going to teach them about Jesus that day? I instantly started to cry all over again. I told her I didn't even have a Bible. She answered me by saying, "I will be right back, I am going to go and find you one." She took off down the stairs and then across the open bay where all the tables were located for us all to eat in the common area. Then she went down some additional stairs and disappeared. I then looked around to whom were all standing in front of me.

All the women were so good to me; telling me to not be afraid, and don't cry, it will be okay. I did not understand how these women could be telling me that everything was going to be okay; none of this looked to be okay to me. This is when I noticed the women whom had taken off a few minutes before was back and she now had a Bible in her hand and she handed it to me.

It was a King James Version Bible with no concordance and half of Revelation missing. I was told later that when inmates would run out of cigarettes they would burn lettuce or banana peelings in the microwave and smoke them using the Bible pages. They use the ones at the end of the Bible normally and that was why a lot of Revelation was missing.

The enemy is full of ways of keeping the truth from God's children. Think of the one who would get this Bible and not be able to read the end as God wrote it. And this was the Bible that I had been given to use to teach these women God's Word. When she handed it to me all I could say to her was thank you; and I will try.

One of the women in the group I recognized from the day before. It was Diana the women from the cell in Fort Lauderdale. She was the one who stood up and said "praise the Lord we have been praying for someone like you to come in here and teach us about Jesus," after she had asked me what I did for a living. Now that I was up in the unit and it being my first day, she took charge to help me get settled. She told everyone to back up some and give me a minute to get use to where I was. Diana said to me "you have to be hungry, I know you did not eat much yesterday while you were being processed."

She then proceeded to tell me that we were having a great breakfast, bagels and cream cheese. All I wanted was a cup of coffee, food was not even on my mind; I had no appetite. Some of the women with me had bought coffee, cream and sugar off of commissary and they shared what they had with me. I ate and drank several cups of coffee while the ladies informed me of all the rules. They were explaining to me the rules of the unit, the ones the officers don't tell you.

You have the rules that are governed by the officers and then you have the rules or what you may call, the hidden rules or the way things are done inside. Knowing these rules were the ones that would help you keep peace with all the other inmates. I would have to remember them all in order to get by inside of prison.

Understanding how the showers work, the laundry, even how to live with your Bunkie and not upset her were all valuable things to know and understand; I needed to learn it all and quickly. For instance, remember we didn't have mirrors in our rooms. You could buy a mirror from commissary and it had a magnet on the back of it. Each door to the cell had a long rectangular window that the officer could look in and seen everything you were doing; they did rounds every two hours, twenty-four hours a day. Whenever a Bunkie would like to have some privacy they would take a long piece of toilet paper and use the mirror with the magnet on the back to hold it up over the window in order to have some privacy. This would tell the roommate to not come in to the cell at that moment. She could be using the restroom or dressing after a shower to mention a few things, she would be sending a message to her Bunkie that see needed some private time. This was hard to get in prison, it was also valuable and both Bunkie's had to cooperate to be able to get any privacy at all. You would be able to use this method as long as the officers were not doing rounds.

If the officer would see the window covered, he or she would open the door and remove the mirror. Many times if the Bunkie on the outside would see the officer getting ready to do round and come by their room, she would then go and notify the other Bunkie nicely; each Bunkie would rather be warned by her Bunkie than the officer. I was still overwhelmed with this all and I was trying to remember as much as I could. Diana noticed my frustration and said "don't worry we will all help you with everything, you can't remember it all in one day, it will take some time and be patient with yourself."

After we had all talked for a while and eaten, I was then told that a volunteer would be coming in soon to teach a Bible study from one of the local churches. Boy was I glad to hear that; I needed to be fed from the Word of God at this time in a big way. Diana told me to go back to my cell and use the restroom and clean up as well as I could and she would be up to get me in a few minutes. I went upstairs and walked into my cell. I had not met my Bunkie yet, she was asleep when I was woken up by the crowd at my door that morning, and now as I went back to my cell to clean up she was still not in the cell; I would have to meet her later. I noticed the mirror on the door that I had been told about. I took the small comb and straightened my hair some and washed my face. I had been crying most of the morning and my eyes and face were still red and swollen. I did the best I could to clean up and then Diana was at my door.

I was then led to the chapel; I learned that this was where the woman that had brought me the Bible earlier that morning had gone to find one for me. It was a small room; it appeared to sit about forty. It had chairs and a shelf full of Bibles and song books. The other women that I had been with earlier that morning were already in the chapel setting up the chairs for others to sit in once they had arrived. I went over to a chair in the back and sat down. I had with me the Bible that had been given to me earlier that morning.

Everyone looked so happy and full of joy, even in this place; prison. I could not understand why all the women were so happy. Diana came over to me and asked me if I was ok, I looked up at her and asked her, how can you all have so much joy being here in prison? She looked at me with a small tear in her eye and said "God answers prayers even in here Lanette, He brought us you. We are all excited in what you will teach us. Don't be frightened with it all, take a day or two and get used to where you are. God will give you what you need, we know this and we all are praying for you." Tears rolled down my cheeks even more, oh God how can I teach them, when I feel so unstable myself. I cried out to the Lord saying," Lord, I stand before you in need to hear from you and you teach me. How can I teach them when I feel so overwhelmed with everything? Lord, please help me," I cried.

Then the volunteers' came in, it was two women and they started with a prayer and then worship. One had brought in a guitar and I was so blessed by the music and being able to worship the Lord. I sat and listened and soaked in the entire message, I felt God touching and comforting me. Once it was all over, the volunteers prayed for us all and told us when they would be back again soon.

Then it was time for count. This meant that we all needed to get back to our cells. As we all were walking out of the chapel, you could hear the officer yell out "count time, count time." We all then moved quickly to our cells to be counted. This would happen several times a day. Each time before lunch and dinner, and we were all counted in the morning before the officer would unlock the doors for breakfast. We were also counted at night before lock down.

Meeting My Bunkie

I walked up the stairs so I could go to my cell for count time as instructed by the officers. As I walked I saw many of the women that I had been with earlier that morning and in the chapel. They all smiled and encouraged me that it would be okay, and they would see me later. As I stepped into my cell, my Bunkie was already in the cell preparing for count time. This was the first time that the both of us would meet. I was nervous. We were going to be living together in close quarters and it would help a lot if we both could be friends. She introduced herself and I did the same. She was nice and pleasant and we did become friends during the short time we would be together.

This was my first count time that was being done while I was awake. The officers counted us during the night while we slept, but I was unaware of it. My Bunkie instructed me in what to do. She told me to sit quietly on my bunk and once I heard all clear, I could then move around and talk. She said you can read or write while you wait, but she instructed me to make sure I did not move around. I had to be still so the officers could see me and would not be distracted by any movement by me. She was a Muslim and this was her prayer time. She was allowed to be moving around while she prayed. While you are in prison you cannot be withheld from doing anything that is required of your religion. Muslims have specific times to pray, and it was now during count time, and she had to be allowed to pray and pray the way her religion instructed her to do so. I watched her intensely as she prepared the room to pray.

She first put one of the chairs over the toilet, and then she washed her hands and put water on both of her feet and on her head. She then put a scarf over her head and a prayer rug on the floor. Then as count was being conducted by the officers, she started to pray. She did not pray in English, so I could not understand what she was saying. She was praying in the language of her faith, Muslim. I did notice that she was repeating the same prayer over and over. She would stand, and then kneel, her hands would go up and then down. But even the movement she was doing was the same each time; she would repeat the prayer several times. Even as count was called all clear, she was not finished praying. I remained in my bunk until she was done.

After she was done I asked her then, "do you mind to explain to me what you were doing and the reason for all the things you did?" She answered me, "not at all." She explained to me that she was making herself clean and also the room as much as she could. The toilet would be offensive to her god; this is why she covered it with the chair. I could see her passion in what she was doing. Without me knowing it, I had opened a line of communication with her. It was only the beginning of us both sharing our faiths and the differences in them both.

I had no idea how God was going to use me to minister to her. She was so lost and sad with what was going on in her life. She was one that did not share a lot with others; I was told this later by the ones who knew her best. Since we were in the cell together for long periods of time due to lockdowns etc, she opened up to me about many things. She was a Christian before she was a Muslim; she became a Muslim once she was in prison. She told me they were the only ones who embraced her when she came into prison. Her husband had done the same thing when he was taken into prison; she felt it was her responsibility to follow his example. She had been raised in the Christian faith as a child. Her mom led Bible studies and my Bunkie even went with her mom when she would teach. My Bunkie told me she would even help her mom with worship. She then told me she used to work at the airport and her husband had her help him bring drugs in on airplanes. This was the reason they were both in prison. She did not tell me the full story because she was still trying to get her sentence reduced. She had two children, a boy and girl. She had something like twenty years and she had only done about five.

We stopped talking while she put her items up and returned the room back to the way it was. I could not help myself to think about my Jesus in how we can come to Him just as we are. We are not able to clean ourselves up without Him. In having Jesus as our Savior, He forgives us and wipes us clean and we are not offensive to our God at all, My Lord casts our sins into the sea of forgetfulness and remembers them no more.

God loved us even in our fallen state, full of sin and dirty. He loved us first. I had such peace in knowing this as I remembered her ritual that she had gone through to be able to pray to her god. We have such an open door to our Lord because of what Jesus did for us all. I prayed for her every day that she would find her way back to Jesus; she even let me pray with her on a few occasions during my stay with her in the cell. I never did see her come back to Christ but it did not stop me from praying for her.

Surrendered All To God

After I had watched my Bunkie pray for a little while during count, I then went to my God. Count took about 30 minutes or longer, so I first prayed for my Bunkie and then asked God to remove anything that would distract me from Him or hearing Him. I then took the Bible and the small pencil with no eraser, and a small yellow tablet that had been given to me earlier that day. I sat in my bed and bowed my head and prayed to God. "I can't do this, God," I cried. I continued to cry out to God saying, "This Bible is not even a study Bible and it doesn't even have a concordance. I have no Bible dictionary or commentary. I certainly don't have a lap top with a Bible software program. My Lord I don't know how to teach these women with only these items. I can't do this Lord," I cried. Then as my heart was broken and I found myself in a place that was lower than I can ever remember being, this in when these words came out of my bosom to my Lord, "but you can Lord. I surrender it all to you God, if you would only do this through me, I am here Lord, and have your way with me." I have to admit I had no idea to what exactly God was going to do with me, but from that day on God gave me a Bible study to teach the women in the unit every day.

I taught everyday unless we had another who had a study to share with the ladies in the unit or a volunteer came in. I lost track to how many women came to Christ or turned their life back to Jesus. It became clear to me that we stand in the way of God more times than we would like to admit. God needed me to trust in Him completely and not lean on my own understanding, but His.

In this situation, God had me in a place that I had to let go and let Him do it all. I asked myself and asked God at the same time, "Why did it take this entire situation Lord for me to learn this? Why could I not learn this without this storm?" I would learn the answer to this question as I Journeyed behind prison walls, but I had a new appreciation to the patience of God and that He never gives up on us to teach us what we need to learn to be in His perfect will.

I prayed everyday for God to use me and help me to grow with Him. God knew my heart was genuine and that was why God was able to use me the way He did. It was not easy and I felt the spiritual warfare daily going on inside of me. The devil did not want me to listen to my Lord and follow Him. I had to stay in prayer and God's Word in order for God to do what He did in me and through me. God wants to use us all in and out of the storm. Are you allowing God to use you right where you are today? I encourage you if you are not being used or it seems to you that you are not being used, go to God in prayer and ask Him to use you, and He will.

The very first time I taught in Miami, I had only been in the unit about twenty-four hours. Using the Bible that I had been given on my first day and the small tablet and the small pencil with no eraser, I sat down and prepared a study. I was amazed in what God did. Even in what to teach. It was so clear what God wanted me to teach the women. I was in the book of Genesis studying the life of Abraham.

That first night that I was going to stand in front of all the ladies, I thought I would be uncertain, but I was not. Here I was out of my element and trusting completely on God. Now don't get me wrong, I had already been teaching God's Word for a long time, but this was different. It was more complete, a new level as you may say. There was nothing of me involved, all God; yes, this is how it is supposed to be all the time. But until it is revealed to us how much we are in the way, we don't normally know or understand that we need to get out of the way. This is what God was showing me, how much I was leaning on my own understanding and not Him. This all needed to change and that was exactly what God was doing in me, teaching me to lean and listen to Him in all things.

As I prepared to go to the chapel and present what God had given me, I stood in my cell and prayed to God. I asked Him to use me and soften all the hearts that would be coming to the chapel that night, so they would hear Him and not me. I asked God to come inside of me and take over and remove anything of me that may be in the way of Him doing His perfect will through me. I asked God to also give me courage, to not let my surroundings be intimidating to me and to help me stay focused on Him.

Now remember, I am also dressed in a jumper that is two times to big for me. Walking in it was not easy; I had to hold it up so I would not trip. Since I had come into prison on a weekend and it was also a holiday, I would not get any other clothing until the following week. I was told that someone would come in and make sure of my size and then they would bring me some clothing. I had to make due until that happened.

Here I was going to teach the first time in this big jumper. Also I am the only one in the unit that was wearing the jumper; I was the only newbie as they called me. Even in this God was using it to make me visible to all who were trying to find the new girl; the one that everyone was talking about that was going to teach them about Jesus. I was approached by many that did not even know my name, but had heard about me and wanted me to pray for them. Some had a question about the Bible;

again God was using something that was uncomfortable to me to accomplish His purpose. I was learning quickly, it was not all about me, but about God and spreading His good news to all who would listen. In this journey, I needed to get use to things not being what I was used to; this was only the beginning of a very long journey, and I had so much to learn.

As I approached the Chapel, I could hear all the voices, the Chapel was full. I was amazed at how many women had come out to hear what God had to say. Only God could do this. See women inside of prison are leery of new people until they get to know them. As I walked inside everyone looked and smiled and started to settle down. I had a woman that was going to be my translator for all the Spanish speaking ladies; I found out later that the number of Spanish speaking ladies was great, and God provided an interpreter for them all. I was told that the word was out in the unit that a woman was here that could teach them all about Jesus, and this was why they had all come out in such great number.

God blessed us with some woman that had a real heart for worship. They knew songs in Spanish and English so all could enjoy and praise God. Once we finished, I stepped to the podium to start the study that God had given me. Remember I was already used to teaching in front of people, but this was different. I felt different; the presence of God was so strong, it is hard for me to even explain what I felt.

As I looked out over all the faces in the room I noticed something I had not seen before, a hunger to hear from Jesus, a deep hunger; deeper than I had ever seen before. They were so hungry to hear from God, and He had brought me to a place such as this to give them Jesus.

God had heard their prayer and I was the blessed one that He was going to use to give them what they needed, "His Word." I did as God had brought me there to do, give them Jesus and the good news they were looking for.

At the end of the study I gave an altar call for anyone who wanted to accept Jesus as their Savior to come forward, so many came forward. I have to say God answered my prayer in my cell; it was like we were not even in prison any more. I lead them all in a prayer and explained what they were doing. We ended in prayer and closed out to go back into the unit or our cells.

But then I was even more surprised, so many came up to me after the service to ask questions and thank me for being there to teach them. God spoke to my spirit so clearly," this is why you are hear, to feed my sheep." I was learning when we say yes to God we have to be willing to do what He deems best. I asked God to increase my territory and to use me in whatever way He chose to; and that was exactly what God was doing, only what I had asked of Him.

But aren't we all surprised when God does that, what we ask of Him? Or better yet, we want to have some say in how He will use us. My flesh was not completely yielded to God, but my heart and spirit was. My flesh needed to be brought into submission to the will of my Father; I did not understand that at first. But so many things were becoming so clear now. I was not only being used to help them with their relationship with God, but mine was also being pruned and polished right along with them.

That night I went to my cell for count, all I could do was pray to God and thank Him for using me and touching so many who were looking for Him. God showed me in that prayer I had so much to learn and I was going to have to trust Him on a level that I had not done before in my life. But if I would only give everything over to Him, I was going to be on a Journey that would change my life forever. I said, "Yes God" and admitted that it would be impossible to go through something like this and my life not be changed. He said, "Yes, but did you think it could be changed for the better and not the worse." I answered in honesty, "I can't understand that right now God, but I will trust you in this, have your way Lord I am yours."

How about you, are you at a crossroad in your life that is similar to what I was dealing with, with a choice to make to whom you will follow? It may not be the same situation as mine behind prison walls, but the journey is for the same reason. I encourage you to look deep into the place you are right now. What is God trying to show you and teach you? Everything that we go through in life is for a reason; it is all up to us to seek out God in all things and learn whatever it is that God is trying to teach us.

When I woke up the next day and went down for breakfast, I was approached by a lot of the women who were at the teaching the night before. They asked me if I would mind to go into the Chapel after lunch when no one was in there and go over some questions they had. I told them I did not mind at all. After lunch was over and once we were all allowed to come out of our cells, we would then have free time to do whatever we wanted.

I went to the chapel and found about ten to fifteen woman there. A lot of them could not speak English, but God even then provided an interpreter. The questions started to come and we went into the Word to see what

God had to say, not my opinion but God's. Questions were from marriage to baptism. God also used this time to show me what some of our future studies would be on. I was surprised that this became a daily event, and the numbers grew even in this.

Chapter 4

First Trip Outside Prison As An Inmate

Part of the processing at Miami FDC was to do all the medical screening that you needed before you were transported to the prison that you would be assigned to. I remember being told that I would have to have a Mammogram due to my age, and I would have to leave the prison to get this done. I had not been in long when I was told this, and I was not looking forward to going out into the community as an inmate. When I was wakened early one morning and told to get ready to go down stairs to be processed to go to the hospital for the mammogram, I prayed for God to help me through it. Once downstairs, I was taken back into the intake/outtake area where I had been when I first came to Miami FDC after sentencing. The emotions of that first day at Miami FDC all came back to me. I was taken into a holding cell to wait for the officers that would be taking me out for the x-ray. The holding cell I was put in was the same one I was in when I first came to Miami FDC.

I could remember all the emotions that went through me when I was in that cell before. A lot had changed since then, but a lot was still the same. I was still at a place that I wanted a closet to hide in. I remember God saying to me that we would be working on that; but that had not happened yet. The officer that was going to take me to the hospital came into the cell and took me into the strip search room; this was also the room that I had been strip searched when I first came to Miami. I was going to have to be searched prior to leaving and once I returned.

I would also have to put on different clothing, travel clothing as they called it. I was told later that this was done so inmates could not hide something inside of their clothes and leave it on the outside; like a written message to someone.

After the strip search was done and my clothes had been changed, I was put inside of a van. I did not have hand cuffs or shackles on and the officer that was transporting me explained why I did not have to wear them as I did when I first came to Miami FDC. When I first came to Miami FDC, I was transported with a lot of different security level inmates.

I was camp status and it was not required to transport me with hand cuffs and shackles; it was up to the officer that was transporting me to use them or not, and my officer for this trip said she had decided it was not necessary to use handcuffs and shackles with me. I was thankful to God for the blessing that I would not have to wear shackles or handcuffs. As we drove down the highways and roads in Miami my heart saddened as before when I was being transported to Miami FDC from the Fort Lauderdale courtroom after sentencing.

I looked out the window as I had done before and again I could see all the people in their cars driving past going about their business with dreams and a life; and I still felt like mine were all gone. I had a lot to work on still. God was with me and I prayed for Him to help me in what I was feeling so I would not be crying once we arrived at the hospital.

When we arrived at the hospital, the officers got out of the van and went inside, leaving me inside of the van alone. It was only a few minutes before they came back for me. I was escorted to a reception desk to check in.

Even though I was an inmate, I still had to sign the consent forms for myself to be seen; this gave me joy in a strange way; I did still have some say in what happened to me. Once all the forms were signed, I was escorted by a nurse to the back, without the officers; that was strange to me, but it felt good. The nurses did not treat me any differently than if I was a patient off the street.

Again this was a blessing; I began to enjoy being at the hospital for the x-ray; something that I had been dreading turned out to be a blessing. I was instructed to remove all my upper garments and put on a gown and then I would be taken into the x-ray room. Once I had removed all my upper clothing and let them know I was ready, I was taken in the room to do the x-ray.

The x-ray tech was nice and polite to me; she treated me with gentleness and kindness. I was thankful to God for everyone that I was coming in contact with; from the officers that were escorting me to the employees at the hospital. I was nervous about this trip and it turned out to not be hurtful but a blessing. I actually enjoyed it. Once the tech was done with all the x-rays that needed to be taken I was asked to have a seat and they would let me know when I could get dressed.

It was not long when the tech came back into the room and informed me that all the pictures were good and I could get dressed. Once I was dressed, I was taken back outside to the officers, who put me back in the van to take me back to Miami FDC. This time the ride back to the prison was not so bad. I was still sad, but I was able to deal with it a lot better. God had blessed me at every turn of the day and I was too busy thanking God for the events of the day to be sad about my situation.

Even in this trip to the hospital, God was teaching me a valuable lesson. It is and can be a lot easier to endure the trials of today if we would only focus on the blessings of God instead of so much of the situations we find ourselves in. My situation had not changed but my perspective had. I realized that I was living out what it says in James 1:2-4.

James 1:2-4 *Consider it all joy, my brethren, when you encounter various trials, 3) knowing that the testing of your faith produces endurances. 4) And let endurance have its perfect result, so that you may be perfect and complete, lacking nothing. (NASB)*

What I was going through was not a surprise to God; He knew where I was and what was ahead of me. God's plan for me was not that I would fall but that I would learn to count it all joy in the midst of the trials in my life. The testing of my faith would produce patience if I would only allow it. I could sit down and have a pity party, or I could decide to find my joy in Jesus and what He was doing for me even in the midst of this situation. God was blessing me at every turn. God was trying to help me let my faith in Him have its perfect work; this would bring me closer to being perfected and complete lacking nothing. Trust me, this was not easy, I had to stay focused, on God and in His Word. I found myself falling into despair every time I would allow my attention to be distracted for even a moment. I was learning to be diligent in my attention on Jesus and not my situation.

In the book of John it tells us that we will have tribulations, but we are to be of good cheer because Jesus has already overcome the world. Many of us read the Word of God and do not allow it to have its full work in our lives. I am guilty of this also, but this Scripture was ministering to me on a whole new level now. I did not understand completely why God allowed this situation in my life; but I needed to trust Him and allow it to accomplish in me what God intended and not allow the devil to distract me with his craziness. For this to happen for any of us, we have to stay focused and not let our guard down; my peace was in Jesus and only Him.

John 16: 33 *These things I have spoken to you, so that in Me you may have peace. In the world you have tribulation; but take courage, I have overcome the world. (NASB)*

I had a lot ahead of me and this was a valuable lesson for me to learn early in my journey behind prison walls. I had no idea at the time how much I was going to have to trust God and allow Him to guide me, and more times than I would like to admit; to carry me. At this point of my journey I was still under the understanding that I could go home any day on bond, which was not going to happen; but I did not know that. But for me to have the peace that was needed for this journey, I had to hold John 16:33 close to my heart and allow it to have its complete work in me, and I did. Yes, I had a lot of difficult nights, but I was amazed in how much peace and joyfulness I had on an everyday basis; it was all because of my relationship with Jesus that made this all possible.

As we take this journey together I encourage you to focus on what is going on in your life, are you allowing the Word of God to have its perfect work in you? The trials and tribulations will come and go; the Word tells us this. But we have to decide for ourselves what we will allow the trials of today to produce in us. My prayer for you is that as you take this journey through prison walls with me that it will change your perspective on life and all that God has for you in it. The devil only has the power you give him; it's time for him to lose his hold on you and for God to have the full glory in all your situations; good and bad.

Life In Prison: Learning To Be Alert At All Times

God kept showing me to do as He led me and they would come to hear Him. In all the studies God showed me to always do an altar call, make sure that all understood how to come to Him and be saved. I learned from the women in the unit that a lot of them did not understand how to come to Jesus and be saved. They all came from so many different religions and mixed up teachings that the basics of Salvation was what they needed most. I could not even keep track of how many women came to Christ or rededicated their lives to Jesus, making Him Lord not only Savior.

I was so blessed to see so many lives changed for the glory of God. I was also able to watch them walk with Jesus in their everyday life. When I was out in the unit, watching the flow of the unit as you may say, God blessed me to see the many that had come to Him in action with others. I was able to watch them share what they had learned, how they were going by the rules and even their attitude with the officers had changed.

I was being extremely blessed everyday to watch God work in so many lives. But my heart was still heavy. I missed my family and I wanted to go home. I had to ask God daily to help me with my fear and the longing to go home; the nights were the hardest for me. When the unit was quiet and we were all locked down in our cells for the night, I would cry for several hours before I would be able to go to sleep. My Bunkie would ask me in the morning if I was okay because she could hear me crying for most of the night. I would respond to her that every night was hard for me and it doesn't seem to be getting any easier. I would tell her if it was not for my Jesus, I don't think I would get any sleep at all. My Bunkie told me that after a while I would get use to being in prison and I would be able to sleep better soon; I found that hard to believe.

The everyday routine in prison was a constant reminder to where I was. Monday through Friday we would be wakened at 5:30 AM for breakfast and to clean our cells. We were all required to get up at 5:30 AM when the officers turned on the lights and unlocked our doors Monday through Friday if we wanted to or not. Weekends and holidays we could sleep until count time and skip breakfast if you wanted to; count time was at 10:00 AM.

At count time on the weekend, we all had to have our rooms clean with our beds made to specifications and dressed ready for count time. We did not have to dress in our uniforms on the weekends. Our shorts or jogging suits were allowed.

During the week was a lot crazier. We had a room inspection every day. In preparing for inspection, we were all required to clean our cell from top to bottom, including the walls and the floor. Each room had been given an old towel to use as a rag to clean their room; we had plenty of mop sticks but no mop heads. To mop the floor we would use the old towel and a mop stick by pushing the towel around the floor with the mop stick; this was better than doing it by hand and on your knees.

To get any cleaning supplies to clean your cell, you had to get them from the orderly that had been put in charge of giving out the supplies. My Bunkie knew everyone and we were able to get everything we needed easily. I was learning that inside of prison what you were able to get and do depended a lot on who you knew and how well you were liked. Many times there were no cleaning supplies for anyone to get.

We then would use our shampoo to clean our rooms. At 8:00 AM Monday through Friday an officer would walk by and inspect each cell. Being ready meant that you would have your room clean and dressed in your green uniform with your shirt tucked in, standing in front of your cell at attention, with no talking.

We all also had a red foot locker that had to be left open and ready for inspection. The locker had to be well organized and not have anything within it that was not allowed.

I was not a morning person when I first went into prison. I had been praying for God to help me to become more of a morning person. I thought to myself this is a strange way for my prayer to be answered, but it worked. I got to the point that I woke up before the officers would turn on the lights and unlock our door. Our God answers all our prayers. It may not be in the way we think He will, but God answers.

This part of my day was not bad; I actually appreciated how everyone was made to stay on top of keeping the unit clean; I had heard horror stories to how dirty it was in prison and this was a pleasant surprise. My Bunkie was one that did not like anything out of order or dirty, I was thankful to God that I was given such a clean Bunkie, we took turns in cleaning our room, I would clean the room one day and she would clean it the next; we got along well together.

Each month we would also be inspected by the warden and our officer. During the inspection was the time if you had any complaints about any of the staff or wanted to bring anything to the wardens attention in reference to anything that was going on within your unit, you would bring it to the wardens attention during this inspection. But you had to be careful to what all you said. It could come back against you later depending on whom your complaint was against.

This was why most of us kept quiet. I was warned about this when I first came to the unit by my Bunkie. I did see for myself what my Bunkie meant when I watched one of the women in the unit present a complaint against one of the staff members, life was made very difficult for her in many ways.

For example, her family was not able to get in for visitation for no reason at all, even though they had been in before to visit her. She was not able to get her phone calls to go through and even her mail seemed to stop for a while, then one day she would get all her mail at one time; she could tell by the postmark to how long ago the letters had been mailed.

There were many ways that the staff could make your life difficult inside of prison if they wanted to. Most of us dealt with the issues that would come up together and prayed through them and did not take them to the warden.

I kept so many things before God in prayer, including all the inmates and even the staff. God was showing me the staff that works in prisons from a different perspective. All the staff that worked within the prison system put their lives in danger every day. I started to pray for their protection and even their peace of mind and of course their Salvation. It was not easy for them to work under the stress that they had to work under every day.

You could not blame the officers for keeping to themselves, keeping a distance between them and the inmates most of the time. Many came up against inmates that if they were given a chance would hurt them or even kill them. God showed me they needed our prayers.

When I started to pray for the officers, I noticed a difference in me, in how I looked at the officers and what they did for a living. My respect for the officers grew everyday as I prayed for them. They did not only watch over us all to make sure we were going by the rules and present for count; the officers were also keeping us all safe.

Because of what God had showed me during my prayer time in praying for the officers, I started thanking God for all the staff and the sacrifices that they all made every day when they came to work.

After all the inspections were over and count time was clear, we all had to deal with the everyday life of prison. Trying to get your laundry done was an event by itself. The washers and dryers were free but you had to wait your turn. We had two washers and two dryers in the unit; you had to put your laundry bag on the floor in a line with other laundry bags waiting to be washed also, then you waited for it to be your turn; but not everyone would go by the rules. You could be fifth in line when you first placed your bag in line and come back to check on the status later, and you would find your laundry bag would then be ninth in line.

What were you going to do; some would fight and yell at each other over their bag being moved. This would get ugly sometimes and a full fledged - fight would break out. Then you would hear the officer yelling; "lock down; go to your cells." This meant for you to stop whatever you were doing and go to your cell; you could even be in the shower. The first time it happened to me, I was quite frightened. The officer in each unit has a panic button on their person. When something like this happens, they push their panic button and officers from outside the unit come running from all over the prison, yelling also, "Get to your cells."

Depending on where you are in the prison, this can be very alarming because you may not even be in position that you can see the fight. You may or may not even be able to hear the yelling. The first time it happened, I was in the chapel. We had a door to the chapel that we were allowed to close while we were in the chapel; it didn't lock, of course.

We had the door closed so we could not hear all the commotion out in the unit, until someone came in and told us to go to our cells, there was a fight. We all knew that this meant that we may not be able to come back out of our cells that day except to eat, so whatever we were all talking about and studying may have to wait for another day. When we stepped out into the unit, we were all yelled at by all the officers, "we said get to your cells."

We were not allowed to explain that we had been in the chapel and that we had just found out that we were to go to our cells; the officers did not want to hear anything from anyone; we all needed to move as fast as we could and get to our cells.

Officers were everywhere yelling and pointing; "go to your cells now." I was terrified. I had not experience this kind of yelling by the officers up to this point at all, and I was not sure what was going to happen next. I was actually relieved when I reached my cell. When I stepped into my cell I found my Bunkie sitting on her bunk reading. She looked at me and could tell I was frightened. She assured me to not be frightened "things will calm down, but prepare to be in your cell the remaining of the day."

Anytime anything would break out in the unit, like a fight or a disruption by anyone, the whole unit would be punished. This would cause even more problems within the unit between inmates and even the officers. While we were on lockdown, we would not be allowed to use the phones or even take a shower; not to mention to do our laundry. If commissary was to be delivered on the day we were on lockdown, we would have to wait for it the following week unless the officer allowed it, and this made many mad.

Visitors would be turned around and told that our unit was on lockdown and was not allowed to have visitors; this did not apply to attorney visits. Once we were allowed to come out of our cells, you had to be careful in how you handled others, walking on egg shells would describe the atmosphere of the unit.

I learned that you had to be careful all the time in what was going on around you in the unit. Even though we had many coming to the chapel trying to turn their lives around and seeking Christ, this only accounted for about fifty women within the unit. The unit housed one hundred and twenty five women, which left a lot of women not trying to live a life for Christ at all.

Now yes, there were other faiths in the unit, and we all had to be careful to respect each other's boundaries. But for the most part the other religions were not trying to cause any trouble either. But that only accounted for thirty to forty more women, which left thirty five to forty five women that were looking for something to entertain them. Sometimes they were only mad at the world looking for someone to take it out on. I had to be careful of the ones who were mad at everything because they would try to start something with me and the other women who came to the chapel.

They would accuse us that we thought we were better than them, they would call us miss goody two shoes and try to entice us into a fight. When this happened we would walk away and go to our cells or to the chapel and pray; we knew this was the enemy trying to attack us and the only response was prayer.

Every day I walked out of my cell, I had to pray before I would even leave my cell. I had to be alert to all that was around me at all times. I learned this fast with the help of my Bunkie one day. I was being brought back from medical and when I walked into the unit I did not pay any attention to all the commotion going on downstairs at the front door leading into the unit. Everyone in the unit was on lockdown and I was told to go to my cell.

Once I had walked through the front door of the unit, an officer walked with me to my cell and opened the door and locked it behind me once I was inside. Once in the cell, my Bunkie asked me what was going on down stairs with the girls that were being taken to the shoe; and who was being taken. "Shoe" was what solitary confinement was called. I told her I did not notice who it was. I told her that I did not even know you all were on lockdown until the officer approached me and told me to go to my cell.

My Bunkie looked at me in a stern way and then spoke to me in a concerned voice telling me I would not last long in prison if I did not learn to pay attention to what was going on all around me. I could get hurt or caught up in the middle of something only because I was not paying attention to what was going on around myself. It scared me that I was so oblivious to what was going on around me and that I had not even seen the women at the front door that were being taken to the shoe.

I thanked my Bunkie for being straight forward with me and helping me to wake up. I did not even realize that I was allowing myself to withdraw from what was going around me. I climbed up on my bunk and went to the Lord in prayer; I asked God to help me to be observant to the things around me, and also asked God why was I doing this?

God showed me that I was detaching myself from many things that were going on around me, because it hurt too much to face it all. But this was not what God wanted me to do. It could have put me in harm's way, but I would also miss opportunities to learn what God was trying to teach me; and even miss opportunities to minister to others. I had to surrender everything to God, and I thought I had, but it was clear that I had not.

This was a valuable lesson that God taught me and it was a lesson that needed to be learned in the early part of my journey behind prison walls. It changed my outlook on many things. So often we are doing things that we are unaware of that hurts our relationship with God and hinders how we can be used by God. God used my Bunkie to show me a weakness that I had allowed in my life. Was I doing this only in prison? I am sure that I had been doing this on the outside also. I thought to myself, how much of life have I missed Lord?

God came to me and assured me that I did not need to waste my time on what was in the past, but to focus on what was now and in my future; these were the only things that I had any control over. I made my mind up from that day on that I would make an effort to be more aware of my surroundings; I even asked my Bunkie to help me and make me accountable to what was going on within the unit. She was happy to help me.

Chapter 5

A Touch From God, When We Needed It Most

I had been at Miami FDC for about three weeks and unable to see my family. My family had come to see me every weekend only to be told that they could not come in. They were told that the paper work had not been done yet. I had been told on the other hand by my counselor that all the paperwork had been done and my family could come to visit me. I then told my family they could come and visit but to make sure they brought an ID that all the paperwork had been approved. We lived in Coral Springs Florida and for them to come and visit me in Miami took them a good forty five minutes to an hour to get to the prison. Not to mention that my family had to get up about 5:00 AM so they could get to the prison early enough so they could get in line to be able to get in; only a certain number of visitors were allowed in and if you did not get in line early, you may not get in at all. I was told by my daughters later how hard it was for them to come and see me. The treatment from the guards was rude and mean. They said they were treated like they were criminals. This broke my heart when they told me this, but I was not surprised.

But God had a reason for everything we were going through. We all learned a lot. To trust Him no matter what, love the unlovable and let His light shine no matter what we were feeling inside. I learned that I was not only going to be able to minister to the inmates, but also officers. You never know who is watching and who God may be using you to bless or touch for Him; we must trust Jesus in all things. This was not easy for me, but I believe that it was even harder for my family. They had to go on with everyday life once I was taken from them – working, taking care of the family, and coming to see me and take care of what little needs they could help me with from the outside of prison. I could see what I was faced with, and I was frightened. But my family had so much left to mystery still, and the imagination can play tricks on you if you are not careful. I prayed for my family all the time and God kept telling me that He would take care of my family, for me to be busy about His work and leave my family in His hands. I had to do this daily; it was real hard for me to trust that they would be okay; I wanted to be able to see it with my own eyes. God's Word would come back to me when I felt like this. We walk by faith, not by sight; I had to trust God and He was helping me to learn to trust Him on a whole new level.

I was now not able to be with my daughters' everyday like I was used to. My daughters and I were real close. We would see each other three or four times a week. My youngest daughter Faleasha worked with me in the ministry, meaning I would see her Monday through Friday, and I would still see her and her family on the weekends. My daughters and I had never been apart from each other for any stretch of time; this was the hardest part for me and them, being apart. My husband had been in the Army for most of our marriage, and we were all used to him being gone for long periods of time. I think this made the bond between my daughters and I even stronger. We had to depend on each other a lot over the years. We had moved many times over the last fifteen years to places where we knew no one, but we always had each other; but now we were being separated and our dependency on God had to grow for us all.

My husband was not the rock of our family, unfortunately, as my daughters would tell you, it was me. I was also the spiritual leader of our household, not that I wanted the job, but my husband never would take on the role. I really believe that God was trying to get my husband's attention in many ways, to bring him into a relationship with his Lord that he had never had. Maybe I was in the way, and now he could step up to the plate and be the head of our family, as all men are called to be by God. God would reveal many things to me during this journey behind prison walls; I would learn my husband's decision much later.

The third time my daughters tried to come and visit me they were turned away again. They were told that the paperwork was still not there and the officers could not let them in. My youngest could not believe this was happening again, and before they left they were outside trying to think to whom they could call or who could they ask to see. One daughter was sitting on the curb crying and the other was walking the sidewalk back and forth fit to be tied.

Now at this time an officer came walking down the sidewalk and asked them both a question, "Are you both okay? Can I help you?" The daughter that was walking the sidewalk answered quickly from what I was told of this situation later. My youngest daughter, Faleasha, answered the officer, "Yes sir. This is our third time that we have come to see our mother. She was taken from us in the courtroom and we have not seen her since. She is not in good health and we understand she is not getting all her medication, and we are concerned for her and only want to see her to make sure she is alright".

The office asked; "what is your mom's name?" Lanette Black, my daughters answered. The officer then started to smile. The youngest daughter asked; "why are you smiling?" "Let me explain", he said. "I am on my way to work now. I work in the pod your mom is in. Let me explain to you what your mom is doing in her unit. First your mom is doing fine; she is the one that makes my job easier, everyday your mom is teaching the Word of God to all who will listen. If she is not teaching she is praying with anyone who has asked her to, or she is talking to the women one on one about any question they may have about God's Word. The rest of her time she is reading and studying her Bible. I assure you that your mother is fine; she is busy about God's work."

"I am a Christian also," he stated. "I am not able to talk to her about what I see her doing and how good it makes me feel, but I can tell you. I don't know why you are not able to get in to see your mother, but I will look into the situation, and I will make sure you are able to visit your mother next week. I will also look into your mom's medication and make sure she is getting everything she is supposed to be receiving," My daughters thanked him for sharing everything with them and they were able to go home with peace in their hearts that I was okay.

Once the officer came into work, I was called into his office. This was done by calling my name over the intercom; this was not normally good news when you were called into the office. When I heard my name over the intercom, I was concerned to why I was being called by the officer to his office. I was still dressed and ready to be called for visitation, but my name had not been called for visitation all day. I could not call my daughters and see if everything was all right, since they were not allowed to bring cell phones inside the prison; I would have to wait and call them later. Now I was being called and I knew it was not for visitation. When you were called for visitation your name was called followed by; "you have a visitor." I said a prayer prior to walking downstairs to see what the officer wanted with me.

Once in the office I was asked to sit down, then the officer began to speak. I was still dressed for visitation; when you get a visit, you iron your clothes etc. Some of the other women even put some makeup on me. I did not have any of my own makeup at the time and the women in the unit wanted me to look good for my daughters so they would not worry so much about me. The officer looked at me and said with a smile; I met two interesting women outside. I knew then it was my daughters. The officer explained to me that he had been told by my daughters that they had not been able to come in to visit me and today was the third time. The officer told me that he told them he would find out why they had not be able to get in and make sure they got in next weekend. I told the officer thank you, as a tear rolled down my face. I realized I was not going to be seeing my girls for another week, this was disappointing.

The officer then said, "I am also concerned about something else your daughters told me today," and he asked, "Are you getting all of your medications that you are supposed to take while you are here." I took a minute before I answered him; you have to be careful in how you say things in prison. You have to remember even if one department is not doing what they are supposed to, you have to say it in a way to not attack that department or it could come back to hurt you later. I answer saying, "yes, I am missing a few medications; but I think it is due to me taking so many different kinds of mediation. I was going to give them a few more days and then go back to sick call." I told the officer, "My daughters worry about me a lot. The visit today I had been praying that it would have put them at peace once they saw me and could see with their own eyes that I was okay. I guess that will have to wait for another week." The officer then said, "I think they have some peace after talking to me today that you are okay. I am sure they will tell you all about our conversation when you see them next weekend." The officer then asked me to give him the names of the medications that I had not received yet. He then told me to look for the medications in pill line that night. He continued to tell me, "If you don't get them at pill line tonight I want you to let me know." I thanked him for everything he was doing for me and my daughters. He then gave me a gentle look that was different than before and then he said, "Mrs. Black, keep doing what you are doing; it is noticed by more than you think."

Once out of the office and back in my room, I went to God in prayer and thanked Him for what He had done for me and my girls. God then reminded me what He had promised me, "you take care of my sheep and I will take care of yours." This day God allowed me to see that in action. I was so thankful and it put me at peace inside. I did not worry so much about my family; I knew they were in good hands.

I had many come to my room trying to find out what happened, remember hearing your name over the intercom is not normally good. You also have to be careful to what you share in prison. I did not want to get the officer in trouble that had shown so much kindness to me and my daughters. I shared with all the women who came to me, that God was good and even though I was not able to see my daughters today, I will see them next weekend. This was a private blessing God had given to me for the moment; God knew how much I needed it. There would come a day I would be able to share it with many, this was not the time

Visitation: Bitter/Sweet

Visitation is a time of mixed feelings, due to what you have to go through before, during and after. My first visitation was from my lawyer. I was not even expecting him when they called my name for visitation. When you have a visit, the officer will call your name over the intercom and you must get dressed and then come to the dining area where you will be picked up by an officer from downstairs. You have to wear your green uniform and not your sweat suit or shorts, which is what most of us wore most of the time. Other than from Monday through Friday from 6:00 AM to 5:00 PM we all had to wear our uniforms, for room inspections and other things that would take place during this time. I was not dressed in my uniform when they called my name so I had to get dressed quickly, I did not have time to do any makeup or my hair, so I did the best I could and went downstairs.

I had no idea to who was coming to visit me since this was during the week and not the weekend. This was also my first visit. I had been told by the other women what to expect, but it is not the same as experiencing it. I had prayed in my cell as I had gotten dressed, asking God to help me get through this first visit. I went downstairs to wait and then the officer came to get me. Anytime when we would go into the elevator with an officer we had to face the back of the elevator looking at the wall and not looking at him or her. I prayed and asked God to help me with the emotions I was feeling.

We picked up some other inmates from other units that also had visitation and we all proceeded to the visitation room. We were taken into a room that looked like a waiting room with chairs on each side of the room. The officer left us in this room locking the door behind us. The other women with me then started to tell me what to expect next. They had already asked me if this was my first visit, I had told them yes it was. I think they could see the fear on my face and they were going to be used by God to help me get through this. We were then asked to come into another room with a desk and a women officer sitting at it. She told us to all strip and she was going to have to search us and our clothing. I had not gone through this kind of search before with other women in the room. The only time I had been strip searched was when I went out to be x-rayed and when I first came to Miami, and I did not do well with either time. I cried through the whole thing both times. I was trying so hard to not cry, I did not want my eyes to be red for my visit.

The other women started to joke around with me and tell me what to do and how. The officer said to us all, "I don't like this any more than you all do. Let's get it over with, so you can proceed to visitation." One of the other women told the officer that this was my first time, and I think she is a little afraid. The officer was very kind to me for the rest of the search. She started to explain everything she was doing and why. I had already read the rules on the wall that was posted in the waiting room. She was going over them again for my benefit. Being searched was hard for me due to my back ground as a child. I had been raped three times before the age of sixteen and getting undressed in front of others was not easy for me. The first time I was strip searched I was alone, and I cried through the whole thing, now I had three other women with me and an officer. I was not comfortable at all; God was the only one getting me through the whole thing.

It was like God was holding my tears back, but the look on my face was telling a different story; from what I was told by the women who were with me. The women who were with me in the strip search room tried to comfort me and put me at ease. The women told me, "It's not a big deal. We are all women here and none of us are paying attention to anybody else. We are all trying to get to our visit the same as you. It will be okay, don't even think about it." The women with me were all sweet and their words did help me a lot, but I knew in my heart that it was really God that was helping me. Once the officer had searched our clothing and us, we where then all allowed to get dressed. Once we were all fully dressed the officer released us to the visitation officer.

The visiting room was big, full of men, women and their visitors. We, the inmates, were not allowed to get up from the table once we sat down. We were also assigned a table and our visitor was already sitting at it waiting for us. Once I walked into the room, the officer took my badge and kept it and told me once my visit was done, I was to pick up my badge and then I would be allowed to go back to my unit. Once I was given the table number that my visitor was sitting at, I was then allowed to go to the table. Once I was given my table number, I looked up to find the table and who was my visitor. I looked across the room and before I could find the table number I saw my lawyer standing, waving at me to come to where he was; it was my lawyer who had come to visit me.

I walked over to him and gave him a hug. You were allowed one hug in the beginning of the visit and one at the end of the visit, no kissing at all even it you were married. The visiting room was full of vending machines of all kind of things to buy. Once I sat down my lawyer asked if I would like anything and I said sure. He brought me something and we began to talk. He was overwhelmed he said to how good I looked. I did not feel like I looked good. But he continued to tell me how I had a glow all around me.

My lawyer was a Christian and He knew how I loved and trusted God. But he had never told me that I glowed, and we now had known each other for about two years. I told him thank you, but he could not stop looking at me with amazement.

He asked me again, "how are you doing?" I began to share with him how God was using me in the unit that I had been assigned to.

He then said, "That doesn't surprise me and now I understand why you are glowing." He proceeded to tell me he was in the area visiting another client and wanted to check in on me. I did share with him that I had not heard from my appeal attorney and my family had no idea to what was going on.

I was told before I came in that I would be bonded out on an appeal, this never happened. My lawyer told me that the appeal attorney had open heart surgery, but he was of the understanding that he had taken care of all the motions before he went into the hospital. He said he would look into it for me and my family and he would call my daughters with an update. We talked a little longer about what I was doing inside and my lawyer then did something that surprised me, he began to cry. He did this in the courtroom and other occasions when he and I would talk.

He looked at me and said; "Lanette, there is something about you that I have not seen in anyone else."

My lawyer continued to tell me how on many occasions he had not been able to stop himself from crying when he was around me.

William continued to tell me, "Lanette, the Spirit of God is on you so strong that I can't help myself to feel His presence. You are here and should not be and it's all my fault, but you are still serving the Lord with all your heart. It makes me think about where I am in my own relationship with the Lord."

He continued to tell me what was going on in his heart about my case. He told me, "you are innocent; you were my first client that I knew without a shadow of a doubt that you did not do what you were being accused of. Through the whole trial I kept praying for God to help me help you. But I let you down. You are in here because I failed and it hurts me to my heart, I can't get it out of my mind."

I looked him in the eyes and told him "do not let the devil do this to you; this is bigger than you and me. God has a plan and had one throughout the whole trial. I don't understand it alright now myself. I can only trust God and I need you to do the same. I know it will all work out for God's glory in the end, and is even now."

As tears rolled down his face, he said to me, "there you go again. I came here to cheer you up and you are cheering me up. I thank you, Lanette. I needed this. I will be praying for you and your family. Please call me or your family if I can help you in any way."

We said our goodbyes and I went back to the officer to retrieve my badge in order for me to go back to my unit. I had to wait until a few more women were also done with their visit. Once there were three of us we were all asked to go into the same room as before to be strip searched. I was still not good with it all, and again I cried. I was not with the same women as before, and I am not sure what they thought of me and I did not care.

I knew God was with me and He had showed me how much with what my lawyer had shared with me. But being in prison was still hard, and there were still many things in me that needed to be healed and smoothed by God.

I did realize that the visit with my lawyer did help me to prepare for my daughters' first visit that was coming up in only a few days. I was able to better prepare for my visitation with my daughters now that I knew what was involved in the visitation process. I had several women explain to me what to expect, but it is not the same as walking through it; I now felt that I would be able to walk into the visitation room to see my daughters without crying.

Daughters' First Visit

The day that my family was coming to see me for the first time since I had come into prison, I was nervous and excited all at the same time. My daughters and my husband would be coming to see me and I had not seen them since the day I had been removed out of the courtroom in front of them all after sentencing, with them all crying and screaming. I was not sure how emotional this visit was going to be; I had been praying for days along with many other women in the unit for myself and my family that our first visit would be enjoyable and not emotionally overwhelming. I was leaving it all in God's hands.

Finally the day was here that I was going to see my family. It was not hard for me to get up early; I barely slept the night before due to being so excited. I did not have any makeup so some of my friends allowed me to use theirs. I ironed my uniform and fixed my hair. Some of my friends helped me put on the makeup. They laid hands on me and prayed for me and my family.

Then I heard my name called over the loudspeaker, I was really going to get to see my family. I had to stay focused and try not to cry during the strip search. I did not want my family to see me for the first time crying and with red eyes. My family was unaware of all that I had to go through in order to see them, and I was wanted to keep it that way; I knew it would upset my daughters if they knew everything that I had to go through for visitation; and I wanted them to be at peace and not worry about me.

I was dressed and ready and my name had been called. It was time for me to go down stairs and wait for an officer to come and escort me to visitation. I was not the only one going to visitation.

Many others women from within my unit also had visits. Since it was the weekend many of the ladies within the unit would have visitors come and see them because family would be off work and able to come. This was the reason that my family made sure they would get to the prison early, so they could get in line to make sure they would get in. Visitation was only allowed for a certain block of time for each unit.

If you did not get to the prison early and get in line you may not be able to get in for visitation at all. This was why my family came early before it was even time for visitation to start; to ensure they would get in to see me. This time I was going to visitation with women I knew from my own unit. It gave me a lot of peace. Once we were all down stairs we were all taken into a waiting room; it was the same room that I had been in before when my lawyer had come to visit me.

It did not take long before an officer opened the other door and asked us to come into the strip search room. I kept focusing on God and not thinking about what was happening; it was the first strip search that I made it through without crying. I gave all the glory to God for getting me through.

Then the door was opened and I was about to see my family. I went to the desk to give my badge to the officer and get the table number I was to be assigned to. I did not need the number; I could see my family standing and waving at me with big smiles showing me exactly where they were. I walked over to them and gave each one a hug, it was so hard to let them go; but we all knew we had to because of the rules. They too had been briefed before coming in what the rules were and they knew the visit could be called to an end by the officer at the desk at any time if he did not see us going by the rules. As we all sat down my daughters' asked me if I wanted anything from the vending machines and then they went to collect some items for themselves and me.

They left my husband at the table with me so he and I could have a moment to talk alone. I could feel that something was not right with him, but was not sure what it was. He asked me if I was okay and was anyone hurting me, I told him that I was okay and not to worry about me being hurt; God was with me and He was protecting me. He shared with me that he missed me and this was harder than he could have ever thought it would be. I told him to take the same approach that we had done when he was in the Army.

Anthony went away often when he was in the army for long periods of time, I encouraged him to do as I did when he was gone; and we would get through this as a family like we had always done. The only difference this time was that he was left behind to take care of things and I was gone. I told him that the family needed him to be strong and he could do this, but he was going to need to trust God and call on Him to get our family through this; I told Anthony that he could not do it without God's help.

He then started to tell me what the family and the church had done when I was taken away from the courtroom after sentencing. About this time the girls were coming back to the table. The girls wanted to know first how I was and also was I being hurt by any one, too - many movies! I told them what was going on and how God was using me.

I told them also some of the things I could use in reference to study material including a study Bible. They said they would let my friends from church know because they had been asking what they could do to help. My girls did say they would send me a new Bible that week themselves. They had asked could they bring in my old Bible and was told they could not; it had to be sent from the book store brand new. Now with this all out of the way, they started to tell me what happened the day when the judge had sentenced me and I was taken away in shackles and handcuffs right in front of them all.

The family had a tradition when someone dies; they all go over to the immediate family's house and have a fish fry. They bring all kinds of food and feed the ones who are hurting the most due to their loss. My daughters told me that when they took me away, it felt like they had lost someone to death, like going to a funeral that never ended. When they all got home from the courthouse and were sitting around wondering what to do next, family members started to show up with food and began to cook and play around with them all to help them cope with the situation. This was what they all needed. They were hurting so much they needed a lot of TLC. I believe it was sent straight from heaven.

I was taken from the courtroom on a Friday, and I did not know, that the Sunday that followed, the whole family went to church at Hopewell Missionary Baptist Church in Pompano. This was our family's home church, even though I went to Calvary Chapel a lot, this was my home church. The pastor, RC, was used by God in a great way to help me and my family, and even the ones who worked in the ministry with me to get through this time in our lives. I will always be thankful to all of them at Hopewell for letting God use them the way He did.

Once the family arrived at church, they were greeted by everyone with condolences and reassurances that they were in their prayers. All wanted to know how I was doing and had they seen me yet; of course, they had not at that time. As soon as the pastor came to the pulpit after worship, my family was asked to come to the front and the whole church prayed for them and me.

My daughter could hardly keep the tears from coming as they told me how much this meant to them. My daughters did not go to this church on Sunday. They attended different churches, but Anthony had asked them if they all could go to church this particular Sunday together and they all agreed to go. The love from Hopewell filled my family with warmth and peace that they were not alone in this storm.

As my family told me, of all the events and how they all transpired it brought tears of joy to my eyes. My God was doing as He had promised me, "I will take care of yours." They then told me of the weekend prior, and how they had met the officer out front of the prison and what all had happened. I then was able to tell them what happened once he came inside.

I could not tell them on the phone because all the phone calls from within prison are being listened to by officers. I did not want to draw any attention to myself or the officer that had shown kindness to me and my daughters. We all laughed and as it came closer to the time for them to leave; I had to work real hard to hold back the tears. They kept saying they could not get over how good I looked. I told them this was all God's doing, and to tell everyone their prayers are being answered. I was able to share with them what God was doing and I was thankful that God was using me. I told them that I was not sure how this was all going to turn out, but I encouraged them to do as I was, one day at a time; and to let God help them. We all hugged and said our goodbyes.

I could tell it was hard for them to say goodbye as much as it was for me; but they would be back next weekend and I missed them already.

As I went to the desk to retrieve my badge and let the officer know I was ready to go back to the unit, again I was instructed to sit and wait until a few more ladies were ready. When you have a visit you are given two hours to visit. If you go over in your time you would be yelled at by the officer that your time was up.

My family and I watched the clock closely so this would not happen to us, but this happened to many others that did not seem to keep track of their time. Then the officer would yell at them and bring their visit to an end. If this happened to you in visitation, you were not given any time to tell your family good bye. You would have to end your visit and walk away from the table as soon as you heard the officer yell at you. If you did not, you could be punished by not being allowed to have a visit for a period of time. I did not want this to happen to me and my family, so we always watched the time closely.

My family and I did not have much control over anything during this time in our lives. We could control this one area when our visit ended, and in doing this it gave us some joy.

As I went into the room to be strip searched I started to cry. The officer asked me, "Have you not gotten use to this yet?" I told her, "I don't think I ever will." I went through the process as tears rolled down my face. I was happy to see my family, but it was so hard to know they were going home back to their lives and their dreams that I use to be a part of with them. I felt so bad that when I got back to the unit, all I wanted to do was go into my cell and cry. I was not bothered by any one, and I think it was because they all knew what I was going through and that I needed some time alone with God.

I went into my room and curled up on my bed and cried out to God some familiar words, "I can't do this, and you have the wrong one." God knew I was going to feel like this and I know He was not shocked by my words. I felt God come into my cell and wrap me in His arms and hug me and soothe me. He did not chastise me. He did not say a word, and He comforted me and let me cry. I was expecting to be scolded; I thought that God would say something to me like, "you should know better, what have you learned up to this point?"

But God did none of that. Jesus loved on me; this ministered to me more than anything could have, and my God knew it was what I needed. I was full of emotions and I knew that God was with me and had not left me, but seeing my family for the first time since I had been in prison was a lot harder for me than I thought it would have been; and God was there for me to fall into His loving arms as my daddy, not only my Lord.

We all have days like this, when we are lower than low and the enemy tries to come in and make us feel even worse and inadequate in all we do. God knows this and if we would only let him be not only our Lord but our daddy, He will come to our aid and help us through the storms in our life. But we have to first submit to God as it says in the book of James.

***James 4:7-8** Submit therefore to God. Resist the devil and he will flee from you. 8) Draw nigh to God and He will draw nigh to you (NASB)*

This was what I did, I was resisting the devil and calling out to God and He drew near to me and comforted me. So often when we are low we listen to the lies of the devil and let him cause us to fall even lower. I was spending a lot of time in God's Word and it was fresh on my heart. The enemy did not win this battle, but it would not be the last. I was teaching that night and the enemy did not want me to continue to do what God had called me to do.

The enemy will try to stop us in any way he can. We have to be alert and ready for the devil's attacks. All we have to do is draw to God and then we are able to resist the devil, and God will do the rest. I was learning this more and more everyday that I could not let my guard down for even a moment. As soon as I thought I had it all together I would find out how much I really didn't.

God is patient and He was with me, every day I had much to learn. My Teacher, Jesus, never stopped teaching me. My responsibility was to surrender and listen. I am so thankful that I was able to figure this out early in the beginning of this long Journey behind Prison walls, it is what made it all bearable and even a joy most of the time. Yes, I said joy! God can and will make even our worst situation joyful if we let Him. I am thankful that He did this for me; He will also do it for you if you let Him.

Chapter 6

Studying God's Word "Communion"

We studied many topics while I was at Miami FDC, but the study on communion I will never forget. God blessed us all through the study and brought us closer together as a body of Christ. There were so many women that had been raised Catholic and due to some of their choices in life, they had been kept from communion based on their Catholic belief. I watched God heal and restore during this study in what the true meaning of communion was established for. Once we finished the study in what the Word of God had to say about communion, it was now time for us all as a group to share in communion together.

We set aside a tentative date that we all agreed on that we would all come together and have communion; we started the planning. Being in prison, we could not go out and prepare for communion in a few days. It would take much longer; it was something we all had to plan for so we could acquire all the items that we would need. We had crackers and grape juice on Commissary, but you could only order your items once a week and you would then receive your order the following week. Not everyone had money on their commissary account.

God moved on a few to step forward to buy the items for all. We needed one more thing that we could not buy on commissary, small cups. We had many women including myself that went to pill line daily to get their medication. In prison, you are not allowed to keep your medication in your cell; you have to go to what they call pill line. A nurse comes into the unit at designated times to give out medication to all who are on the list. In receiving your medication, you are given a small pill cup. You are then required to take the medication in front of the nurse. There is a small trash can next to the drinking fountain where you are to discard the small cup that your medication was given to you in. You have to understand that anything in your possession that is not bought off of commissary, or not given to you to keep, is considered contraband. Under the rule of contraband, these small cups that medication was given to you in, if kept would be considered contraband. The cups would be perfect for our communion, but if the cups were found in our cells they would be taken and put into the trash.

We prayed for God's protection and set the date for our communion once enough cups had been collected. In this preparation time, I was able to talk to many ladies in what this meant to them. Many of the ladies had not taken communion in many years. One I remember particularly. She was divorced and had not been able to take communion for 12 years. She was actually frightened to do so even as we prepared. She did not want to bring judgment on herself. We went into the Word of God, and I watched God bring her full circle in the beauty of communion, and the forgiveness that Jesus provided for us all on the cross.

Finally the day for communion was here; we had collected all the items and prayed for several weeks for God to have His way in this service. We first had praise and worship and then we opened the Word and reviewed the Scriptures on communion again. We then all stood up and moved all the chairs by stacking them up and pushing them up against the walls. We then all sat on the floor in a circle and started to pass out all the elements. Everyone in the room had some part to play in the preparation of this day. It made us all really close and as one body.

In prison they try very hard to keep you separated. It is all about you and your case and you are encouraged to not get close to anyone. But at this time and place, we were a true body of Christ all coming together in communion with God. In looking around the circle, I could see the peace, joy and happiness on every woman's face in the room. It ministered to me in a way that I will never forget. What else really matters? At this place and time we were all sitting in God's presence and He was touching every woman in the room in a special way that was only for them personally. I thanked God to myself for allowing me to be a part of this day with all of these women; my sisters in Christ.

After all the items had been passed out, I started to explain all that Jesus had gone through, before He had gotten to the cross, and while he hung on the cross, and even how He died on the cross for us all. I instructed everyone to go before God and make it personal. Ask for forgiveness and talk to God about anything that they felt they needed to give to God. Then I told them, we would all come back together and take communion together and then close in prayer as a group. There was not a dry eye in the place, including mine. God's presence was so thick in the room that after we were all finished none of us wanted to leave.

The young woman that had not taken communion for twelve years had a glow about her and an overwhelming peace all around her. I was blessed to watch her walk with the Lord as she prepared for sentencing and designated. I had no idea at the time we would both end up at Coleman Camp together, and I was going to be blessed to be able to watch her as she became one of God's shinning stars.

So often we allow others to teach or sow into us false doctrine, we have to read the Word of God for ourselves and make sure that what is being taught to us is in the Word. If we don't, we are allowing strongholds in our lives and these keep us from receiving the freedom that comes with our Salvation. We are still saved, but we don't walk in boldness, and we are hindered in many other ways. This was what had happened to this woman who had not taken communion for twelve years.

She was in bondage and sin had a hold on her, but it was sin that Jesus had already forgiven her for. But, due to others and what they had told her, that she was not worthy of the things of God due to her sin, she would not approach God's throne room in communion and many other areas. It interfered with her prayer life and everything else she would try to do in her walk with God. Now she was free, and God blessed me by letting me have a front row seat in watching her win this victory in her life.

When we all left the chapel that day, we were all different. Every one of us had a closer relationship with God; our relationship with God had gotten more personal. I love that about God; how He meets us right where we all need Him. This day, after we had all taken communion together with the true understanding in what we were doing; we were not ever going to be the same.

Sacrifice/Blessing

One of the other areas that many of the women in the unit started asking questions about was fasting. While we were in prison, we were not allowed to fast, at least not a fast that would require us to miss several meals. We were allowed to miss a meal or skip desert, but if we missed several meals, we could be accused of being on a hunger strike. This could cause someone to go to the shoe for punishment, and we did not want that to happen. Fasting was one of the areas that I was not strong in myself. I had done a few fasts before coming into prison but none that were much longer than twenty-four hours.

I went into the Word and God gave me a study for the women in the unit and myself. As I opened the Word and studied everything that I could find on fasting, I was amazed to how much I did not know. I believe that God blessed me more in the preparation of this study than anyone could have been once I taught it; but God did this all the time with me in all of the Bible studies that I prepared for the women in the unit.

God blessed me amazingly in every study I prepared, then God would bless me all over again when I taught it; I was always double blessed. God was teaching and blessing me in so many ways. As we all studied about fasting, it was brought to my attention that we should do a fast as a group to put into action what we had learned. We all prayed, and we all came to an agreement that we should do a corporate fast together.

When we all agreed to do the fast as a group, I reminded everyone that we were not allowed to miss many meals in prison and if we did we could be accused of a hunger strike. If this happened to any of us, it would not glorify God, and some of us could even go to the shoe. The shoe is the same as the hole or solitary confinement.

None of us wanted that to happen. As we talked about what we could do as a fast and not break the rules of the prison, it came to me that we could do an all liquid fast.

We all agreed to pray about it and come back together the following day and see what God had shown us all. As I prayed, God showed me how we could fast within the rules of the prison and still be blessed by the sacrifice. The next day when I met with all the other ladies in the Chapel, I shared with them what God had shown me. We all agreed to do a fast for one week, and we would partake of only liquids.

We made a list of everything that we could drink; the list also included the soups that were given to us at dinner time; this would keep us within the rules of the prison. In making the list we were careful to include something from each meal that was given to us in order for it not to appear that we were not eating and this would keep us within the rules of the prison. We also made a list of all the things that we were fasting and praying for as a group. The list was copied and each woman was given a copy. Each woman in the unit including myself also had a more personal reason they were doing the fast, and we all had no idea how God was going to bless each of individually.

Remember we had studied what it meant to fast and what to do during a fast, so we were all on the same page. As we started the fast, we as a unit were also preparing for an ACA inspection. This is a certification process that prisons go through that reflects the standard of cleanliness within that prison.

Now all the cleaning had already been done weeks before the inspectors were even at the prison, but the week we were to start our fast was the same week the inspectors would be coming through to inspect. During the week that we were being inspected, our meals were better than they had ever been since I had been in prison - chicken and potatoes with all the fixings - every meal was good and full of surprises that none of us were used to seeing; and this was the week we started our fast.

Many of the women in our group could not take the temptation of all the good foods that were being given to us at our meals and had to stop their fast. We encouraged them and asked them to keep praying for those of us that were still fasting; we also encouraged them to keep praying for all the items on the prayer list.

During the fast we would all still go to every meal and we would give the part of the meal we could not eat away to other inmates in the unit. God did a cool thing through all of us in giving our food away. The ones we were giving our food to were mainly the unbelievers. Only God could set up this kind of witness. But without us even asking, the women we were giving our food to then gave us the part of their meal we could eat. We did not require this from them as a trade. Oh no! They gave it to us all on their own as they learned what we were doing, and what we were allowed to eat. They shared it with us.

One of the things on the list was to pray for every woman in the unit. We shared this with them when they asked, "What are you all praying for?" We would answer; "you!" We all watched God minister to all of the women in the unit through our fast. Since we were eating something from every meal, we did not draw attention from the guards. But I have to say, I did notice them watching us. I knew God ministered to them as well.

Food carries a big importance inside of prison. It is used to trade and even gain favor. And here we were doing this by choice and not requiring anything in return as we gave the food away. Many did not understand it at all. This caused them to ask many questions. This gave many of us a great opportunity to share our faith in Jesus Christ with others in the unit that normally did not come to the Chapel. My joy was great in watching the many ladies that had sat in the Bible study and had learned what fasting was all about and why we do it as Christians. Now I was watching them answering questions proposed to them about their faith; and they were all sharing Jesus with anyone who would listen. I could see in their answers that they had listened and learned what the Word of God had spoken to them about fasting and many other areas we had study. As much as I did not want to be in prison and away from my family, God gave me great joy and peace in watching what He was doing in each woman that had come to Him. I had come to a place of understanding that I was where I was supposed to be, not only for the women in the unit, but also for myself and my growth in my Lord Jesus.

It had only been about a month and I was already not the same person that came into prison, but I was still under the understanding that I would go home soon. The appeal would go through and I would get to go home to my husband and my daughters any day. Staying in prison for three and a half years was still too much for me to even think about doing. I had no idea what God had ahead of me, and it was probably for the best that God did not share it with me at that time. I don't think I would have been ready to hear it. But that is God; He knows what to show us and what to keep from us; and I am thankful that He does.

Inspections And The Fear They Brought

Now everyday life was a challenge for all of us in prison, but when we had to go through inspection from anyone outside of the prison, it was even more challenging. Our cells were real cold. I was on the top bunk and this put me right in line with the air duct. It would blow right on the top of my head all night. I would get so cold sometimes; I would get down and sit on the floor to try to get warm. The cold would bring on an asthma attack, and I had them often at Miami FDC. Because of this, I did have a few concerned guards that would ask me if I was okay and keep an eye on me as they did their inspections and rounds.

We all had to be on our toes with the inspectors in the prison. You never knew if they would come back your way. I started to have a bad asthma attack and the officer called for medical. That meant they would come and see if I needed a breathing treatment. When they did not come, the officer had to call them again. Everyone was afraid for me and all the ladies that came to the Bible studies were praying for me.

When medical finally came after an hour had passed, they took me upstairs to medical to be evaluated. I hated this due to how we had to travel. Remember we could not talk to the officer and, in the elevator; we had to face the back of the elevator looking at the wall with our back to the officer.

Everything was about humiliation, and I was there. Once in medical, one of the attendants there tried to accuse me of faking. Now this upset me so badly that I started to cry. Trust me, that is not the thing you want to do when you are having an asthma attack. I then became frightened and started asking the medical personal, "Are you going to give me a breathing treatment, or let me die?" I was sitting in the hall, but no one had given me a treatment yet.

Then all of a sudden every one came running down the hall trying to calm me down. I was confused. Then I noticed all the inspectors coming down the hallway. It was the inspection team for the ACA accreditation, with the warden. They even stopped to see me and asked if I was okay and was I being taken care of. The medical personal that were responsible for taking care of me were now responding quite quickly. Their response to the inspectors and the warden was, "she is fine, and we are about to give her a breathing treatment and she will then feel much better."

God shows up in the strangest way sometimes. I was then put into an office to see a doctor. They had never done this since I had been at Miami FDC. I knew now that they had to do everything right on my behalf, because the inspection team may use my case as an example to how the prison responded to an emergency, since they were there while it was going on.

The inspection was not only about cleanliness, but also how they treated the inmates and responded to emergencies. Now I was an example on a report, and the medical team knew this; I received the best medical treatment since I had been at Miami FDC, including follow up appointments.

Everyone in medical took real good care of me from that day forward. I was even given some medication to help me sleep that had been denied to me before. They were even going to look into my cell being so cold and how they could correct this problem or get me additional blankets, due to this being one of the main reasons I was having so many asthma attacks. They were also going to look into why I had been assigned a top bunk. With all the medical problems that I had coming into prison, I was not supposed to be on the top bunk, but a bottom bunk. Everything that I had been trying to take care of since I had arrived at Miami FDC in reference to my medical situation was now being taken care; I gave all thanks to God.

I had a lot of attacks like this in Miami, many times was due to us being searched. When the officers would come in to the unit to search, they would come in with about fifteen officers at a time without any warning. When they came into the unit, they would start yelling "come out the cells and go into the exercise yard."

One time I was on the toilet and one of the male officers came right into my room and told me to get outside. I told the officer that I was trying, but he only yelled at me more. I knew this was not good being asked to go into the exercise yard since this was where everyone smoked. I am allergic to smoke; I could never go out in this yard due to all the smoke. This was not outside exactly; it was a big concrete room with a basketball court within it. There were some small windows at the top with fencing on them, but the smoke lingered in the exercise yard for a long time. They put me out in this yard during searches along with everyone else, even with me telling them that I was allergic to smoke and could not go in the yard. It would cause me to have an asthma attack.

Three different times I was put into this yard during searches and each time I had an asthma attack and medical had to be called in order for them to give me a breathing treatment due to the attack. Finally after the third time with the assistance of a concerned officer who had watched me have these attacks every time I was forced to go into the exercise yard. It was approved that under no circumstances was I to be forced into the exercise yard. I was allowed to sit within the common areas at a table. Now these searches could go on for hours. It all depended on what they were looking for and what they found.

We would sit or stand and watch as they would go from cell to cell throwing everything on the floor or out in the hallway. I found out later this was also used to keep you submissive to who was in charge. But the feeling inside was so much harder to deal with. I felt violated every time they would come and search. So did the other women in the unit. We did not have any privacy as it was; our rooms were our homes. We did not like to look at prison as our homes, but it was the truth. I had been a victim of my home being vandalized, and you feel violated when this happens to you, thinking of someone going through all of your things would send chills up and down your spine. I felt these same chills every time the officers came in and searched our cells. I knew it was done to keep the unit safe and free from weapons, etc. Although my room never had anything in it that was not supposed to be there, my room was trashed as bad as the ones who did.

Once we were allowed to go back into our rooms we would then have to clean them and put them back in order for inspection the next day, and sometimes we would even have to have the room ready for inspection within a few hours depending on the time of day the search had been done. Now remember, we are two to a room, items are tossed all over, both roommates have to go into the cell together and figure out what belonged to whom. This could be hard sometimes since we all shopped at the same place. You had to know what you had in your foot locker at all times.

Not all Bunkie's would get along with each other, and when they would be allowed to go back into their cells they would argue with each other as to what belonged to whom. Many women would give in to their Bunkie's in order to keep the peace and not argue. They did not want to get in trouble and sent to the shoe. This was a stressful time for everyone. I prayed during the inspections that the officers would finish quickly and once we were all allowed to go back into our cells that we would all be able to put our things back together without any incidences.

Depending on what the officer found during their shakedown, as they called it, we could all be put on lockdown for the day or several days; even if it was only one person in the unit that had something in their room they were not supposed to have. I was blessed to have a quiet roommate; whenever we were put on lockdown, I would use the time to study God's Word. I was always working on a Bible study to present to the women in the unit. I was always in the Word of God when I was in prison.

I look back on it now and I can see why I get weaker now more than I did then. I am now out in life dealing with many things that come up daily, so much to do and so many things pulling me in so many different directions. I don't have the time I used to have when I was behind prison walls to spend in the Word of God. Inside you have a lot of time to yourself; this is where you have to decide how the time will be spent. I chose to spend my time with God and in His Word. I know with all my heart that is what got me through it all.

But it is also something I have to decide to do on a daily basis now that I am home, outside of prison walls. I work on this daily, making time for God and His Word. I may not be able to sit down and spend hours like I did behind prison walls, but God blesses me in the time that I am able to put aside for Him and me to spend together. It is a matter of making up our minds that God is important and that we will make the time for God. I know when I do, my days are better and I am blessed at every turn.

How about you? Do you make time for God in your everyday life? Do you go days or weeks without reading the Word of God? I encourage you to sit down and rearrange your schedule in order for you to have time with God daily. I can guarantee if you do this, you will not be disappointed; God promises us if we seek Him, we will find Him. And I don't know about you and how your days go, but in mine, I need God daily guiding me and showing me His will for my life not to mention His protection for the many things of this world that we all need protection from. Seek God first every day before your day starts, and you will not face your day alone; there is nothing we can't do with God as our helper and guide. He is waiting on you to call on Him; don't keep Him waiting. Maybe you did not start your day with God today. I would like to encourage you to stop right now and go to the Lord in prayer and ask Him to guide you and help you through the rest of this day and watch God move on your behalf.

Chapter 7

An Encounter With Officers That Was Not Expected

The time for me to leave Miami FDC was getting close; I could feel it in my spirit. It all became so clear to me during the time we were studying about baptism. When we finished the Bible study on baptism, I had about twenty women approach me and inform me that they wanted to be baptized. Being in prison, I was not sure how to direct them to get this done.

You have to remember when you are in prison things are more complicated to get done than on the outside. You are not able to do something because you want to. So many of us take for granted our freedom in how we are able to walk freely and do the things we do. Even as Americans, we are able to do so much more than other in other countries.

Some can't even worship God openly without the fear of being killed. I realized at this time, how good we have it as Americans; but at the same time how much we take what we have for granted. Even those behind bars lose many freedoms that are not luxuries, like the problem we were being presented with in getting the women baptized.

Many of them were going to be deported and wanted to be baptized before they would leave, being that this would be harder for them to accomplish, according to them, once they were home. The reasons varied from women to women to why they wanted to be baptized right then and not wait; it was personal between them and God.

We first went to the chaplain and he denied the women from being baptized. He said they could wait till they got out of prison. He was a Catholic priest and this was not a priority to him. It could wait, in his opinion. But the women had learned the call by Jesus for all to be baptized and they wanted to be obedient to the Word. They understood it had nothing to do with them being saved, but it meant a new beginning, a fresh walk with Jesus. It was important to them, so it was also to me. I went to God in prayer and He asked me a question I did not know how to answer at first. "Why don't you baptize them?"

My answer at first was because I am a woman and not a pastor. Then God led me to His Word to find exactly where that was a stipulation in His Word. I could not find it anywhere. I went back to God in prayer and asked "tell me Lord what you would have me do in this matter."

I was instructed to baptize them myself, so I proceeded to baptize anyone who wanted me to do so. I was surprised when I approached the women. All who had signed up wanted me to baptize them. But in my investigation to why they were so willing I was again surprised. All the women interested in being baptized had already gone into the Word themselves to research why I could not baptize them. They all shared with me that they had learned in the Word, there was no reason that I could not baptize them.

God even gave me confirmation fully in what I heard Him say and what I had read in His Word. I was so blessed to see how all these women had grown with God and His Word and depended on what God's Word said and not me or man. They were all learning from God and understanding to see Him in all things, to go to His Word for all answers and not man. I was so proud of all of them in how much they had grown. I cried out to the Lord and thanked Him for allowing me to be a witness to all that was going on in each of these women.

We all agreed that I was not doing anything wrong in doing the baptism. It was God that was doing the actual baptism of the women, not me; I was only a vessel He was using. God showed me if we were in a deep jungle and I was the only one available would I not baptize them then? I was only being used by God because there was no other willing or available to baptize His daughters.

I understood and proceeded. I was always very careful while I was inside prison being used by God, to not do what I was not called to do or should not do. It was not all about me, but God. The women I was with came to me often and thanked me for being so careful. I always reiterated to the ladies, "It is not all about me, but all about God. He can use all of us if we only would let Him." I would tell them, "I am only a vessel that God had chosen to use at this moment. Once I leave from this place He will choose to use one of you that will be left behind, and you will have to be ready and willing to let Him."

The question at hand was how was this to be done? We discussed with the women who wanted to be baptized how they wanted to do this. Sprinkle in the chapel with a glass of water, or in the shower with a bucket of water? It was unanimous they wanted to be baptized in the shower; it was the closest thing to be dunked under water to them. I did explain to them the method that we use is not where the power is. It is all in your willingness and surrendering to the will of your Lord, and in your obedience in being baptized. They all understood and they all still wanted to

A Journey Behind Prison Walls

use the shower. We all were given a shower dress when we first came to Miami FDC. Most of us never used them, but now we had a use for them.

The women would were the shower dress, and I would get a small trash can, clean it out, of course. I would then fill it with water and pour water over their head once the question was presented to the one being baptized. Now being in prison we are not allowed to gather in crowds or groups unless it is in the designated places, like the chapel where we had our studies. In my eyes at the time it would have been a lot easier in the chapel, but it was not what the women wanted.

Praying to God, He showed me do as they asked. This had to be done discretely and not drawing any attention to ourselves. I had one helper to fill the trash can and hand it to me, and then only I and the woman to be baptized would be in the shower. All the other women from the Bible study group would be waiting for me and the woman that had been baptized; once we were both done, we would then join everyone in the chapel for prayer.

We could only do one at a time to not draw attention to ourselves. All was in place and the first woman was in the shower, I asked her if she believed the Word of God and that Jesus was her Savior and that Jesus died for her on the cross and was raised on the third day.

Her answer was, "yes", and she added, "I wish to live and walk with Him as my Lord."

I then said, "I baptize you in the name of the Father, the Son and the Holy Spirit." I was then blessed to witness the Holy Spirit in a way I had never seen before in my life. I was able to see the Holy Spirit descend on the woman that was being baptized. She was glowing with the Spirit of God, and began to sing softly.

I left her immediately, even though I did not want to leave, I needed to go to the chapel in order to not draw attention to both of us. Once in the chapel, all wanted to hear how it went. It was hard to put into words what I had witnessed. I explained to them the best I could. I had been blessed to see the Holy Spirit fill our sister in Christ with His Spirit, and in her obedience, God blessed her with a blessing and me in being one that was able to witness it.

The women in this prison were taking a chance by doing this in the shower. It was their choice, not mine and God was blessing them. We had not been told that we could not to do this, but, due to where we were, we knew it could be something we could get in trouble for because we were gathering together in the shower; this was why I did not stand long in the shower.

Once the woman who had been baptized came back to the chapel in dry clothes, she was still glowing and singing with joy. We all gathered around her to pray for her. But she first wanted to share with us all what she had encountered with God. She said she felt God all over her. She felt great peace and joy and could not stop singing His praises. The rest of the women wanted to go and be baptized right then, but we could only do a few a day, and one had already been scheduled for later that afternoon, remembering we could not draw attention to ourselves. We would find out later that we were not successful.

We all circled around her and laid hands on her as I began to pray for her. Many of the women in the room also lifted up prayers for our sister who had been baptized. We all left the chapel with an overwhelming peace and joy, and for a brief moment we all even forgot that we were all in prison!

I was only able to baptize two more women before I was called into the office. My name was announced over the loud speaker to come to the officer's office. As I walked to the office the officer on duty was known to be mean and not very understanding. I also understood her to not be a Christian. She and I had a few conversations that led me to this understanding, I was trying to plant a seed within her, and I was not sure to how much had been accomplished. Once I arrived in her office, she asked me to be seated. You always waited, to be told to be seated when you enter the officer's office.

She then asked me a question. She did not beat around the bush; she got right to the point of why she had called me into her office. "Are you baptizing women in the showers Mrs. Black?" I answered her, "yes, I am, is that not allowed?" I asked? "No, you are not, like a doctor is not allowed to practice medicine once inside of prison, you are not allowed to be a pastor once inside of prison either."

I responded to her, "I am not a pastor and not trying to be one." I then informed her that we had asked the chaplain and he declined to baptize the women interested. We did our best to not make a disruption or bother anyone.

She then said, "I have called you in here due to someone coming to me and complaining, so someone was bothered by what you are doing. You have to understand where you are, Mrs. Black. You are in prison and everyone in here is watching you, and not all who say they are with you are. I have to ask you to stop. If you don't, you will be punished, do you understand?"

I answered, "Yes, I do." But I could not get out of my mind what she said, "Everyone is watching and not all who are with you are with you."

We can find this also in the Word, as Jesus walked this world as a man, even he was betrayed by one of His own disciples. This opened my eyes even more. I had to trust and lean on God even more. The enemy would not be happy with what God was using me to do here; I could not take anything for granted and always keep my eyes on God. Again here I was learning a very important lesson. I kept learning that in everything, bad or good, God is teaching us always. We always have to pay attention and learn whatever it is that God is trying to teach us.

In leaving the office, I went directly to my room. Many women were coming to me concerned and wanted to know what I was called into the office for. Remember it is not normally a good thing to be called into the officer's office. I asked them to give me a minute and I would be right back out to explain. I felt the great need to go and pray and spend some time with God first. I needed His guidance in what this all meant, and what was I going to do with the remaining seventeen women who still wanted to be baptized. Crying and confused due to what had happened, I was feeling so many things, "who complained God?" That was when God reminded me that not everyone is of Him, even in our group. Wow, this was what the office had said to me also. God showed me that this was not an attack on me but Him "God," and an attempt to keep His children from Him. But not to worry, it would not keep them from Him. I was assured by God to rest in Him. This too had a reason, I was to wait and do nothing, I would see it all unfold and all would make sense soon.

Now I don't know about you, but this is hard for me sometimes - the waiting game. I have to tell you that during my time in prison, I learned to wait on the Lord. It was what kept me in peace. I learned quickly that I could not trust my understanding of things. I had to trust God completely. He knew what was ahead; I did not. If I even tried to think about what was ahead of me, I would get overwhelmed with fear. I had to take one day at a time. This was something I was known for telling everyone I encountered. "Take one day at a time. We are given enough grace for today. Do not try to borrow from tomorrow." This was the only thing that got me through, and I was thankful that God taught me this early on my journey behind prison walls. I was so glad He did. I needed it so much and I still live by it today.

When I left my room to comfort the many women who were concerned for me, I have to admit, I had a heavy heart. I did not know who complained and with what God had shown me it could be even one that was close to me. I trusted God to lead my words and I began to speak to them all. As soon as I walked into the Chapel, I was asked, "What happened? Is everything okay?" "Yes, all is okay," I answered, "but we will have to stop the baptism for right now." "Why?" they asked? "I know we all tried to not disturb anyone but someone did go and complain. I have been told that I most stop or I will be punished. Before I came to you I went to my room to pray, and God has given me peace that this will all work out in time. We have to trust Him and keep ourselves in prayer."

I went on to explain to the women who wanted to be baptized but had not been yet, "I want you to know that not being baptized right now will not keep you from

God. God sees your heart and knows your desire, and God will provide a way for you to be baptized in due time, even if it is not here. We must have faith and trust God even in this." Many were upset and many had questions and I tried to answer them all to the best of my ability with God leading me. At the end, I asked everyone to join me in a word of prayer to ask God to give us all a peace with all that had happened. Once we all prayed God gave us all a peace to wait on Him.

We did not have to wait long before we all were able to see what God was doing. I was asked into the counselor's office the next day. This was the woman who did all of our paper work for visitation, etc. She was not liked by many due to her unavailability and she was not good at getting the paper work done for any of us. My visitation problems with my family, not being able to get in to see me, were all stemmed from her not doing her job correctly and in a timely manner. I found out later that my situation was not an isolated incident.

This happened to most of the women in the unit; she caused a lot of difficulties for many women within our unit. She was not a Christian and was not one that spent a lot of time with anyone. When I walked into her office, she asked me to sit down. She then looked at me and asked, "What is this I hear about you baptizing women in the shower? You are one of our best behaved inmates; you go by all the rules and encourage other to do the same. I was not expecting to get a bad report come across my desk about you. I have to admit that I was surprised by this, Mrs. Black," she stated.

I began by explaining that we had asked the chaplain to baptize the women and he had refused. We tried to not disturb anyone and be quiet. I only learned that we had disturbed someone once I was called into the officer's office. My Counselor then responded by saying, "first I will have to check into why the chaplain refused, this would be his job, but what I want to know from you is why it is so important that you baptize these women now?

What is the big deal about baptism anyway?" she asked, I could not believe what I was hearing. I had been given an open door to share the Gospel with a person I would have never thought I would have been able to. I began by sharing the whole Gospel with the counselor; I could not explain baptism without explaining the Gospel first. I then proceeded with the importance of baptism; this took about an hour and a half. I could feel the presence of the Lord in the room. Once I was done, she said she understood why it was so important for this to be done. She did not accept Jesus right then, but I was at peace that a seed had been planted. Now all I could do was to pray for her that she would find her way to Jesus. She again told me that she was going to check into this being done by the chaplain first and find out why he had refused. This was his area of responsibility. She then told me she would allow me to continue if the chaplain still refused. I was in shock; I could not believe in what had happened.

Not even that I may be allowed to finish the baptisms if the chaplain would not, but that I was able to share the Gospel with this women that I am sure did not go to church or seek out God in any way. All I could think and say to the Lord was, "Lord you are so amazing in how you make sure all your children will have a chance to hear of your goodness and mercy and the Salvation that is available to all who accept your son Jesus Christ."

I left the counselor's office with so much peace inside of me, I was in amazement. The officer that had spoken to me did not have to forward this report to my counselor. She had already handled the situation, and I did not resist her in any way. Once an officer handles something like this, it doesn't normally go to the counselor or anyone else unless the inmate that is being corrected would not respond to the request made by the officer.

But God was not finished with this situation. I should not have been so surprised in what God did. God had told me to wait on Him and even this situation that looked bad to all of us had a reason - one that would glorify God and His purpose. What I had seen as a failure, God turned into victory. This was a lesson that was going to be played out many times over and over again on my journey behind prison walls. I did not have any idea to what magnitude at the time. There was so much more ahead of me. The time spend at Miami FDC was being used by God to strengthen me and root me in His Word and in Him, no matter what things looked like - bad or good. I was learning to trust only God and walk with Him no matter what others may say or do. The enemy was going to try to derail me in many different ways. I had no idea to what all was a head of me. My journey had only begun.

Once back in my cell, again I had many women coming and asking me if I was okay. I informed them that everything was fine and as God had promised, He had a much bigger reason for allowing everything to take place the way it had in reference to the baptisms, and everything had been revealed to me in my meeting with the counselor. I was careful with my words, remembering I was in prison and anytime you talked about a staff member, you had to be careful in what you said and how you said it.

Now I was aware that not everyone in our group was a part of us, or a follower of Christ. I wanted to minister to all of the women in what God had done, but I also wanted to minister to the ones who did not have Christ as their Savior or Lord. I wanted all to hear how God used this situation for His glory, even the one who reported us to the officer; what they meant for bad God used for good. I was careful with my words so they would not go back to the counselor and embarrass her or make her mad.

I don't know why I felt like I needed to be careful, but I trusted my spirit. I let everyone know that God had showed up and showed out in my meeting with the counselor, and that we all needed to keep the counselor in prayer. I certainly got some strange looks on that comment; remember no one liked the counselor.

I used this as an opportunity to remind everyone that Jesus loves us all even the ones that we may not like. I explained to them that God could be using this as an opportunity to teach them how to love the unlovable; everyone in the group smiled and agreed. I did tell them that she would be checking with the chaplain to, see if he would baptize the remaining women and if he would not, she would allow me to finish.

This brought great joy to all. I reminded them to be patient with the system and know that God is at work on the behalf of us all. Our ways are not His ways and as we saw in this current situation, God can use anything to make sure all hear His Gospel. I was then asked by one of the women in the group why I was in the counselor's office for so long. She stated that everyone had been praying for me and that they had all been worried because the counselor never talks to any one as long as she spoke to me.

I proceeded to tell them all how God had provided me the opportunity to share the Gospel with our counselor. She asked what was so important about baptism and that opened the door for me to tell her not only the importance of baptism, but Salvation. I reiterated to them all "see how God used something that looked bad to us, for His glory." I then said with boldness to all who were present, "whoever told on us, I don't want any of you to be mad at whoever it is, because they were used by God to fulfill God's purpose; we all need to pray for whoever this person is that they will be used by God even more."

Again I received some strange looks, but I did notice a look on one face that was different from any other in the group - it was her - the one who had told. God was ministering to her. I was not sure what this all meant to her or what she may do next, but I knew that God knew her heart and He was working within her. I now knew who had told, but better yet, it was not about her telling, but that she was struggling with God, and I needed to pray for her and ask God to give me an opportunity to talk to her one on one. I had no idea how quickly God was going to answer my prayer and give me the opportunity to talk to her. It was the next day after lunch.

The next day I was sitting at a table in the common area all alone, which was not normal in itself. Every time I would go downstairs to sit at one of the tables in the common area, I never would sit alone for long, but this day, I was; and the women I had noticed to be the one who had told the officer about the baptism had approached my table and asked if she could join me.

A Journey Behind Prison Walls

She looked at me in the eye and said to me, "I am not sure if you know, but I am the one who told that you were baptizing women in the showers, and I felt like I needed to come and talk to you today." I looked at her and smiled, and said, "Yes, I already knew it was you, and I am glad that you have come and sat with me today." She smiled at me and said, "I am not surprised that you knew, but I am not sure why I had to come and sit with you today; I knew I needed to." I then asked her, "Why did you go to the officer and tell them we were baptizing in the showers?" She then told me that she did not like the fact that I was doing the baptizing, that she did not like how much everyone looked up to me and gave me so much attention. "You are not God," she said. I calmly looked at her and told her I understood that the way we have to do things while we are here in prison is not how we would normally do things on the outside. I asked her, "is it because I am not a pastor?" She answered "no;" and then said, "I don't' think that it is necessary for anyone to be baptized at all; at least by you." I looked at her and asked her why? She responded that she did not believe in baptism and she felt I was only doing it to lift myself up, so all would think I was special.

I noticed that as she spoke to me that her face took on a completely different look, dark and sunken is the best way I can explain it. At this time, one of her friends came to sit with us. She said to me, "you don't mind if my friend joins us do you?" I answered, "of course I don't." I introduced myself to her friend because I had not noticed her in the chapel in any of our Bible studies, and I did not know her. I had only seen her around in the unit.

This was when things began to make more sense to what was really going on. The young woman that joined us, her friend, explained to me that she was involved in Santeria, and she had been encouraging her friend to stop going to the Bible studies that were being held by me in the Chapel. I asked her why? She responded that she felt that I was trying to be God, and I had been lying to everyone and she did not want her friend to be misled from the truth. I asked her then, "What is the truth?" She proceeded to tell me that they believe different than I do, they believed in spells and curses and many other things that she was not going to go into with me.

As her friend was finishing her statement, we were then joined by two other women asking if it was okay for them to join us. It was the voodoo queen and her daughter; they had both come to Christ during one of our Bible studies in the Chapel. I remember when I first came to Miami FDC, and I was warned by many women within the unit to be leery of these two women, because they were into voodoo and may do me harm. I met the daughter first and I was told by her that her mother was a very powerful priest, and was looked up to and even feared by many in the realm of voodoo. I was so blessed the night when they both came to Jesus.

When they started to come to the Bible studies, I was surprised. I don't know why since I had been praying for them both and God is faithful. Even in this, God was teaching me to pray and trust Him. There were many women of different faith in our unit and I had to respect all boundaries; but the boundaries did not stop me from trying to plant a seed.

In trying to reach out to the voodoo queen and her daughter, God showed me to go and visit them in their cell. No one in the unit would ever visit them or even associate with either one of them, due to fear. As I visited them often, they both started to relax and open up to me. On many occasions, I was asked to join them for lunch or dinner.

They would fix me food and I would share with them about my faith as they would share theirs. I would get scolded often by many of the women in our Bible study group, because I was eating the food that the voodoo queen and her daughter would fix for me.

Out of fear, they were frightened for me that the food that was being fixed by the voodoo queen and her daughter could have a curse on it. I would use everything as a lesson whenever I had a chance. I shared with them that God is my protector and they had no power over me. I went to them with Jesus and He who sent me would protect me. I was not afraid. I trusted Jesus.

I believe with all my heart that because I was willing to go to them, they were willing to come to me. In turn, they were coming to Jesus and He had plenty for them to hear.

Now, as we all sat at the table together, God was getting ready to bless me again. I had been praying the whole time in my spirit while I sat at the table for God to help me to reach the two women who were sitting in front of me. In my response to what had been said by the friend of the women who had told, I wanted to ask the two of them one more question. My question was going to be directed to both women, but the question was really for the one woman that had been in our Bible studies and had on many occasions asked me to pray for her and even asked me questions about the Bible. I looked at her in her eyes and asked her this, "how does your belief work with the Word of God, because I know that you have been reading the Bible and have even had question for me in reference to it?"

I had listened to them quietly and patiently. It was now time to get back to the Word of God. This was when the one who had told on me to the officer that I was baptizing women in the shower spoke up. "I will tell you" she said, "I write the Scriptures on a piece of paper and put it in my shoe and walk on it.

This is how we get our prayers answered, not how you teach everyone." I started to respond and was interrupted by the voodoo queen. She looked at both of the women sitting in front of me and said, "Do you not know that the woman you are criticizing is anointed by the true and only God to teach His Word, and you are bringing condemnation on yourself by attacking her; because you are not attacking her, but God? Be careful to what you do, I know of your spells and tricks. I have used them also. They are of no good, but evil. God has showed me what you both had planned for Lanette when you sat down at this table with her; and I am here to tell you, you will not succeed."

Once these words were spoken, the two women sitting in front of me got up from the table and left. I looked at the voodoo queen and her daughter in amazement. They could tell I was confused as to what had happened. I did not even have to ask them to explain. They both proceeded to explain to me the story behind what the mother had done. The mother looked at me and said, "Lanette, we were both in our room when we felt God tell us to come to the common area, Lanette needs you. Once we reached the common area and saw who you were sitting with, we were then instructed to join you at the table. God showed me that the two women sitting with you had composed a plan to get you into a fight and get you sent to the shoe. Even if you would not fight, they would, to make sure you would be sent to the shoe. You know, as we do, no matter whom starts the fight, all involved are punished. They did not care if they were punished as long as you were also. God brought us to your aid to protect you."

I looked at her with a tear in my eye, not because I was sad; but thankful. God had brought both of these ladies full circle from where they used to be in voodoo, they were both serving the Lord now and God also used them to minister to me and protect me. The daughter then spoke up and said, "Lanette you gave us the good news of Jesus Christ. In doing this, we have been saved from an eternity in hell; we were honored when God called us to protect you." The mother then said, "You see we have the background and the understanding in what both of these women were involved in, and the both of them were still afraid of us from what we used to be. They don't believe in Jesus and His changing power so they didn't believe that we were any different from what they had known of us and our past. God used our past for His purpose today, which makes us both feel good, that God was able to use our past for His purpose and to protect you at the same time." As the tears rolled down my cheeks, this caused them both to ask me to please stop crying and assured me that no one was going to hurt me. I responded by telling them my tears were not of fear but of joy for them; this is when they started to cry also. We all hugged and I thanked them for being obedient to the call of God in what He had called them to do that day. I encouraged them to be mindful of God's voice; it would not be the last time that God would call on them. I reminded them that God can use everything for His glory, even our past no matter how dark it was.

Chapter 8

Oklahoma Detention Center "Con Air"

One night as I was preparing a Bible study for the ladies in the unit, God showed me I would be leaving Miami FDC soon. I was a little disappointed because we were still waiting to hear from the chaplain in the matter of baptizing the remaining women who had requested to be baptized. It looked like I would not be around to hear the decision or watch how God was going to provide for these women to be baptized.

But I remembered quickly what God had told me, "He would make sure the women were baptized." I gave it to God and left things with Him. That night after the study, I shared with the women what God had shared with me. I would be leaving soon. Many started to cry and say, "It can't be so." I reminded them that God had brought me there due to their prayers, and that God had been preparing some of them to teach and minister once I left, to the ones who needed to hear God's Word.

I reminded them that we are all here at Miami FDC for only a short while, and then we are all transferred to wherever we are designated. "Remember this, we all have to be mindful to prepare and lift up the ones that will be left behind when we leave, so they can also continue to teach the good news of Jesus Christ. This is what I have prayed for God to do with me in all of you, and He has answered my prayers. Many of you are ready to teach the Word of God, now it is time for you to trust God and do what He has called you to do and take a step of faith."

I reminded them that I was not the one they needed to depend on, but God.

Miami was only a transient prison; we all knew we were not to be there long; we would only be there long enough for our paper work to be processed in order for us to be designated and then we would move on to where we had been designated to. Once this was done, we then would be transferred. We had a few women at Miami that were waiting to go to court still, but there were not many. Most of us had already been to court and sentencing. We were only waiting for our paper work to be finished. I knew I was going to Coleman, Florida; this was in the Orlando area. It was only three days later when my name was called to pack out.

When you are going to be transported, you are only notified the day before, for security reasons. You then have to get all your items ready to pack. This is called pack out. All of your things are then put into boxes in order for them to be shipped to your next destination. You are not allowed to pack out everything. Any open items such as shampoo, lotion etc. You were not allowed to pack out and most would leave these items behind for the ones who were not able to buy things off of commissary. When you are called to pack out you are not told where you are going or what time you will be leaving.

You may know where you are to end up from what the judge ordered, but you have no idea where you may have to go to get there. If the particular prison you were assigned to happens to be full, you would be sent somewhere else. I was to go to Coleman, Fl in order for me to be close to my family. This was still a 3 ½ hour drive for my family, but it was the closest federal camp in the area.

A Journey Behind Prison Walls

I found out later it was also the best; even in this God was taking care of me.

I was mentoring several women during my stay at Miami FDC in how to study the Word of God and how to do Bible studies allowing God to lead them. They had done several Bible studies while I was at Miami FDC and I assured them that they were all ready and that they would do fine. All my things were packed, and it was my last night that I was going to be at Miami FDC. I stood up in front of all the women that I had come to know and call friends to do my last Bible study. I was full of emotion, bittersweet as you may say.

I taught on listening to God and trusting in Him. At the end of the study and after the altar call, I opened the altar for anyone that needed prayer. I was surprised to see every woman in the place come forward. I prayed for every woman who came. I looked up and noticed that the voodoo queen and her daughter were in line. They had both blessed me on many occasions while I was at Miami FDC. They both had become not only my sisters in the Lord, but my friends. I had to trust Jesus in reaching out to the both of them and because I did, I was being blessed to watch them trust and reach out to God even as I was leaving.

God was again teaching me to trust Him with everything. This was all by His power not mine; I was only the vessel He was using. Now they were both coming for me to pray for them before I left. I was so blessed and emotional by watching them walk with Christ. The daughter stepped forward first; and I asked her what she was seeking prayer for. The daughter wanted guidance from God in how to weather the time ahead of her and the sentencing pending against her. I shared with her to be honest in everything she did, and leave it all in God's hands. We do have consciences that we must walk through due to the decisions that we make. But when we give our lives to God and trust Him, He will give us the grace that we need to make it through. I explained to her that I know that sometimes we go through things that we can't see what we may have done to cause the storm, and other times we know what we have done and are praying for mercy, but even in that we must trust God's love for us and know that He wants only good for us and accept whatever it is that God allows. "There is something to learn in everything we go through," I told her, "but we will only learn it if we surrender it to God and listen. God is doing this for me and He will do the same for you. You have to trust in God in whatever sentence you are given and ask God to help you walk through it."

As tears rolled down her face she looked at me and said, "Lanette, I wish I had met someone like you before my mother and I had gone through this situation; we may not have even been where we are today if we had. Our choices may have been different and the road we are traveling today could have been a different one." "I assured her that I too had gone through these kind of thoughts, but to be careful looking back on what you should have done except to ask God for forgiveness; it can throw you in to a tail spin if you ponder too long on things you can't change." I continued by telling her, "ask God for forgiveness and receive whatever is ahead of you, and watch God bless you and your mother."

As the daughter stepped away, the mother stepped forward and her request was very different. She was asking God to help her with the burden as to what she had gotten her daughter into. It was tearing her apart inside to watch her daughter go through everything they were going through. She felt it was all her fault, and she did not think she would ever forgive herself; and how could her daughter ever forgive her. I shared with her that she also was going to have to be honest in everything concerning the case, no matter what she thought the consequences may be. She was going to have to surrender everything to God, and He will be faithful to give you the strength you need to walk through everything; but you must trust God with the outcome no matter what it may be. After I had prayed for them both, they walked away together hand in hand. I could see a strange peace come over the both of them. I knew this was God. Even though they had a long journey ahead of them, they were not alone now, God was with them both.

As I finished praying for each woman that had come forward, one by one each woman was calling out to the Lord in a very personal way, but also each one was similar because the time for each woman was the same. As I needed God to help me get through this journey behind prison walls, they needed God to do the same thing for them. This was why God was able to use me; I was only able to help them because I myself was in the same situation as them. God was giving me an understanding of their situation by me living it myself, and because of this, I was able to help them; this was only because God had first taught me. So often when we are caught up in a storm, we are only consumed with ourselves.

We do not learn much because we are so consumed, and, because of this, we are not able to teach anyone anything because we have not learned it first. And if we do learn anything, most of the time it is not everything that God intended us to learn because we were not submissive to Him completely. And then, because of the condition of our heart, what we do learn is short lived; it doesn't stay with us long enough to produce any fruit. This is not the intention of God; a storm is not to destroy us but to bring us closer to Him. So many times we want the testimony without going through the test, this is not possible. I would like to encourage you in your storm. Seek out God and He will not let you down. God was with me every moment during my Journey Behind prison Walls and He will be with you on your journey through your storm if you let Him. But it is up to you. Surrender and let God have His way. He will not let you down, all you have to do is trust Him and sit back and watch God work it all out for His glory.

My life verse is

Roman 8:28 *And we know that God causes all things to work together for good to those who love God, to those who are called according to His purpose.* (NASB)

This verse was my life verse before I went into prison. But now the verse was taking on its full meaning to me. We have to trust God in all things no matter what it looks like. I knew I loved God, and He loved me, so I had to trust Him and believe that this was all going to work out for His glory, if I would only let Him have His way. This was not easy for me. I had to put it on the altar daily and ask God to help me with my faith and my fear. Being in prison caused me to have a lot of fear, which is understandable. I was not sure what was going to happen from day to day, I had to trust God in a way I had never trusted Him before, not only day to day but sometimes moment to moment. This was what I had tried to leave with the women of Miami FDC before I had to leave them. In what I had witnessed on my last night at Miami FDC, God had answered my prayers. The women that had been with me in the Chapel on my last night at Miami FDC - it was clear to whom they were trusting - it was God. This gave me peace and great joy as I prepared for my journey to leave the next day.

As I went back to my cell after the service, my last at Miami FDC, I could not help myself to look back over all that God had done through me and in me. You have to understand that, yes, many were blessed by the teachings that God gave me, and even saved. But what God had done in me was much more of a miracle. Yes, I had been changed in many ways. I had learned so much while I was at Miami FDC, and I had no idea at the time how much more God had for me on this Journey through Prison walls. There was so much in me that needed to be removed and healed, and Jesus had a plan already to help me with it all. All I had to do was surrender and let Him have his way; I was learning how to do that every day. Again how about you? Is God trying to get your attention within the storm that you may currently be in? Things that need to be removed or healed in you, but you keep ignoring His call and make excuses. I would like to encourage you as you read about my Journey, that you allow God to guide you and direct your path into a new awareness of Him and what He is trying to do in your life. Trust me you will never regret it. God's Word tells us He will never leave us or forsake us

Deuteronomy 31:6 *Be strong and courageous, do not be afraid or tremble at them, for the Lord your God is the one who goes with you. He will not fail you or forsake you."* (NASB)

He is waiting for you to let Him in and bring you to a better place with Him. He did this with me, and, most of the time, I did not even understand what was going on. I surrendered and then one day, when I looked in the mirror, I realized I was not the same. I did not hurt the way I used to; my pain was beginning to diminish. It was not all gone yet, I still had many things to work on and I am thankful to the patience that God had with me and still does. We are all under construction, and, if we would only start everyday with the expectation in letting God make us a little better than the day before He will never let us down; key here is letting Him.

The officers came in to my cell and woke me up about 4:00 AM, along with some others that were also leaving that same day. Now all of us were not going to be on the same transport, depending on where we were going we could travel by plane or van; we would not know until we were loaded. I had been told that the women going to Coleman, Fl most of the time would travel by van. The officers could even choose to not have us in shackles or hand cuffs due to our camp status. Camp status meant low security risk, once at the camp we would not even have a fence or locked doors to hold us. We were on our own honor system to not leave. I was not sure how I was going to be traveling since we are not told until the last minute, van or plan "called con air" but I was praying for it to be by van.

Due to not knowing how I was going to be traveling and how long it would be, I decided to not eat anything for breakfast, so I would not have to use the restroom; I only drank enough water to take my medication. I was only allowed to travel with my travel papers and my inhaler and contact container. I had written all important phone numbers on the back of my travel papers so I would have them with me. Everything else was in the boxes that would be shipped to my destination. I had been told that it could take up to three months to catch up with you.

Now the contacts that I had been wearing were disposable. They were to only last only two weeks. I did not have my glasses with me and my daughters tried to bring them to me, but were not allowed to do so. I had been at Miami FDC for almost three months; it was only by the grace of God that my contacts were lasting as long as they were. I did buy a pair of reading glasses from the commissary for a dollar. I used them a lot to give my eyes a rest from the contacts, but they were not that good. I could not bring the glasses with me either that I had bought from the commissary since they were not prescription. I could not see well without the glasses or contacts. Because of this, I was very careful in taking care of both. Once they were gone, I would not be able to read or write at all. This was a big concern of mine. They do have eye doctors inside the prison system, but I was not able to get an appointment. I was told that it could wait until I reached Coleman Camp. I had to give this also to God, again drawing me closer to Him and trusting in Him.

The officers took us all downstairs to the intake/outtake; it was the same place that I had been processed in when I first came to Miami FDC. I had only seen this place one other time, when they took me out to have a mammogram. This time would be different. I would only be around other inmates and officers, not sure why that was more comforting to me, but it was or at least I thought it was going to be at the time. We were all taken into a room and told to strip so we could be searched. We then were give different clothes to travel in, all the way down to our underwear.

We were then escorted back into a small cell to wait for further instructions. I am not sure how many of us there were, but the cell was full. All the other cells were full of men. We had one woman in our group whose husband was in one of the other cells. The officers keep yelling at them both to stop communicating with one another. She was crying, and I could tell she was afraid; I was not able to talk to her to comfort her because she only spoke Spanish. One of the other women in the cell that knew her explained to me the situation and why she kept trying to talk to her husband even with the risk of getting in trouble from the officers. Her husband and she were both being transported to prison, and they were not going to be able to talk or see each other for many years, neither of them cared if they were yelled at by the officers, due to the time they were going to be apart from one another; this was their last chance to talk, and they were taking advantage of it no matter the risk. I told the woman, who had been explaining their situation to me, to tell them that I would be praying for them. The woman, with tears in her eyes knowing she was not going to see her husband for many years, said thank you.

We had another young woman in the cell with us that one of the officers came and pulled her out of the cell in order for the doctor to see her before she was transported. She was being transported back to the state that had initiated the charges against her. She had not even gone to court to hear the charges or be able to post bail yet. She had been unable to speak to a lawyer either. She was in

Florida for a visit of some sort and was arrested at a friend's house. All I remember about her charges was that it had something to do with an old boyfriend. She was not even seeing him anymore, and had not seen him within the year. She told me that she had no idea what the prosecutor was talking about in reference to the charges, but they would not to listen to her.

The officers brought her back to the cell and she was crying. She came over to me and sat beside me. She was one of the women that had been in our Bible study, and I knew she loved God and was trying to trust Him in the midst of this storm she was going through. She looked up at me and said, "I am pregnant, and they want me to have an abortion." She looked at me and said, "They want me to kill my baby. I don't belong here, and I want to go back to my life. I have not been found guilty of anything and they want to kill my baby." I took her by the hand and looked into her eyes and told her, "They cannot make you do anything that you don't want to." I told her to trust God and He will get you through this and to not let them intimidate you. She showed me the paper work that they had given her; it was paper work to give them permission to do an abortion.

She said she did not want to sign it. I told her, "Do not sign it then." I asked her if I could pray for her and her baby and she said yes. When women are found to be pregnant once inside of prison they have to be tended to completely different and the prison has a lot more liability on them on behalf of the child. She was taken from the cell and was not transported that day with us. I prayed for her often during the next week that God would strengthen her and keep her and her baby safe; she and I never crossed paths again.

We all were dressed and ready to go, as ready as we could be that is. All the men were loaded into the buses first. I learned that we women, the twelve of us, were going to have to wait a lot for the men. There were about 200 of them, and it was policy to process them first due to the large number of them, for security reasons. Once the men were all loaded, then the women were loaded into two vans also. We had not been told where we were going or what time we would arrive, security reasons again. We were all given a bag of lunch to eat later that day during the trip. We all had a sandwich, cookies and a carton of juice and cheese crackers.

Remember, I had not eaten anything that morning due to not wanting to have to use the restroom. I had taken my blood pressure pill that morning, and it was a diuretic. I was concerned about the availability of a restroom on this trip. Inmates are not allowed to use the restrooms whenever they felt like it while being transported. We had to go through a process. It normally called for us to wait, and this was an area of weakness for me. First of all, we had to ask permission, and then you had to be taken and supervised, and, depending on how we were traveling, this could pose a problem. I was nervous to where and how we were traveling and what kind of facilities were going to be available. Until these concerns were answered, I chose not to eat or drink. I kept the sack lunch to have something to eat once these concerns were put to rest.

We started to drive, and I noticed after about thirty minutes that we were driving up on to an airfield. I could see the buses with the men in them pulling onto the airfield ahead of us. I thought to myself, we all must be traveling together on a plane. This was a small airport, not the big ones most of us fly out of. I then saw a lot of officers standing on the airfield with shotguns. This, in itself, brought tears to my eyes. Those are for us, I thought to myself. Inside of the prison you can separate yourself from the embarrassment of being labeled an inmate. You can even limit how much contact you have with officers, and I did. It was like a community inside. You live everyday with the task to do and don't think about the outside, the best you can anyway. It makes it easier and you don't miss the outside as much, but you do have your moments; you can't get away from it all the time.

But once out in the public, and face to face with officers yelling at you and holding shotguns to protect the public from you, you cannot escape the humiliation of it all. I was feeling all the humiliation overwhelming me all at one time sitting in the van. I did not know still where we were going, and why did I need to go on an airplane to get to Coleman, Fl. I was beginning to get nervous, and I could not stop the tears. The men were loaded first, of course, then us women. When we were told to get out of the van, we were constantly yelled at by the officers nonstop. We could not determine what we were being yelled at for because we were all doing everything that we were told to do; but we were yelled at anyway. "Keep your eyes forward, don't talk" was what the officers yelled at us every moment, even though we were not doing any of it. I know now that it was only to intimidate us and keep us submissive to their authority; it worked.

The wind was blowing terribly hard; we were not allowed to have hair ties in our hair while being transported, so everyone's hair was blowing everywhere. All the women with long hair were trying to hold their hair out of their eyes in order to see where they were walking. They were yelled at by the officers to "stop. Let it blow, let it go," they would yell. Many of the women did not understand the instructions of the officers because they only spoke Spanish and other languages. The officers did not care; they yelled louder, women began to cry.

This is when some women within our group would try to motion, in hand language to the other women who did not understand what the officers were telling them to do. These women were yelled at also. Then they started to cry. This was all familiar to me. Remember the van I was in, in the beginning going to Miami FDC when all I did was cry? Here we were again. I am not sure what all the other women were feeling at the moment, but I felt like an animal with no value. I prayed for God to help us all through all that we were going through and all that was ahead of us.

I tried to hold it together but it was not easy. Once on the plane, we could not buckle ourselves in. We had to wait for the officers to come by and do it for us. The men were all in the back of the plane and us women were upfront with the bulk of the officers. This was okay unless you needed to go to the restroom. The restroom for inmates was located in the back of the plane, and to get to the restroom you had to walk by all of the men. The restroom in the front or the airplane was for the officers only. Once on the plane we were all told the rules, and it was simple - no talking and if you have a question raise your hand and an officer would come to you. This was mainly in the case if you needed to use the restroom.

Now all the women that were in the front of the plane were told they could talk as long as they kept it low and did not get out of hand, but under no circumstance was any of us to talk to the men behind us. We had one man up front with us; he had what they called a black box on his hands. I was told by one of the women sitting next to me this was used for inmates who in the past had tried to escape. He did not seem to let it upset him. He thought everything was funny. He kept the officers upset with him the whole trip and he looked like he enjoyed every moment. The woman who had a husband in one of the other cells back at Miami FDC, that was in trouble for taking to him all the time was also on the plane, and was sitting close to her husband. They got in trouble a few times for talking and then the husband was eventually moved to the back of the plane.

One of the women, who spoke Spanish, told me more about the husband and wife who were on the plane together. The wife was frightened because her husband was everything to her. He had always taken care of everything for her, and she was not going to be able see or talk to him for more than five years. She did not know how she was going to make it without him. She was in this situation because of him and what he had done, but she did not seem to care, she was not even mad at him.

I saw a lot of this inside of prison - women caught up in something due to the activity of their husbands or boyfriends; being in the wrong place at the wrong time with the wrong person. It reminded me of what God's Word says in reference to the importance of the heart of the man who is called to be the head of his house. It is so important that the men of our homes are centered on Jesus. If they are not, the whole family can fall apart. I was witnessing this right before my eyes. The enemy is attacking our homes, and it is starting at the head; our men. It makes sense. If the head falls, the rest of the body will follow, referencing the family unit. I was witnessing so many women who had chosen the men in their lives for all the wrong reasons, and they and their children were now paying a high price for her choices. Life can be hard at times, and God tells us in His Word that we will have trials and tribulations, but, if we would only trust God in everything we do, we would not have to go through all the storms that many of us go through.

This reinforced the importance to me of being alert to the enemy, and that he will try to attack at any weakness he can find in us. We have to be alert and centered on Jesus Christ at all times in order for us to not be fooled by the devil's foolishness. Christ will shine on all the darkness in our lives that the enemy tries to bring about, but we first have to invite Christ in, and surrender all to Him. I prayed for that woman as I sat in my seat, but after the plane ride would come to an end I would never see her again. I began to notice that God was allowing a lot of people to come into and out of my life for only a brief moment. I was being called to intercede for them in prayer. God was teaching me about the importance of intercession. This was not all about me, but all those who needed a touch from God; I was being blessed in the midst of it all in being used by God to pray for them. I was also realizing that it did not matter how big or small the task was that God called us to do. It was all important.

On the plane, I was sitting next to a woman that was on her way to a drug rehab boot camp. She was concerned if she was going to be able to make it at the camp due to her large size. After talking to her for a while, I found out she loved God and was putting it all in His hands. She, too, was answering charges due to an old boyfriend and the activity he was involved in, but she admitted that she did notice he made a lot of money. She knew he had to be doing something wrong to make all the money he had, but she enjoyed the money and turned her head. She had not been doing drugs for a long time. Then she slipped, and started doing them again; this was why she was going to rehab.

This was an old case, which she thought was all over. It looked to her like she was not going to be charged. But then the charges were brought against her all of a sudden. She shared with me that she believed it was all God, and He was saving her from walking down the wrong path again with drugs. She had been praying that God would help her get back on track and clean again, even though she had to answer to old charges that she thought were gone. She was also going to rehab which was going to help her get a fresh start without drugs. We don't always get our prayers answered the way we think they will be, but God will answer every prayer one by one, but in His way and what is best for us. When she finished the boot camp she was going to be allowed to go home on probation. All she had to do was stay off drugs. She had her second chance. I prayed for her, and once we reached our destination, we would have many more conversations about our Lord and how to trust Him in all things.

I asked one of the officers if he was allowed to tell us were we were going yet, and that is when I was told that we were on our way to Oklahoma. I was in shock! What in the world would I be going to Oklahoma for? That is a long way from where I was supposed to go. All kinds of things - started going through my mind. Maybe the paper work had gotten messed up and I was going to be sent to

Oklahoma to stay and not go to Coleman, Fl at all. The system had messed up other paper work before, why not mine. The devil will attack us in many ways. I lowered my head and started to cry. I tried to stop the tears, but could not. An officer came over to me and asked if I was okay. I told him I was supposed to go to Coleman, Fl, not Oklahoma. I would be so far from my family, I would never see them. He looked at me and told me that a lot go to Oklahoma, and then they go to their place of designation. He told me to go to the officer in charge once I was in my unit and ask them to check if my designation had been changed.

I was still frightened but the officer's words did help. He was kind and compassionate to me; he treated me like a human being, and I needed that at that moment. That is when the Lord started to talk to me. "Why are you frightened? Did I not tell you I would take care of you? Do you not trust me still?" I did not know how to answer. All I could say was, "my Lord, you are correct. Please help me with my fear. My fear causes me to doubt you Lord when I should not." When I was finished with this short prayer, I felt peace come all over me and my spirit was at rest, even though the tears still flowed. All I had to do is acknowledge my weakness to God and ask for His help, and He came in and helped me with it. The fear was consuming me that quickly, but, because I called on the Lord, I was no longer consumed by the fear. Christ shined a light on a place the devil was trying to make dark. We will feel fear, but we don't have to allow it to consume us; but we must ask God to help us with this and not try to face it alone. I was learning that I could not let my guard down for one moment. If I did, the devil would be there waiting to punch.

I was still concerned with where I was going and why and what would happen once we arrived in Oklahoma, but I was able to control my emotions somewhat in reference to it all because I was leaning on God. I continued to pray to God, "Oh my Lord; thank you. Please forgive me in my weakness and show me how I can grow in this area." The tears then stopped, and I was able to raise my head and endure the rest of the trip.

I started to talk to the woman that was sitting next to me again. She needed to use the restroom, but could not use the one on the airplane due to her size, she could not fit. I could see the fear in her face. Was she going to make it? I asked her could I pray for her again and she said yes. Once I was done praying for her, she smiled at me, and it looked like God had given her the peace she needed. She was resting on her Lord, Jesus Christ.

I had come to the point in the trip I had been dreading. I needed to use the restroom. Now I had done pretty well up to this point. It was late in the afternoon and I had never gone this long without using the restroom before due to the medication that I was on. I know with all my heart it was because of my Lord. "Thank you Jesus." I had no idea to how much longer the trip would be before we would land. I needed to go ahead and have an officer take me to the back of the plane where the restrooms were located. I raised my hand as we had been instructed to do in the beginning of the flight, an officer came over to me, and I told him I needed to use the restroom. He told me to wait one moment and he would get a women officer.

A women officer came over to me and asked me again if I needed to use the restroom. I said yes. She loosened my seat belt and disconnected me from the metal loop that my shackles were connected to on the floor of the plane, in order for me to stand up. We were all shackled to the plane so we were not able to move much. Remember, I am also handcuffed and my hands are shackled to my waist and my feet have shackles on them also. Moving was not that easy, and I was already wondering how I was going to use the restroom with all this on me. I was thinking to myself, maybe they will remove it for a brief moment so I could use the restroom. This was hopeful thinking anyway. The officer instructed me to keep my eyes looking forward and to not talk to any of the men when we walked to the back of the airplane. As I walked the long aisle to the back of the airplane, I could see the men looking at me from top to the bottom. It made me nervous and uncomfortable and I tried to walk as fast I could without falling. I kept thinking to myself, don't fall. The walk seemed to be as long as a mile. I was glad once we reached the back of the airplane. It was not long that I had my answer if they would remove anything so I could use the restroom - the answer was no!

The officer instructed me to not lock the door and to knock on the door if I needed any help. She was not allowed to remove anything because it was policy. I understood even though it did not make me happy. Once in the restroom, tears started to roll down my face. I did not have any idea how this was going to work. I started by first undoing my shirt, going back and forth with one hand to other lifting it upwards. Once this was accomplished, I took a short breather and then started on the pants. Using the same method I pulled them down going back and forth between hands. I finally was able to sit down, and use the restroom. I sat still for a moment, saying a little prayer and asking God to help me with this also. It was overwhelming for me and I needed His help. My asthma had not been good with all the stress and I would get winded easily. I was also dreading the walk back to the front of the airplane.

I had rested enough. I had gotten my wind back and now it was time to get everything back in place in preparation to go back to my seat. This was much more difficult, I started with the pants. I had to take several breaks, because I was getting quite winded due to my asthma. It seemed like I was not getting any where. I would pull up one side and then go to the other side. This is when I would notice that the side I had already pulled up had gone right back down. I was making a lot of noise going back and forth inside of the small restroom. This was when the officer knocked on the door and asked if I needed any help. I answered, "Yes, please," and she opened the door. She stepped into the small restroom, but left the door ajar. She then helped me put my clothing back in order. Again, I was humiliated. I could not even dress myself without help. But God gave me peace and He used the officer to do that. She looked at me and said with a smile, "you did pretty well. You did not need my help as soon as most do. Don't feel bad. It is impossible to put your clothing back in place with all of these shackles and handcuffs on you." She then stated, "Don't feel bad. This is why I am here to help you, not only guard you. If that was the case, they could have used a male officer. Remember we all are only doing our job. It is not personal." I felt much better and was actually laughing some inside. The walk back to the front of the plane was much easier; God had heard my prayer.

The Lord will answer your prayers always. It may not be in the way you or I think He will. I did not even consider that He would use the very guard that was watching me to give me peace, but He did. I felt much better. I had faced one of my fears that I had on this whole trip - going to the restroom. God helped me, even in this. I now could eat my food, and boy was I hungry. I was able to sit in peace and enjoy my small lunch that had been given to me. I heard God say, "you could have had this a long time ago, and if you will only trust me this journey will be a lot more bearable." I smiled to myself and answered, "Yes, Lord."

About an hour later, I heard an announcement over the intercom. We were all being told to get ready for landing. "What is next, Lord?" I cried. I was learning quickly that I needed to take things one minute at a time. I could not predict in any way what I was about to encounter from one moment to the next. We didn't really have anything to do to prepare for landing. We all had been seatbelt in once we were seated on the plane from the start, and we could not undo the seatbelt ourselves. But the announcement did tell us we are finally at Oklahoma. My stomach was full of butterflies in wonder what was ahead of us all now. I had no idea to how long it was going to take to process us up to the unit that we all would be assigned to. We all had not had much to eat other than the bag that was given to us at the beginning of the flight. None of us had any water all day, we only had the carton of juice that was in our lunch bag, and I had given that away to someone early in the day, because I knew I was not going to drink it. I was hungry and thirsty, but there was no telling to how long it would be before we would get anything to eat.

Once we landed and the doors were opened, of course, the men were unloaded first as we women waited. Once the men were all out of the plane and taken to cells, then we women were told to stand to our feet. When I stood up and stepped into the aisle way, I was behind the only other women that came from my unit at Miami FDC and her name was Malone. She did not speak much English and she looked as frightened as me or more. We were told to get in a line and follow the officers inside. This is when I noticed how big the prison was. We were not at an airfield as before. We were stepping off the plane directly into the prison. We were walking right through a tunnel connected to the plane and the prison, like you would see at an airport. Once out of the tunnel we stepped into a large hallway. It looked like something in the movies. You could hear all our shackles dragging on the floor. The sound engulfed the hallway and rang in my ears.

Once to the end of the hall, there was a small step to step up on. Then you were able to walk onto a long ledge of wood that would put you up high enough for the officers to remove your shackles. Malone was in front of me and the officer was telling her to spread her legs so he could remove the shackles. She did not understand what the officer was telling her to do, and the officer yelled even louder at her. She began to cry. I motioned to her and showed her with my body what he was trying to tell her to do and she complied. Once the shackles were removed and handcuffs off, we were all taken into a small cell to wait to be processed. The women were in one cell all together and all the men had to be separated into many cells. You could hear the men yelling, and the officers telling them to be quiet.

The cell we were in had two long metal benches up against the walls, one toilet and a sink on other wall. This cell had no divider by the toilet to keep you from being seen while using it. The woman that had been sitting next to me on the plane needed to go so badly but had not been able to due to her size. We all let her go first. We all noticed that we did not have much toilet tissue. We all had to share and only use a little. I have to say that inside of prison there is a sisterhood among the women inside to watch out and help one another, no matter your background or faith. Each one of us took turns using the restroom while others would watch for officers since we had no cover for privacy, and the officers that were overseeing us were all men from what we could tell.

Within an hour, we were all brought a bag of food for dinner. It was about 7:00 PM and we had been traveling since about 9:00AM. We were all hungry, but once the bag was opened, it was not much to look at. We all had two slices of bread and one slice of cheese, some crackers and a carton of milk. We also had some kind of cookies for dessert. We all did not care what it was; we were all hungry and ate what was given to us. Most of us had learned to eat what was available. In prison, the food was not normally really good. You learn to eat for nourishment, not enjoyment. The officers did bring us in some bottled water, and that is what I wanted the most and I was happy and thankful for it. We all ate and drank what we had been given and some even shared what they did not like or traded with others that were willing to trade.

Once we all had eaten, we all started to talk and shared where we were from and where we were supposed to be going. We had all been on the plane together, but we all could not talk to each other. We were only allowed

A Journey Behind Prison Walls

to talk to the one that was next to you on the plane. Each woman introduced herself and where she was from, the prison that is, and where she was on her way to. This is when I learned from some of the other women with us, that the prison we were all at was one of the largest transient prisons in the country. Prisoners from all over would come through the Oklahoma prison, and only be there for a few days or weeks and then on to their destinations. Many of the women with me in the cell had been at Oklahoma before and were preparing the rest of us in what to expect.

One of the women in the group was from Coleman, Fl. She had gotten on the plane when we made a stop. We had made one stop someplace - not sure where we were. Some inmates got off and some inmates were brought on to the plane. She was one that got on; she was on her way to Miami for a hearing on a motion that had been filed by her lawyers. She had cancer and they were petitioning the court for early release. If she was not granted the petition, she would die in prison. She told me all about Coleman, what to do and not to do. She told me it was nothing like I had seen already, to keep trusting God, and it would be a lot better once I was at Coleman. She sang in the choir at Coleman and was very active in the church there. I enjoyed talking to her, but I could see in her eyes, she did not have much longer to live. She was only in her forties. I asked her could I pray for her and she said she would like that a lot. She had a peace over her; she knew where she was going - to heaven. She was only trying to go home before she died for her family's sake. She did not want them to have to deal with losing her while she was in prison, but at home with them. This is what I prayed for her, along with healing.

I did find out later once at Coleman that she had made it home. She had many friends at Coleman and her family was keeping them all informed of her progress. The judge did grant her motion to let her go home early. This is not done often - God heard our prayer. It was not much later that I heard she had passed away and gone home to be with the Lord. It was hard on many at Coleman that knew her. I thanked God for allowing me to meet her and pray for her. Again God was showing me the importance of intercessory prayer, and to not ever take for granted even the brief encounter that we may have with anyone. We all have to be aware that God will and can allow brief encounters with others in our life, only for the reason for us to pray for them. We have to be aware of everything around us at all times. If not, we will miss an opportunity to be used by God to bless one of His children and be blessed ourselves in return.

Now that we were all together, one of the other women, who spoke English and Spanish, could translate for Malone and me. I was so happy for her. I could see the fear in her eyes earlier when the officer was yelling at her. She now thanked me for helping her. I let her know that we were here together and for her to let me know if she needed anything. "You are not in this alone," I told her. She smiled and gave me a hug.

We all had been at Oklahoma for a long time in the same cell and no one had come and told us anything. We were all cold and tired, and we were all relieved when a woman officer came into our cell finally. She instructed us to follow her. She took us all into a large room to be strip searched and gave us all some clothing to change into. Yes, here we go again, even though we had been in the custody of the US marshals all day, on a plane, we had to be searched again. Once searched and dressed, we were then taken back to the same cell we were in. Then one by one our names were called to be seen by the doctor. Each time you go into a new facility, you have to be seen by the doctor of that facility for your medicine to be reviewed, in preparation for them to be able to give you your medicine while you are at their facility. Once we were all seen by the doctor, we were all then taken upstairs to the unit we were assigned to.

We all stepped into the elevator and walked to the back of the elevator and faced the wall. The officer noticed what we had all done and responded to us in this way, "we don't do that here ladies; you can turn around and face me." We all turned around and faced him at the same time. He then told us this, "we here at this prison give you respect and you in turn give us respect. We don't know why you are here, and it is not any of our business. But we believe everyone deserves respect no matter what you have done or not done. All you have to do is go by the rules while you are here and your stay will be pleasant and uneventful." We all looked at each other in surprise. This was a nice thing to hear coming from an officer - something most of us were not used to. He told us that we only had thirty minutes until lockdown. Once we were in our unit, we needed to take care of whatever we needed to quickly, or it would have to wait until morning. He told us where the showers were located in case any of us wanted to take a shower before lockdown, but we would have to move quickly or it would have to wait until morning.

Once we reached our unit and the door was opened, it was amazing to me. It was even bigger than Miami, three tiers, and there were women everywhere. The officer told us what cells we were all assigned to; and again I was on the top bunk. I took my assignment and went off to find my cell. I put my things on the bed and my new Bunkie was not in the room at the time, I would meet her later. I went downstairs and asked the officer "where can I find a Bible?" He told me that there were a lot of them on the book cart over on the other side of the room. I walked over to the book cart and could not find one. I looked all over, up and down, and then finally I found one in the back on the bottom of the shelf. "Praise God," I said to myself. I then heard the officer yell, "lockdown; everyone to your cells." I took the Bible and went to my cell; it was upstairs back by the showers. I found out that each cell had its own light switch within it, and we were allowed to keep the light on as long as we wanted to as long as both women within the cell agreed to leave it on. This was different from Miami FDC. The lights there were turned off at 11PM and if you wanted to read or do anything after lights out, you had to buy a nightlight off commissary and it ran on batteries. It could get expensive to use.

Now in using the light here after hours, both roommates had to agree to leave it on or it would have to be turned off. My Bunkie came into the room, and I introduced myself and she filled me in on a few things that I should know. She also told me it was okay with her to keep the light on as long as I wanted to. The light did not bother her, and she could sleep with it on or off. We both talked for a while, and I learned she was also a Christian but she did not read the Bible much, but she understood she needed to. She was back inside on a probation violation and was waiting to be shipped back to the prison she had been in before to finish the rest of her time due to the violation. It looked like she and I was going to get along fine and maybe God could use me to help her find her way back into God's Word, so He could help her on the rest of her journey. I could tell by talking to her, she did not have much of a relationship with God, but she knew she needed to but did not know how. It was late and I could tell she was tired. She and I would have time in the morning to talk. I said goodnight and climbed up into my bed with the light on and my Bible. I prayed God would give me a chance before she left to help her lean on Him.

A lesson learned, with a gift of coffee

As I sat in my bed, I looked around the room to get equated with my new surroundings. I was not sure to how long I was going to be at Oklahoma, but I had to make the best of things no matter how long I was going to be there. The cell was equipped with a toilet, sink and even a mirror, of course one that could not be broken. There was also a small desk located over by the cell door. I could see my roommate had all ready taken it over because all her things were scattered all over it. I also noticed a chair at the end of the bunk beds.

This, too, had some of my Bunkie's clothing hanging on it to dry. My cell was located at the end of a hallway on a corner, with the showers only a few steps away. I had noticed this before I had even stepped into the cell. As I sat and looked around the cell, I could hear the guards walking up and down the halls counting. I could hear their footsteps, but most of all I could hear their keys. This would ring in my ears for hours. As they came to each door to count, they would also lock the door. This is a sound you would think you would get used to after a while, but I had not gotten used to it yet. It sent chills down my spine every time I would hear the clang of the door being locked.

To take my attention off of what was going on outside of my door; I picked up the Bible that I had found downstairs on the book cart. It was a red Gideon Bible, the kind you would find inside nightstands in hotels. In opening the Bible, I did something I do not normally do. I turned to the back and looked at the cardboard backing and read what was written there. When I opened it, I noticed something was written in red and it said "the reason you are here is read Isaiah 61:1" I felt an overwhelming urge that I needed to read this Scripture right away. And this is what I read.

Isaiah 61:1 *The Spirit of the Lord God is upon me, because the Lord has anointed me to bring good news to the afflicted; He has sent me to bind up the brokenhearted, to proclaim liberty to captives and freedom to prisoners;(NASB)*

Now as I read this, I could feel the presence of the Lord in my cell, it was breathtaking. I had chills all over me; all I could do was praise the Lord right in my prison bunk as tears ran down my face. It was so clear what God was saying to me, not that I had not heard this from God before, but God was making sure I understood what it was that He was calling me to do. I was to proclaim His good news to all who would listen. So many were prisoners, and God was not referring to the prison bars and shackles that held us all currently within prison. God was referring to something much more important - our souls - our relationship with Him!

After I had read the Bible a little while longer, I climbed down from the bunk and removed my contacts in preparation for bed. My Bunkie was already sleeping and I could see out the window of my cell door that all the other lights were already turned off. I did not know how long I had been praying and reading. All I know is that I had an overwhelming peace and joy within me.

I climbed back up into my bunk, and my first night at Oklahoma was spent sleeping well, all due to the time I had spent with God in His Word and the red writing on the back that I had found. I was no longer frightened or concerned to how long I was going to be at Oklahoma, or what was ahead of me. Now nothing had changed, but again I had. God had touched me again in such a special way my first night at Oklahoma. I was so thankful for His touch and guidance, and I had no idea to how much I needed it until He had given it.

As I lay asleep in my bunk, I was woken by the noise of the officers opening all the cell doors. As I rolled over and looked down from my bunk, I could see my roommate standing at the sink and brushing her teeth. She said, "Get up Lanette, breakfast is served in a few minutes. If you are not present to receive your breakfast when it is being passed out, you will not eat until lunch. No one is allowed to collect it for other; you have to be there yourself." I was definitely hungry; I had not eaten much the day before. And I was hoping, from the bottom of my heart, that we would be given some kind of coffee.

I jumped down from my bunk, and did as my Bunkie - brushed my teeth quickly and combed my hair and put my contacts in and out the door to join all the other in a very long line. As I walked down the stairs, I could see Malone already in line. I did not dare join her where she was in line. Others would not have appreciated me cutting in before them. Eating time was the highlight for most in prison. You learned quickly to go by the rules and take your turn - first come, first served. I would catch up with her after I had gotten my breakfast.

Once I had gotten to the front of the line, the officer handed me my breakfast trays. It was two trays and a bag of milk on top of it. The two trays were one for cold and the other one was for hot food. The milk was in a sealed bag. This was strange to me, and once I had joined Malone, I asked some of the other women sitting with her why the milk was in a bag and not a carton. They told me that it was due to the way milk was given to the prison here.

It comes in big vats. They put it in sealed bags because it is the easiest way to transport it to us, and the cheapest. As I opened my cold tray first, I could see some cereal and fruit, along with salt and pepper and plastic ware to eat with. Then I found the prize - a small package of coffee. I was so excited. I paused a moment and thanked God for hearing my prayer, even for coffee. In the hot tray there was eggs and bread. The breakfast looked to be really good compared to what I had been used to in Miami. Things were looking good so far!

The women sitting with us told me where I could find the Styrofoam cups and hot water to make my coffee. Along with the coffee, I had two bags of sugar and one creamer. As I was about to stand to my feet, and make the long awaited cup of coffee that I had prayed for, again I was blessed by God and His provisions. Before I could even stand to my feet, a Muslim woman was standing in front of me. I knew she was Muslim due to the black head scarf she was wearing.

She was tall and thin and was standing in front of me, looking down at me. I did not move. I only smiled at her

A Journey Behind Prison Walls

and said hello. She did not reply, but she took my hand and opened it, and then she laid approximately eight packages of coffee in my hand. She then said to me, "Here, pastor, these are for you." Before I could even say thank you, she turned around and walked away as quickly as she had come to me.

I looked to one of the women who was sitting with me and asked her, "Why did she call me pastor? I am not a pastor." She told me that was what Muslims call any one in other faiths, that they recognize as a teacher of that faith, a pastor. The one package of coffee that I had would have only made a half a cup of coffee, and it would not have been that strong ether. I like strong coffee and I would usually drink about three cups every morning. Now I was happy and thankful with the small half a cup of coffee that I had been provided with, but God went over and beyond what I had expected. God had not only given me enough for myself but also enough that I could share with others and I did.

When I bowed my head to thank God for what He had done for me and how He had blessed me, He spoke this to me, "trust me in all things, I will take care of yours as I have already promised, but I will also take care of you and all your needs, and even some of your wants. Do not be afraid I am with you." Again I felt the presence of God all around me. I was truly being blessed by God, and it was becoming perfectly clear why I had to come through Oklahoma on my way to Coleman, Florida.

Every day the same woman would bring me coffee. Each day, she did the same thing that she had done on my first day. She never allowed me to minister to her or say thank you. She would step away before the words would leave my lips. God showed me again, that he will and can use anything or anyone to bless us and fulfill His purpose; even those who do not serve Him, He can use even them to bless His children.

Prior to getting in line for breakfast, one of the reason I was last in line; I walked over to the book carts where I had found the Bible the night before. Now no-one had been by them all morning. They were all eating and trading whatever they could from their morning breakfast. But once I was standing in front of the book cart. I noticed there were many Gideon Bibles to choose from that had not been there the night before.

It became clear to me that the Bible that I had retrieved from the cart the night before was meant for me and the message it contained. Again, I had to thank God for all He was doing and showing me here at Oklahoma. I could not help myself to look back on how frightened I was to come to Oklahoma, and, all along, God wanted to bless me and teach me something that I was going to need in the days ahead. I am so thankful that God works things out His way and not our way.

We all put prayers before God. We even give details to how and when we want God to answer our prayers. I was beginning to learn that I needed to pray for God's will and for the Lord to help me in trusting Him in whatever His will was for me. This was what gave me great joy and peace. God knew this. The devil wanted to keep me from it. I was learning everyday to surrender to God on a whole different level than I had ever done before, and God was going to use me to teach others how to do the same.

If we could only trust God in everything, He has something to teach us in everything that He allows to come our way. I did not understand this before I walked the journey behind prison walls. When I read Romans 5:3-4 it became very clear to me.

Romans 5:3-4 *And not only this, but we also exult in our tribulations, knowing that tribulation brings about perseverance; 4) and perseverance, proven character; and proven character, hope;(NASB)*

Chapter 9

This is what we do in prayer. Not a wish, but we have faith with expectation. This happens when we spend time with God and read His Word. In the midst of a storm, God will produce perseverance; and perseverance, character; and character, hope. Notice that every time I felt frightened in what was going to happen to me next, I was consumed in what was happening. I was not focused on God. I was only able to gain peace, joy and hope by going into God's Word and spending time in His presence. God never let me down when I did this. The devil wanted me to be consumed by my situation; God wanted me to be centered on Him. I was only able to do this by spending time with God and His Word; because of this my relationship with God grew stronger along with my dependency on Him.

John 16:33 *These things I have spoken to you, so that in Me you may have peace. In the world you will have tribulation; but take courage; I have overcome the world. (NASB)*

God was working out a lot in me. I had a lot of things in me that needed to be healed and polished, but I did not know it at the time. God helped me grow in my faith and trust in Him. But even more, a lot of the residue from my past was being removed, only because I was seeing it through God's eyes as He revealed it to me one thing at a time. Remember the disciples in Matthew 14:25-27, were in a storm and could not see anything good coming out of it. How about you and your storm? Is Jesus approaching you, but you can't hear His voice because you are not even listening. I had to look to God and His Word to not miss what it was that God had for me. He wants to do the same for you, but you have to seek Him in the midst of the storm and not wait until it is over.

When the disciples first saw Jesus, they were afraid, but when they heard His voice, they were no longer afraid. Is Jesus trying to talk to you in your storm? Are you missing the voice of Jesus in your storm because you are not even looking or listening? You many have already decided that nothing good can come out of your storm. I want to encourage you to think again. The disciples did not recognize Jesus until He spoke to them. All it took for them to not be afraid was to hear the voice of Jesus. Are you missing the voice of Jesus in your storm?

When Jesus got into the boat with the disciples, their fears had already been put to ease by hearing His voice, but Jesus was not finished working on their behalf. He also calmed the storm once He was in the boat. I don't know about you, but I sure needed my storm to be calmed, but before this could happen, I had to invite Jesus into my boat - my storm. Storms will come and go. The difference in them is how you and I will weather them, and what you and I will or will not learn while we are in them. If you would only give Jesus a chance, He will show you the good He has planned for you in your storm, as Jesus was doing for me.

I spent the rest of my time at Oklahoma in Bible study with others and praying for anyone who asked me. Since we had three tiers, I also spent a lot of time walking up and down the stairs and hallways for exercise. As I walked, I would sing a hymn called "Hallelujah" over and over again in a low voice. God would also lead me to pray for many as I walked. It was not easy being in Oklahoma, but it was not as bad as I had made it out to be in my mind either.

One of the hardest things for me being at Oklahoma was that I was not able to talk to my family as much or have visitation with them. We did not have our commissary accounts available to us while we were at Oklahoma; this meant no money for phone calls. The phones were located in the unit. We were all welcome to use them as often as we wished, but all calls were collect and the cost to the one that you were calling was one dollar a minute. This was expensive and my family was already having a hard enough time with me being gone. I was not home contributing financially as I was before. My income was half of our budget. Now that I was gone, this was causing my family not only an emotional hardship but also a financial one. Even though my family told me to call as often as I needed, I could not do that knowing what it would cost them. Even this would draw me closer to my Lord. When I wanted to call home and could not, I would go to God in prayer and He would give me peace.

I had put in a request to the chaplain for a study Bible and a concordance in order to study the Word even more deeply. A request in prison is called a "cop out" but this normally takes about three to five working days. I did not know how long I was going to be at Oklahoma, so I put my request in as soon as I arrived. It only took about three days, and I heard my name called over the loud speaker to come to the officer station. This was not done often at Oklahoma since we did not have any visitation and not many of us ever received any mail either while we were at Oklahoma. Reason being, none of us were at Oklahoma long enough for family to mail us anything. By the time family would know where we were in order to try to mail us anything, we would be gone.

Remember, we were not allowed to travel with anything other than our travel papers, and I was also allowed to carry with me my inhaler and contact case, but most did not have any addresses of family or friends with them; it was all packed away on its way to their next destination. We were all given two stamps and two envelopes per week while we were at Oklahoma in order to mail family letters and let them know we were okay. I was able to mail some letters to a few due to the addresses I had with me on the back of my traveling papers. I was so thankful to the women who had told me about writing them on the back of my travel paper so I would have them with me if I needed them. But I instructed everyone I mailed a letter to, not to mail me anything while I was at Oklahoma because I would be leaving soon.

Once I got to the officers station, I then saw what it was that the officer had for me - the Bible and the concordance had came from the chaplain's office that I had requested. I was so excited. I could hardly wait to get back to my room and get started, but I would have to wait until later that night since I was involved in a Bible study with some other women at the time and I could not leave. At the end of the day and as lockdown was called for all to go to their cells, I was off to my cell to study the Word of God with the material that had come from the chaplain's office. I had taken for granted all the reference material that I had when I was at home. We all take so many things for granted until they are no longer available to us. We then appreciate what we had once it is gone. I pray to this day that God will help me stay focused on all that He has given me and that I will not take anything for granted any more. It is so easy to do; we have to keep watch daily for it not to happen to us in our lives. Even in the little things, we need to be thankful.

On my way to my room, I noticed some discomfort in my left eye. Once I had gotten to my room, I went to the sink and took out the contact that was within my left eye. Once it was removed, I noticed that it was torn in half. I am not sure how the contact got torn, but it was. I tried to put it back in my eye, but the irritation was too much to deal with. I was also concerned that my eye would get scratched if I left it in, so I had to remove it. I have what they call mono vision - my left eye; I wear a contact for reading. My right eye, I wear a contact for distance, and the left eye was the contact that I had discovered was torn. This meant I could see far off, but I would not be able to read.

Here I had a new Bible and concordance from the chaplain's office that I was unable to read. I lowered my head and prayed to God. I knew this was the enemy trying to discourage me but I was not going to let him have the victory. As I prayed I told God, "it is okay, I have so much of your Word in my heart, and I am going to pull from that which you have sowed into me, Lord." I told the Lord, "I am going to use this time to sit before you, God, and thank you for what you are doing in my life and also listen to anything that you may be trying to share with me." God and I had a real special time that night; I was not discouraged but encouraged after God and I spent the time together. I thanked Him for my contact lenses lasting as long as they did. I had been using them in my eyes for now almost three months. They were only supposed to last two weeks. I had been blessed by the time they had lasted. I would be at Coleman soon and then I would be able to get some glasses off commissary. I also understood that once I was at Coleman I would be able to see the eye doctor and get some glasses; I needed to be patient.

I had been at Oklahoma for five days, and I was told that Tuesday was the day that the transport went to Coleman Florida. Today was Sunday. I could be leaving in a few days, and if not, God would provide someone to read for me. The next day, God did. I took my books with me into one of the other woman's cell that I had already been studying with, and we studied together using the concordance and study Bible that I had received.

I found out that she had never used a concordance. I could only smile! Look at God! He was now giving me an opportunity to teach someone else how to use the study material that I had received from the chaplain's office. She told me that she had many subjects she wanted to study, but did not know how to find them all in the Bible. She only had a King James Version Bible and her Bible did not have a concordance in the back. She did not study the Bible when she was at home prior to coming into prison; this was something God had given her since she had come into prison - a hunger for His Word. She was so excited, that she put in a request the next day to the chaplain's office to receive the same material I had. I was not allowed to leave it with her when I left; I had to turn it in when I was asked to pack out. But that was okay. We used the material together and she would have her own in a few days, if she was still at Oklahoma. Remember, we all at Oklahoma were only there for a few days or weeks. If she did not receive the material while she was at Oklahoma, she now knew what she needed to look for to help her dig deeper into the Word once she got to where she was going.

You see how God works; the enemy wanted me to be frustrated about my contact tearing and me not being able to read. But this time I was more aware of His ways. I was learning. The devil will never stop; he will only try different ways of attacking. This is why we have to be diligent in reading the Word of God and allow God to fill us daily with His Holy Spirit. If we do not, when the enemy comes to rob, steal and destroy, we will give into his lies. This was a victory the devil did not win. My Lord helped me stand, and I maintained my joy and hope, and God again used something that looked bad at first for His purpose.

Leaving For Coleman, Florida

Monday night, my sixth night at Oklahoma, and as every other night, I was off to bed once lockdown had been called. The next day was Tuesday, the day that I had been told the transport to Coleman, Florida should leave. Here at Oklahoma, you are not told the day before that you would be leaving the next day. You are told the day of, at four in the morning. You are told to get up and get ready; you would be leaving that day. At four o'clock in the morning, I heard a knock at my door and an officer stepped into my cell. I think he knocked to be polite. He did have the key. He did as the women had told me he would. He instructed me to get up and gather my things and come downstairs, I was leaving on the transport that day. Again, he was not allowed to tell me where I was going.

This time I was better prepared. I had done this once already. I knew what to expect on the plane, and I was

A Journey Behind Prison Walls

not as fearful as before. Once we were all together and ready, a woman officer came to get us to process us for travel. We had to go through the strip search again and change our clothes into traveling cloths. Then we were all put into a holding cell like before while we waited for the men to be loaded. We were given a brown paper bag again with our lunch in it, but this time, I would not be so reluctant to eat it. I noticed as we began to be loaded, it was all the same US Marshals that we had traveled with before. This gave me a strange kind of peace - not sure why.

As we were all being led onto the plane, we all noticed an elderly man in front of us walking slowly. He did not look well; I overheard an office mention that he was being transported to a medical facility. As we got closer to the elderly man, we were told to slow down, rules were rules, and the elderly man had to get on the plane first because he was a man, and all men had to be loaded first before the women. This was when I could hear the elderly man and one of the officers talking. I learned that this man had been in prison most of his life. He was now up in his years and was not in good health. According to the elderly man, he was ready to die. He said, "I will never leave this prison system and I am okay with that, but it is now time for me to go home and see my Jesus." This was what I overheard the elderly man saying to the officer that was escorting him to the plane. The officer that was holding a conversation with him responded to him by saying, "You say that to me every time I come and pick you up for transport." The officer continued by telling the elderly man that he was going to outlive them all. I could tell the officer had known this man a long time and was trying to encourage him to get on the plane and stop talking about dying.

The old man was placed up front with us women, and, as we all got to our seats and buckled in by the officers, I then lowered my head and said a prayer for the elderly man. I could tell that he had touched many hearts that day with his words - even some of them were US Marshalls. God was using him even in his weakened and sick state. God can use us all in every situation we find ourselves in, even in dying, if we would only let Him.

As the plane prepared to take off, I felt excitement come over me. I was finally on my way to Coleman. Now don't get me wrong, I was not happy that I was in prison and going to Coleman. I was happy to be getting to my final destination. I was finally going to be able to get settled and get this all behind me, and Coleman was the beginning of the end, and I needed to get there, and it looked like I was finally on my way. I had heard a lot of good things about Coleman, including that it was a lot easier on families to visit. It was nothing like Miami FDC. I was looking forward to seeing my family in a more relaxed environment. This was all so hard on them. We all could use some kind of normality, and not that Coleman was that, but I was praying it was better than where I had been for me and my family.

We had been in the air for some time, when I noticed we were landing. I looked out the window and we were back at the same airport we had left out of when I left Miami FDC before. I thought to myself, "What are we doing back in Miami? Am I going back to Miami FDC?" It did not take long before I had my answer. The doors opened and a few inmates on the airplane did get off, but I was not one of them. A sigh of relief came over my body, and I told the Lord thank you. Then to my surprise, I looked up to see who were all getting on the plane and walking toward me were several women from Miami FDC that I knew.

They all looked at me in surprise, and asked me in a low whisper, "What are you doing on this plane? You should have been at Coleman by now." Once all the women were seated and the officers had come around and made sure all had their seatbelts on, I was then able to tell them that I had been in Oklahoma since I had left Miami FDC. They shook their heads and smiled and said, "This crazy system." But I knew that there was an important reason that I had gone to Oklahoma and I was blessed that I had.

Coleman, Florida: We Arrived

The officers again prepared us for landing. I thought to myself, we were finally here; at least I thought we were. I had no idea that I still had some traveling ahead of me before we would be at Coleman camp. As before, the men were all taken off the plane first. I noticed in looking out of the window, we were again on a small airfield.

There were several buses waiting outside to transport all the men to their destinations, and several white vans to transport all of us women. I was unaware that all of us women were not going to the same place. Some had to catch a connecting plane, and some of the vans were going to other facilities other than Coleman camp. Once off the plane all of us that were going to Coleman camp were loaded into one van. Others were loaded into the other vans.

I had no idea where all of them were going, but as I watched everyone being loaded into the all of the vans, I asked my Lord to give them all traveling mercies and be with everyone wherever they would find themselves tonight. Once the officers got into our van, we were all told that we were waiting for one more to join us, and then we would be leaving.

The officers then left all of us women in the van as they stepped out to talk to the other officers. They did leave the van running with the air on so we would be cool. It was awfully hot outside, and we were all happy to be cool and unsupervised for at least a little while inside the van. We women did not mind this, because now we could all talk freely without every word we were saying being listened to, or told that we were talking too much or too loud. Not that I minded the officers listening. I was not saying anything they could not hear, but the other women that I was with did not trust the officers due to all that they had been through behind prison walls.

Some of the women in the van expressed that they had been through some pretty awful situations concerning officers. They warned me to not trust anyone, inmate or officer. They proceeded to tell me that the world inside of prison is not like anything I had ever seen or lived before and to be careful and keep my eyes open to everything that was going on around me. And I would need to be careful as to whom I called friend and associated with.

As I thought to myself about all that I had seen and been through up to this point, they were all telling me the truth. God had given me protection and favor up to this point, and I trusted Him to do the same thing where I was going, but I took their words to heart.

God was with me and protecting me. He had shown me this already. But I was going to have to also be mindful to exactly where I was at all times, and that this was not like anything I had ever experienced before. God was showing me that I was going to have to trust Him in a way I had never trusted Him before. There was no room for me to be gullible or wander from His presence.

The women that had come from Miami now could catch me up on everything that was going on at Miami FDC. I then shared with them what all God had done with me in Oklahoma. Then the officers came back to the van with the woman that we all had been waiting for. We were then instructed by the officers about the rules and the journey ahead of us. We were told that we could talk, but keep it low. The trip to Coleman was about two hours, and we would not be stopping anywhere on the way. It was about 3:00 PM and we were all hungry and were hoping we would get to Coleman in time for dinner, and not get a brown bag with a cheese sandwich in it for dinner like we had been given before, when we arrived at Oklahoma.

The officers were allowed to remove our shackles and handcuffs while we were being transported to Coleman due to all of us having camp status. This was up to them, but the officers decided, for whatever the reason may have been, to leave the shackles and handcuff on us all for the full trip. I did not mind it this time really. I knew we would be at Coleman soon and they would all be removed. I understood that we would soon be at a place that we would no longer be locked up behind bars or even locked doors; I had waited almost three months to get there, I could endure a few more hours.

The officers pulled out some food for themselves that smelled really good. It bothered some of the women in the van. I tried to distract them by talking about what was ahead of us. We had a few with us that had come from Coleman. I got them all talking about what all went on at Coleman and soon it looked like all had forgot about the food or at least did not let it bother them anymore.

I was learning quickly to not take everything officers did so personally. They were at work. For example, they needed to eat also, and we had no idea to how long it had been since they had eaten last. Should they not eat because they had us in the van? That would not be fair to them; it is not all about us all the time. It is easy in the midst of a storm to be only focused on yourself and your pain. This is not what God wants of us. We are to look around and see whatever it is that God wants us to learn or do. I was changing so much already in how I acted and how I looked at things, but I had to be careful all the time. There was still much in me that needed to be changed by God. The devil wanted me to be consumed with my storm; it was up to me to not let him have this victory. Every minute of the day, God was teaching me something. It was up to me to learn it and apply it to my life and my surroundings.

As we pulled up to Coleman Camp, I started to get nervous, but it was not like before. I was not frightened, but nervous, because this was a new place. I was going to have to learn how things were done here. I was about to meet new staff and new inmates. How was it here at Coleman Camp?

Would the officers treat us like animals or people? I had experienced both in the last three months, but this was the end of the road. I was going to be here for three years. When I was at Miami and Oklahoma, I knew I would be leaving there soon. I always looked forward to the next place being better than where I was.

Yes, this was a false security of mine, but it did give me some kind of comfort nevertheless. Yes it is true that the next place could be worse than where I was, but I did not look at it that way at the time. But now I was at my destination. All truth is about to be presented to me. I was praying that I was ready. Reality was here, and, yes, I was nervous.

The officers stepped out of the van and went inside leaving us all in the van parked outside in front of Coleman Camp. I did not understand why they did this, but again we all had to wait. It did not take long and the officers came back to the van and helped us all out one by one. We were all asked to stand next to the van so they could remove our shackles and handcuffs. This was a real relief to have them finally removed. We had been traveling since about 6AM, and they had not been removed once. It was now about 5:30 PM, and I was happy we were done with the shackles and handcuffs. It is not only uncomfortable and difficult to do anything in them, but it is also demeaning.

We were all then led inside to processing; once inside we were even greeted by a really nice and pleasant officer. She even welcomed us all to Coleman Camp and asked us to be seated. She told us her name and explained to us that we would be with her for several hours, but not to worry dinner was being brought to us. Things were beginning to look up already. We would have several staff members that we would also have to meet with prior to being taken to our unit. But we would start first with this officer. She needed to sign us in and take our picture for our ID.

We were all told that once the ID was made and given to us to not lose it and keep it with us at all times. It would be used to identify us and even used in connection with our commissary account. The ID was also like a debit card. It had a strip on the back that could be read by vending machines and also for doing laundry. The washers and dryers that were located in each unit were not free. You would have to have money on your card to use the laundry facility.

We would all be called, one by one, to have our picture taken for the ID, but while we were waiting for each other to finish taking their picture, the food arrived. An inmate who worked in the kitchen rolled in a cart that was full of food, even dessert.

I looked up at her and asked, "Is this for us, or the officers?"

She said, "No, it is for all of you."

I was in shock; the food smelled good and even looked better. The tray was loaded with salad and vegetables and some kind of noodle dish that looked great. But then I found the dessert - it was banana cream pie!

I asked again, "Is the pie for us also?"

She looked at me and laughed. "Yes it is, and if you need more I will bring you more, you are allowed to eat all you want."

We were all then asked what we would like to drink. The inmate that had brought us the food explained everything that they had to drink.

She said, "We have Coke, Sprite, fruit punch, and root beer, but we also have tea and milk."

We all looked at each other in amazement, except for the ones who had been at Coleman camp before; they laughed and said, "I told you so."

We all then looked back at the women who had brought the food and were going to bring us what we wanted to drink and said, "We have all that to pick from?" "Yes, and this will be available to you every day in the cafeteria," she stated. We then told her what all we wanted to drink and she told us she would be right back.

I was so overwhelmed; I was speechless and so were many of the other women with me. Now the ones who had been at Coleman Camp were laughing at the rest of us. We all sat down and started to eat. The food was great! There was plenty. We did not need to ask for more. I could not help myself from having two pieces of pie. It was real good! It had been a long time since I had any dessert, real dessert, that is. I was thanking God over and over in my spirit. After a long trip on Conair, this was a perfect way to end the day.

When my name was called to get my picture taken, I was instructed where to stand and to look straight into the camera. Once the picture was taken, the officer asked me a question. "Lanette, why are you smiling so big in this picture? Most are crying or at least quite sad, but you are not either one, why? You look like you are happy to be here."

I answered, "No, that is not it at all. You don't know where all I have been and what all I have been through. I am happy to be here at Coleman Camp finally, but not in prison.

The officer then said to me, "I hope things keep getting better for you while you are here Coleman." The officer then said to me, "Remember Coleman is what you make of it. Get involved and listen to your team and go by the rules and you will be fine."

I smiled at her and said, "I can handle that, thank you."

I know that everywhere I had been up to this point, God had used me, and I was happy that He had. It was the only thing that gave me joy, but the rest of the time other than when I was being used by God, I was miserable and spent most nights crying myself to sleep. I had the joy of God, but I was still overwhelmed with sadness being away from my family and in a place that I did not understand why God had allowed me to be where I was. This was where God had to help me conform to His will and not mine. There was so much God needed to teach me, and God would in the years ahead. I had only begun a journey that was going to change my life in many ways, but most of all it was going to change me and my relationship with Him, my Lord and Savior, Jesus Christ.

Once we all had eaten and had our ID's made, some additional staff came in to complete more paper work and give us our unit assignments. Now many of us were waiting for this so we could see if we would be in the same unit together. Malone and I had been praying that we would be together, even if we did not have the same room, at least in the same unit.

Once we were all assigned a unit, it was explained to us that we were never allowed to go into another unit that was not ours. So being assigned together we would be more able to be there for each other. We were there for hours waiting for everything to be completed. We were then taken to our rooms in time for count. Malone and I were assigned to the same unit, F2. I found out later that there were four units, F1, 2, 3 and 4. The camp held approximately 500 women, and there was only one officer on duty after 5:00 PM.

Once we were all given our unit assignment, we were all taken to our unit. There was a woman in each unit that volunteered to help the women when they first came to the camp. A woman from each unit came to processing to assist all of us to our assigned unit. Malone and I were both assigned to F2, and we were thanking God for answering our prayer.

Once we were at the unit we both had to go to our room quickly due to it being count time. We would be shown around the unit after count. My room was the first one as you walked into the unit. My Bunkie's name was Donna Ray, and she was standing at the entrance of the cell waiting for count as I walked in. She informed me to stand by the entrance of our room and be quiet until the officers counted us and left the unit and called all clear.

This was all new for me, how the unit was and most of all how our cells were set up. We did not have an officer assigned to each unit. The front desk was empty. Our cells were not cells at all, but cubicles made of concrete, and we did not even have a door. Within the room was a set of bunk beds and two lockers, these were standup lockers, not flat floor lockers like in Miami. They were also a lot bigger. They would be easier to organize. Each woman had a hook on the wall in order for her to hang up her clothing, and a bulletin board hanging over her locker to display her personal pictures and stuff.

The bulletin board was very important inside of prison; each woman would display her pictures or anything else that was personal to her. It was the only place within the cell that you were allowed to personalize to your liking. As you would go to each cell the bulletin board hanging over each locker would tell a story of the women who lived there. Once my things would arrive from Miami, I too would be able to decorate my bulletin board to tell the story of all that was important to me - my Lord and my family. In the corner was a small metal desk with a pull-out chair. My assignment was for the bottom bunk this time; this was the first time since I had come into prison that I was on the bottom bunk. This made me really happy, due to us living in cubicles here at Coleman. Everyone on the top bunk could see everyone else on top bunks. There was less security here, but also less privacy. Being on the bottom bunk did give me a little more privacy than the one on the top bunk.

Once the officer walked out of the unit, everyone started to move around and look for us new girls to see if they knew us. I was surprised to how many women I knew were from Miami, who were also here at Coleman and assigned to F2. Women were coming from all over F2 to come and welcome me and see what they could do for me to help me get comfortable. Whenever you are shipped anywhere you have to wait for all your belongings to catch up with you, and this could take an additional two months. It was common for others to let you borrow things until your belongings arrived. It was a comfort to me to see so many faces that I knew. Many of the women that knew me told me of the other women in the other units that were also waiting for me to arrive. After count was cleared, we would be allowed to go outside for one hour, and then the compound would be closed for the night. They wanted me to follow them out onto the compound so the others who had been waiting for me could see I was here.

God will give us peace in the midst of our storm and God did that for me when I arrived at Coleman. There were so many from Miami that God had allowed me to minister to. Now they were being used to minister to me as I arrived at Coleman. I learned they had all been praying for me and waiting for me to arrive. Count was not cleared yet. The woman that had come to processing to show us to F2 came back to give us newcomers a tour of F2. I found out later that the woman who was showing us around had been at Coleman a long time - over five years. The unit had a large restroom for all to use and a shower room; all with doors. We did not have facilities within our rooms at Coleman. There was also a laundry room - four washers and four dryers but they were not free like in Miami. They cost fifty cents each. To use the washer or dryer, you would have to put money on your ID card. You could only put money on your ID card when you went to the commissary on your shopping day. Your ID card could be used like a debit card.

The units also had a fund that other inmates were allowed to donate items to for newcomers to have while they waited for their belongings to come in. We were given some shower shoes and hangers to hang our clothes, also some shampoo, conditioner and lotion. Once I got back to my room, I was again greeted with many friends who were waiting for me.

They all started evaluating what all I would need to borrow from them while I waited on my things to arrive. One handed me a Bible. They all knew this was going to be my first request. I was then given some coffee, creamer and sugar along with a cup to make the coffee in. One of the women went to get me a jogging suit for me to wear and a pair of shorts and a t-shirt. There was also a large drawer up front with old tennis shoes for all to pick from. I tried on several and found a pair that would work until my things arrived. We then heard the all clear. This meant count was clear and we could go outside. We had to hurry if we wanted to find everyone that had been waiting to see me. We only had an hour till the compound was closed for the night.

As I stepped outside, it felt strange to be able to walk about without an officer guarding me. It felt amazing! I thought to myself, this is the closest I would get to feeling free for a long time, or at least I thought it was. I took a deep breath in - fresh air! This, too, had been something I had not been able to enjoy. I had not been outside without shackles on for almost three months. I looked around the camp, and there were plenty of trees and grass. I could see the four units and some other buildings. I did not yet know what they were. In the far distance, I could see a track with a softball field in the middle of it. There was no fence of any kind. It was pointed out to me to not go beyond the big bolder - looking rocks; they were placed all around the camp. That was the boundary for us. The rocks! Wow! I was in shock.

As much as I was happy to be at Coleman Camp and not where I had been for the last three months, I could not help myself from thinking, "why are we all here." We literally were on our own honor system; no locked doors, fences, or even guards. We had only one officer to watch all 500 of us. I did not get why we could not be doing some kind of probation or even house arrest. But then I came back to myself and let it go. I could not change anything, and there was no reason for me to get myself all worked up. But God did have a plan for while I was here. This had already been shown to me. Now I needed to seek Him and find out what else He had for me here in this place.

The other ladies instructed me to follow them across the compound. We went to a place that was located in the center of the compound, were smoking was allowed. Under a canopy were concrete tables and benches. Many women were under these canopy's playing cards and getting in a quick cigarette before the compound was closed. They would not be able to smoke again until morning. Here was where we found several other women that had been looking for me to arrive at Coleman.

I did not understand how everyone knew I was coming, so I asked. I was then told that everyone within the camp had to have a job. Inmates working in the kitchen had a list of all who were coming in on the transport that day. They were given the list in order for them to fix a tray loaded with enough dinner for all to eat once they arrived.

Once the ladies in the kitchen knew who were coming in on the transport, the information would travel throughout the camp quickly, as all information did at the camp. Many had been waiting for me to come to Coleman and they knew the system.

They would check with the women who worked in the kitchen every time a transport was expected. Once my name showed up on the list, they then knew I had arrived. Once everyone knew what unit I was to be assigned to, someone within my unit knew to take me out after count to the canopy in order for me to see everyone else that had been waiting for me to arrive.

After I had talked with a few of the women under the canopy I was instructed that there were a few women that wanted to see me, but they were in front of their units.

They did not like the smoke under the canopy. As we walked to the other units and looked to see who was outside we found a few more that I knew. Anita was one of them.

She gave me a big hug and told me how glad she was to see me. She said life was hard for her and she did not know how she was going to make it through. When I last saw her, she was still expecting to get out on bond as I was, but it had not happened yet and it did not look like it was going to, as it did not look like it was going to for me either. I took her hands and asked her if I could pray for her. As we finished praying, we heard the buzzer for the compound to be closed. I told Anita that I would look for her tomorrow or for her to find me. She agreed and we both went to our own units.

This did not mean we had to go to bed, only that we had to go inside and lights out. We could still be up and even up and about within the unit. We were not allowed in others' rooms, because it was bed time for those who chose to go to sleep now. The time was 10:30 PM. The TV room did not close until 12:00 AM, and they were open all night on Friday and Saturday and holidays. The laundry room and multipurpose room were still open and you could even have the lights on within them. Once back in the unit, I found my Bunkie back in our room. She was real nice, and we were able to talk, but it had to be at a whisper.

Donna Ray was much younger than me; she was not much older than her late twenties. She told me how she was hoping that she would not get a roommate because her mom was going to be coming to Coleman soon. They wanted to be bunk together. I asked her once her mom was at Coleman would I be allowed to move into another room and her mom could have my bunk.

Donna Ray smiled and thanked me and said she would ask the counselor in the morning, his name was Mr. Seed. I put my room together the best I could with the items that had been given to me earlier that day, including making my bed. I was even given an extra blanket and pillow from some of the other women in the unit. They all told me that it got really cold at night, and I would be happy that I had an extra blanket, and they knew how my asthma acted up when I would get cold.

I then prepared myself for a shower. I found out that you were not allowed to shower after lights out, but since I had only arrived, it would be okay. Donna Ray told me if the officers came in and asked why I was in the shower to tell them that I had just arrived at Coleman, and they would leave me alone. It was nice to have real shampoo and conditioner and someone even gave me a bottle of shower gel. Once out of the shower, I put on my night shirt. We were all given a night shirt when we arrived. It was a large green t-shirt that went way below my knees. This was to be used to sleep in, and it was quite comfortable, and I was happy to have it.

Once back to my room, I sat down on my bed and took a good look around me. The unit was quiet but you could still hear many that were still up moving around. My Bunkie was in bed already due to her needing to be up early for work. She worked in landscaping, and it was hard work from what she had told me earlier. She was required to work in the sun all day, and this put a drain on her and she needed her rest. As I sat on my bed all kinds of emotions were going through me, I was happy to be at Coleman finally, but I missed my family and wanted to be at home. I thought to myself, "three and a half years to be here in prison. My Lord how can I do this?"

Thinking about the length of time that I was supposed to be in prison would only bring on anxiety and then I would get overwhelmed with my situation. Tears started to run down my cheeks. All I could think, life as I knew it up to this point was gone forever.

While we are in a storm, it is hard for us most of the time to look into the storm and face what God has for us to learn or do within it. We too often look to the past for comfort, stuck in the poor-me syndrome; or we are focus only on the end of the storm and getting it behind us. The past is what we know; it is familiar to us, and this is why it can bring a false comfort to us, even if our past was not a good one.

We have come to grips with it as you may say. We may have allowed it to become our security blanket. It is hard for us to accept change sometimes because of this. The future is what we can control, not our past. Our God wants us to embrace the future, but looking to the past can keep us from living in the present and this can, and will, dictate your future if you let it. This is a trick of the enemy - getting us consumed in our past.

The past can be used to minister to others and even yourself in reference to a testimony, in telling how God got you through. This is not how the enemy wants you to look at your past. The enemy would rather you get stuck in the poor-me syndrome. When we do this, it puts us in a mindset that we are always looking to be comforted and lifted up by others, receiving attention by others because of what we have been through in our past. It becomes our security blanket. But God wants us to heal and forgive and be able to eventually stand with Him and proclaim victory over our past.

In my past, I had many places that caused me pain. I thought I had put most of them behind me, but I was about to learn that there were many things from my past that still held me captive, and God wanted me to be free. How about you? Is your past still holding you captive, keeping you from all God has for you? Trust me, whatever it is that God has for you, He will give, and has given, you everything you need to walk the Journey.

But to walk the Journey, many of us need to let God help us lighten our loads. All you have to do is look to God, and trust Him, and God will help you. Many times we think we have already lightened our loads, but then God allows a storm to blow in, and it reveals many hidden things within us that we thought were gone, or reveals things that we never knew were even there.

This is exactly what happened to me. As I sat on my bunk, many things went through my head, but first and foremost the closet came back to me. I still wanted a closet to hide in. God again said to me, "this is still here. We need to work on this." I did not understand why I still felt the need to run into a closet. I thought I had given this to God years ago. I had not felt the need to run into a closet for many years.

But now I wanted a closet to run into and hide from all the pain and fear I was feeling. I thought I had given the closet to God before, but I had not given all the things that were linked to the closet - the reasons the closet was created to begin with. This was what God wanted to help me with, not the closet itself, but the reasons the closet was ever needed. God was showing me that I had never dealt with the root of this problem.

Many times, we do not work on the root of a problem; we only deal with the symptoms. It was time for me to work on the root. Why did I need a closet to feel safe?

This was the only way for the closet to be permanently removed from my life. In accomplishing this, the closet would not hold me captive any longer, and the load that I was carrying around would be lightened. God wanted me to only need Him to feel safe. Once I was able to acquire this, the devil would lose many avenues to attack me and distract me from God.

As it became clearer to me that the closet was something that I still needed, I did not like the idea that I was still in the need of the closet, and I wanted to do whatever I needed to do to remove it from my life, but at this moment, that was too much for me to think about. All I wanted was a closet and I did not have one. I began to think of a way I could satisfy the need, even without a closet to hide in. I was on the bottom bunk now; I could hang something from the top bunk and let it hang down in order for me to lie behind it.

It was not a closet exactly, but it did give a pretty good illusion. I did not have much to use. I did have a towel, and it would have to do for the time being. This gave me some comfort and also kept the bright light from shining in my eyes. Every unit had red lights that would light up at night, so the officers could see when they walked through the units to do count or check on any activity within the unit at night. There was one red light right over my room, and it would shine directly into my eyes. This made it real difficult to go to sleep. I had a hard enough time sleeping inside of prison without having a bright light shining in my face. The towel hanging from the top bunk looked to me to be a good fix, and solved many issues for the moment; but God was not done with this crutch that plagued my life.

The towel hanging from my bed was not God's idea of how to fix or even address the root of my problem. Don't we all do this? God shows us something we need to work on, and we find a quick fix to get us by. We really don't want to deal with the pain that we may have to feel in order to get to the bottom of the problem, at least not right then; we will get to it later. I am thankful that God doesn't give up on us, even if we try to evade Him and His guidance. God did not give up on me. T

his was not the last in dealing with the issue of the closet and all that was connected to it. I was unaware as to how God was going to walk me through my past and help me heal. I was going to be dealing with it in a very different way than I had ever done before - not with eyes of pain, but a heart of healing! This kind of healing can only be done with God's help and us surrendering to His guidance. But this night, I fell off to sleep with the need of the closet still there, and all of my issues still holding me captive. God had other plans for me that would come later in how I would work on this issue; but God was patient with me as He will be with you.

I woke many times during the night to the officers' keys jingling in the night as they walked the unit. This was a sound that I was going to have to get used to. It happened every two hours. Since we only had one officer on duty for the camp, every time count time came around an officer from one of the other prisons on the compound would come up to the camp and count with our officer. But even if it was not count time, our officer would come around throughout the night checking to make sure everyone was where they were supposed to be. Coleman was the largest federal institution in the US. It had two high security prisons, called pens, also one medium prison and one low, and, of course, the camp, which is where we women were. All the other prisons were for men only. The only facility on the compound for women was the camp.

The officers that were on duty all night were mainly all men. This made me nervous waking up and looking up at men counting us. It was not like before when we had a door between us and them; I felt real vulnerable. I know that most officers would not do anything to any of us, but I had heard some strange stories and because of those stories and my past, I did not trust men watching over us at night while we slept.

Again this was going to be something I had to get used to. I even woke up to an officer standing in my room looking at my roommate on the top bunk; he said he was only making sure she was there. Donna Ray was not a small woman. I could see her with no problem from our doorway. This did make me nervous. Once the officer left the room I was not able to go back to sleep for a long time.

My first night was a restless one; I was able to get some sleep, but not a lot. As morning came, I heard my Bunkie getting up and preparing for work. I went ahead and got myself up and ready to eat breakfast. Breakfast was served in the cafeteria and you had to get there before 7:30 if you wanted to eat.

When I went into the restroom to brush my teeth, I ran into Malone. We went to breakfast together. Over the next few days we were all going to have to go through orientation. We would then be assigned a job. If you found a work detail that you wanted to work on, it was recommended for you to get the foreman from that work detail to sign your request as accepting you on that crew. You would then be allowed to go to this work crew as long as your team approved your request. This was a better way in finding a work crew to work on, unless you really did not care where you worked.

Chapter 10

First visitation at Coleman, a breath of fresh air

Visitation up to this point had been a bitter sweet occasion. I loved to see my family, but I did not like what I had to go through to see them. It also bothered my family in what I had to go through to see them also. Now at Coleman I had been told that the visitation experience was completely different. When I first arrived at Coleman and my counselor met with me, he explained that I would be able to visit my family the first two weeks without all the paper work being completed yet. This would only be good for my close family - my daughters and grandchildren and husband. My family had not seen me for about a month, and they were all eager to come to Coleman and see me and hear what had been going on since I left Miami. When any inmate talks on the phone you have to remember that all calls are being recorded and listened to. Some things you don't share on the phone, you save it for visitation.

Not that I was doing anything that was against the rules, but inside of prison some things are not looked at the same way we may look at them - as blessings of God. For example, all the women that I would pray with and see God answer our prayers and bless them and their families; the staff in prison did not want any of us to come together and become too close, and if they observed any group of women getting together too much, you could find yourself being moved. Even when we would come together and do Bible studies, we had to be careful. We had permission to meet, but we tried not to draw to much attention to ourselves. With this all in mind, all of us inside were careful to what we shared on the phones and in our letters. All of these areas were open to staff to read or listen. When I was in Miami, I could see the staff from my cell window reading all of the inmates' letters. They would pass them around and laugh and joke as they read them. I would pray when I saw this because I knew I was not the only one who could see what they were doing, and I knew how much it hurt the other women who wrote the letters that were being laughed at and all their privacy being invaded.

Many of the letters that were being laughed at were letters to husbands - women trying to keep their marriages in tack by sending letters that were full of graphic language. I knew this because the women would come to me the next day and share with me how hard it was for them to write their husbands knowing that the guards were going to read every word. They were embarrassed and some time the officers would make off-the-wall comments to them whenever they would pass them in the unit. Whenever this would happen, some of the women would run to find me, and I would pray with them. I would explain to them they should not care what the officers think or say. Your concern is for whom you wrote the letter to, and that they understand what you are trying to say to them. Remember the receiver of the letter has no idea that the letter has been read by anyone but you and them. I encouraged them to think about the one they were writing to, and not the officer that was reading the letter. This helped some, but it was still hard for them; this went on nightly. I did not mind my letters being read. They were full of God and what God was doing with me and through me with the other women at Miami FDC. But when I had to write that personal letter on occasion to my family, it did bother me some; this would be that letter that was only meant for one of my daughters who may have been having a hard time. I did feel an invasion of privacy and this did not make me feel good. When this happened to me, I too, had to pray myself through it, and I found it helped a lot if I would not look out the window and watch the guard read our letters. I encouraged all the women to do the same.

But now at Coleman, I was going to have my first visit with my family that I would not have to be strip searched or yelled at if I moved. My family knew that I did not have to go through all the challenges that I had to at Miami and they too were excited. We had no idea to how pleasant it was going to be. All of the women in my unit told me what to expect, and from what I had experienced in Miami FDC, this was going to be great for me and my family. My family had to drive three and a half hours to get to Coleman and my first visit was my two daughters and my husband. It was a Sunday morning and I was up early. I took a shower and pressed my uniform in preparation of my visit. A few of my friends got up with me to help me with my hair and some makeup. I did not have any makeup still of my own, so my friends let me use theirs. I still did not have my things from Miami, so it was still hard for me to see due to me not having any glasses. I had not been able to buy anything on commissary yet, so I was managing with limited eyesight up to this point.

When I came into prison, I did not have my glasses. I was wearing my contacts. My contacts were disposable and only lasted long enough to get me to Coleman. When I arrived at Coleman, I was only wearing one due to one getting torn in Oklahoma. When I went to medical, I was told that I was not allowed to wear contacts unless the doctor at Coleman had signed off on my file that my eyes were bad enough to allow me to wear contacts. If not, I had to wear glasses. This was fine with me, but I did not have any glasses. I was told that I would be put on the waiting list to see the eye doctor. My family even tried to gain permission to mail in my glasses from home, with no response from Miami FDC or Coleman. There were reading glasses on commissary that you could buy, but I had not been able to buy a pair as of yet. Because of me not being able to see well enough to put on makeup, one of my friends put the makeup on for me. She did a real good job and I felt great and even pretty for the first time since I had been in prison. It was explained to me to not take anything into visitation and not to bring anything out, and I would be fine. I sat on my bed and waited for my name to be called.

    I heard my name over the loudspeaker, and off I went to visitation to see my family. I had butterflies all in my stomach. I was going to see my girls and my husband; I was not sure what to say or do first. As I walked into the entry way of visitation, I was instructed to leave my ID with the officer at the desk and when I left visitation, I would then pick it up before returning to the unit. I walked through the door and scanned the room for my family. The first one I saw was my daughter Faleasha - she was a great sight to see! She was so pretty, and I could not get to her soon enough. Once I reached her, I gave her a big hug. We were allowed to hug at the beginning of the visit and at the end. I did not want to let her go, but I knew if I hugged her too long, the officer would ask us to stop. I did not want to draw any attention to us or allow anything to put a damper on our visit. As I let go of my daughter, Faleasha, I then saw my other daughter, Keasha. I took a hold of her and did not want to let her go either. It was her birthday, and she had celebrated it the day before instead of this day so she could come to visit me. It was her first birthday with me being in prison; it was hard for me that she had to spend her birthday without me and with me in prison.

The girls then led me to the outside patio where my husband was. He was lying down on the concrete bench outside. I found out later that there had been a party the night before for Keasha's birthday, and Anthony drank too much and was now hung-over. It was hard for him to sit up due to his head hurting him. I did not let it bother me. I focused my attention to my girls. I shared with them everything that was going on and how much better it was being at Coleman. They in turn shared with me what all was going on with them at home. I could tell the girls were upset with my husband, Anthony, their step father, about something, and it was not that he was hung-over. They did not tell me what it was that they were upset with him about, and they both wanted us three to stay focused on the time we had together; and I agreed. We had a great day; the visitation room had many vending machines that we could eat from. My daughters asked me what did I want and we all ate together. It was not until much later in the afternoon that Anthony began to join us. He kept apologizing for his behavior, but the girls did not want to hear it. He had not been any help in driving to Coleman, and he had not joined in much of the visiting either. The girls were disappointed in him and for good reason.

The visiting room had an area for kids also. My grandchildren had not come on this particular visit, but they would in the future. Coleman had a playroom for them so they did not have to stay seated for the full visit like they had to at Miami FDC. I did not even have to stay in the same seat as I did at Miami FDC. We were allowed to move around from outside to inside and sit wherever we wanted to. The visit had been so much better for me and my girls than Miami had ever been. Even with Anthony not participating, it was a great visitation for me. The day had passed and we had all enjoyed it a lot, but now it was time to say good-bye. We all had agreed that we would not wait for the officers to tell us that visitation was over, we would end our visit on our own. I said my good-bye and gave each of them a hug and told them not to worry about me, they had enough to deal with at home. I could see that my daughters were about to cry, and I had to turn my head and walk to the door I was to leave through so they would not see my tears. I stood by the door waiting for the officer to return my ID, and then I was free to go back to my unit.

I had many friends that were anxious to hear how my visit went, but they all knew and understood that they needed to give me a few minutes after returning to my room to get myself together. Visitation is always an emotional time for everyone involved. It is hard for them to see their loved one in prison, and for the one who is in prison it is hard for them to see their family come to prison to see them. But there is no other way to see each other, so you weather through it. But at the end of the visit, it is hard for everyone. My family was leaving me behind in prison and going back home. I would be able to see them again the next weekend, but I wanted to go home with them and be a part of their lives at home. It was hard for families to leave their loved ones behind also; they too were heartbroken in leaving the ones they love behind in prison. Everyone only wanted to be together, but that would have to wait for a later date. As I reached my room, I sat on my bed and began to pray for myself and my family. I prayed for God to protect them and keep them as they traveled home. I asked God to help them with the emotion of it all and to bless us all with the good memories that we were all able to spend some time together.

It was not long before some of my friends came to my room to check on me. They could tell I had been crying and they understood. They all sat down on my bed and the floor and prayed for me and my family. After the prayer, I thanked them all for praying for me and my family and shared with them all how our first visit went. It was not long before count time was called, and they all had to get back to their rooms for count time, but before they left, one of my friends turned and said to me, "Lanette, the first visit is the hardest. They will get easier." I gave her a smile and thanked her. I knew she was correct, but the emotions of the day was still fresh; I gave it all to God and trusted Him in helping me to get past it all, and He did.

In visiting my daughter, Faleasha, was pretty upset that I did not have any eyeglasses yet. She informed me that she was going to make some calls when she got home to see what had to be done to make sure I was provided with some eyeglasses, since the prison would not allow her to mail me any. I had no idea to what God was going to do in this adventure with my daughter. Faleasha is not one to give up, and she was not going to give up until I had eyeglasses! The next day, she did exactly what she said she was going to do, make a lot of calls. When her efforts to contact the prison system went unanswered, she did something I did not know she was going to do - she wrote her congressmen about the situation! I had no idea at the time what all she was doing, until I was called into the office by the camp manager. Once in the office, it was explained to me what my daughter had done, written her congressman in reference to my glasses. I was asked if I knew she was going to do this. I responded to them that this was the first that I had heard about it, and it was from them not my daughter. I knew she was going to call the prison to see what needed to be done for me to be given some eyeglasses, but, no, I did not know she was writing her congressmen.

The camp manager was not happy with me or my family. The camp manager proceeded to tell me that she had received a letter from the congressmen due to the letter that my daughter had written him, asking about my glasses and why had I not been given any as of yet. I did not say anything at the time, but I was smiling inside because of my daughter's persistence. The camp manager told me to inform my daughter to contact her personally and to not be writing anyone else on my behalf, and if my daughter did write anyone else on my behalf, she may have to move me. This was when I looked the camp manager in her eye and said, "I am sorry, I am here at Coleman and unable to tell my daughter what to do or not do. I am a prisoner, not her. She did not tell me she was going to write the congressman to begin with, so how do you think I can control whom she contacts or not. I know my daughter has been trying to contact someone here in reference to my glasses since I arrived, and no one has ever returned her calls. She is only concerned for me, her mother, and she is free to do as she wishes, and I have no control in what she does or doesn't do."

The camp manager looked at me with anger, but she knew I was correct. She could not punish me for anything that my daughter had done. She was only trying to intimidate me - it did not work! I was told that I could leave. I then returned to my unit. I did not call my daughter and tell her what had happened; I would share that with her on her next visit, but it did not take long before my name showed up on a list to see the eye doctor. I had eyeglasses within a month. God showed up again, this time He used my daughter!

Meeting my Unit Team, and finding a place to work

One of my friends had told me about the plumbing crew. It was outside of the camp and it was not a bad crew to work on from what she told me. They worked hard, but found ways to also have fun. One of the girls who worked on this crew had told me that there was an opening if I wanted to apply. I told them sure. My friend set up a time and place for me to meet Mr. Red in order for me to give him my copout to sign and for him to interview me. When I meet Mr. Red, he asked me a few questions and then said he would let my team know if he had accepted me onto his crew. Copouts are a document that was used by all inmates to communicate anything to the staff. This had to be done for my team to even consider letting me work for Mr. Red. I had no idea at the time to how much power my team had over me in everything I was going to be allowed to do at the camp - this I would learn quickly!

Your unit team consists of your counselor, case worker and the unit manager. The unit team was the ones who had the last say in everything you would be allowed to do at the camp while you were in prison. Each inmate would meet with their unit team every three months. All newcomers would meet with their unit team the first week they were at the camp; this would be the first of many meetings to come.

It was my day to be seen by my unit team. I had not been told much other than to listen to everything they said, and when it came to my restitution payments, I would not have much to say in how much I would have to pay. I was told that I would have to agree to whatever they propose or I would lose many of my privileges. My court paperwork said if I worked for UNICOR, which are factories located within federal prisons, I would pay half my wages, and if not working with UNICOR, I would be required to pay twenty-five a month. There are UNICOR factories at most federal prisons for inmates to work in voluntarily.

While I was standing in the hallway with everyone else, I listened to everyone and their guidance in how to handle my first meeting with my unit team. I knew that this also could set precedence to how I and my unit team got along during my stay at Coleman; I wanted it to go well in order for us to get off on the right foot. I had prayed before I had even gotten into line, but I felt a great need in my spirit to stay in prayer as I stood in line. When my name was called, I stepped up to the door, and my counselor informed me to wait outside the door and they would ask me to come inside in a moment.

As I stepped into the office once I was asked to do so, I then met my case worker and unit team manager whom I had not seen before, and my counselor was also in the meeting. I had only met Mr. Seed prior to this meeting. He was my counselor, and he was the one who helped me get all my paper work done for visitation, etc. I walked over to the table and sat down, I felt and uneasiness in the room. I asked God to help me with the feeling that I felt; maybe I was only nervous in meeting my full unit team for the first time.

They began by reviewing all my requirements of the court and what was to be done while I was at Coleman. There was not much required by the court other than me paying on my restitution. This would be covered later at the end of the meeting. We then went over what they required of me and what all I was to be involved in while I was at the camp. I would take classes in the education department, and they encouraged me to get involved in as many things as I could. I was then asked what would be the main thing I would be interested in while I was here at Coleman. I answered, "Anything with the church." They encouraged me in this and told me that there were many activities to get involved in within the church at Coleman, which I would need to keep a watch on the bulletin board for notices and signup sheets.

We then came to the end of the meeting. Now it was time to talk about where I would be allowed to work. The team did mention at first that they had received my copout with me requesting to go to the Mr. Red crew. They brought it to my attention that I may need to work for UNICOR; I would make more money and would be able to pay more toward my restitution. This was voluntary and they could not make me work for UNICOR only recommend it. There was a sign up list that I would need to put my name on. When UNICOR was in the need of more workers they would call me in for an interview. Then the copout for the Mr. Red crew was brought up and reviewed. They told me I could work for this crew as long as I was medically cleared to do so. I had not yet been medically cleared at this time. I was informed by my unit team that they would have to wait to hear from medical before they could sign off on my copout. At this time, I was not sure to where I would be working. I would have to wait.

Now we had come to my restitution. I thought there was nothing to discuss other than I would have to pay twenty-five a month like my court documents said I would. I was told that they had seen how much money was sent to me in Miami FDC, and they proceeded to show me a formula that they used that would show them how much my monthly payment should be. I asked my unit team, "am I not to pay what my court paperwork says I am to pay? I did not know it was up for discussion." My unit team then answered me, "no, we are allowed to calculate all the money that comes into your account to determine what you will pay every month." This was when things got hard for me. The case worker that was in my unit team was a woman and she looked like she was mad at the whole world throughout the entire meeting. She had not said much, but now she was ready to speak; and she had plenty to say.

She looked at me across the table and asked me, "What do you think you should pay toward your restitution why you are here? " I answered her, "I had prepared myself that I would have to pay the monthly amount my court documents stated I would. I did not understand that it was up for discussion. I did not even understand how I was going to make payments to the court. I was not sure if I myself would make them from here inside of prison or would my family have to make the payments for me from the outside. I did not know the money that my family sent me here to use for the phones and to buy items that I need off of commissary including over-the-counter drugs was used to calculate in how much my restitution payments should be. I have no idea at this time to how much money my family will be able to send me every month. When I was in Miami FDC people from our church helped my family in order for them to be able to send me some money for me to be able to get some of the things that I needed. I guess I did not understand the process at all."

She then looked at me across the table and screamed this at me, "do you think the people you defrauded deserve to buy medicine they need, or things that they may need and can't because you took advantage of them? Do you really think you deserve anything being this kind of person that you are? You are lower than dirt and you don't deserve anything, and what we give you, you should be thankful with that, and you make me sick even thinking you should have more.

Tears started to run down my cheeks, I did not know what to say to her. This was when Mr. Seed intervened and said, "I am going to put your payment at twenty-five for now. But you know at the next team meeting which is in three month from today, we will be using this formula that we have showed you and your payment may be adjusted." I was asked to sign my team paperwork, and I was then asked to tell the next woman in line outside to come in.

As I stepped out of the office, the women in the hallway could see that I was crying. They tried to comfort me, but could not. I was hurting so much inside I needed to get out of the unit and before God. This was when I became acquainted with the camp's track.

The Track, becoming my prayer closet

I went to my room and changed my clothes into some shorts and a t-shirt and headed out to the track. The track outside was rocky and uneven, but it felt good to be outside and away from the meeting that I had just encountered. I was praying the full time walking to the track, "Lord help me to get to the track; I don't feel like talking to anyone right now, only you." The track was located at the far back of the compound. Trees were all around it, with a softball field in the middle. Three trips around the track would make a mile. When I first started, I could do only one mile, but I would soon build up to five miles a day. The track was almost empty due to it being in the middle of the afternoon during work hours. I had not been cleared to work yet, so I was allowed to be on the track during work hours. Others were not unless it was their day off.

As I walked the track I started to pour out my heart to the Lord. I found myself being overwhelmed with everything that had happened to me up until this point. My unit team meeting set off a chain reaction in me that was difficult for me to control; and I knew whom I had to go to in order to gain control back – God!

My prayer to the Lord while I walked the track…..

"Lord you know I am not the person that woman in my unit team tried to portray me to be. You know the truth in what happened, but that is how everyone looks at me now.

God then reminded me of a prayer that I had prayed in the ministry one day while I was sitting at my desk.

God said to me, **"do you remember your prayer?"** *"Which one Lord?"* **"When you asked to spend three years in seminary, to grow closer to Me and gain a better understanding of My Word."** *"Yes Lord, when will that happen?"* **"*That* time is now."** *"I am sorry Lord I do not understand, this is prison not seminary."* **"But it is, this is my seminary, and I am your teacher."**

In the year 2002 around February, I prayed a prayer sitting while at my desk in my office at the ministry that sounded something like this:

"Lord I would love to be able to spend three years in seminary to grow closer to you and have a better understanding of your Word. I know this will never happen. I am needed in my family and here at the ministry too much to be able to take a leave. I seek you Lord. I want more of you and your Word."

In my prayer I stated that I was not able to go away due to how much everyone needed me; I thought I was indispensable. Don't we all think this at one time or another? Yes, my family wanted me, and I was being used by God in the Ministry, but if God chose to move me, He would provide another to continue His work within the ministry, and He would take care of my family. God was about to teach me this in a big way. He could and would keep the ministry and my family while He taught me what I needed to learn and what I was yearning for. I do believe that God was waiting for this to be a desire in my heart, to grow closer to Him. And this is accomplished by spending more time with God and His Word. God's Word says He will give us the desires of our heart, but this only happens when our desires line up with God's will for us, not our will. God was answering my prayer and giving me my heart desire. It was not the way I thought God would have answered my prayer, but God was answering.

I had been in seminary prior to coming into prison, and I was learning so much, and I was growing closer to God everyday. This was causing me to have a deeper longing in my heart for more of God and His Word. My family and the ministry were going to be fine without me, and I was about to learn this. I had no idea at the time to how much God was going to answer my prayer, but He did, not in the way I thought He would. But don't we all have to learn this at one time or other in our lives? Our ways are not God's way, but He will always answer our prayers. It may not look like what we asked for, but after it is all over, we can then see the wisdom of God in it and it was what we needed.

As I continued to walk around the track with tears running down my face, I understood what God was saying to me. But I was so burdened with where I was and looking at three more years being away from my family, all I could do was cry. Tears running down my face, I could hardly see where I was going. I kept putting one foot in front of the other. This was when I looked up and a woman was walking toward me. I had seen her a few times already as I walked around the track and, because she was walking in the opposite direction of me, we kept passing each other. But this time she did not walk on past me. She stopped right in front of me, causing me to stop walking and pay attention to what she had to say.

I did not know her at the time. I had not been at Coleman but a few weeks. I had seen her face in church, but we had never spoken until now. She took a hold of each of my arms and looked right into my eyes and said this to me:

"Woman of God, you know who you are because God has revealed it to you. Do not forget who God said you are. This is a time of preparation for what He has for you. Do not be discouraged, but encouraged. Trust your Lord and listen to all He has to say to you. This is not the end of your life but the beginning. You have been called for a time such as this. Trust God. He has a lot He wants to teach you. Listen, it is all in preparation for what is ahead of you."

She said nothing else to me. She let go of my arms and walked away as quickly as she had stopped in front of me. As I finished walking around the circle, I was close to where the chapel was located. I stopped and went inside; I found the chapel to be empty. As I entered the chapel, I found myself going directly to the altar and falling to my knees, I then began to cry out to the Lord to help me with the sadness I felt inside and the burden that was overwhelming me to go home. I stayed at the altar for quite some time - not sure how long I was there. God then blessed me with a great peace and joy. My tears stopped flowing and I began to smile. There was something different this time in what I had received from God while I was on my knees in the chapel. The peace and joy that I was feeling was not the same as I had felt before. It was not the same peace that I felt when I was teaching God's Word to others or helping others to understand about His goodness and grace. This was more personal for me. I did not want to leave the chapel, but I heard the call over the intercom for all to go to their units for count. I made my way to my unit and the way that I felt did not leave me.

As I waked to my unit, I could not help myself but to smile. I did not understand at the time what all was going on inside of me, but God would teach me soon enough. I was beginning to surrender to God's will for my life and not mine. This was the beginning of many things for me; the seminary I had asked God for in my earlier prayer had begun. Many women who had seen me earlier that day when I left my unit team meeting crying now looked at me with a smile, and said; "we are glad you are doing better." Everyone kept telling me that it would get better; all I had to do was give it some time. They were right in a way, but the time that I needed to give was to God. I responded to them, "I know, God is helping me."

Chapter 11

Why is it so hard to be a kid?

On the Journey behind Prison Walls, I would think about many things. When you are in prison, you think a lot, and I had many things of my past that I needed God to help me heal and forgive, and God had my undivided attention. As I sat in my room after leaving the track and the chapel, I was still in a state of amazement over what had happened between me and God in the chapel. I knew God was trying to get my attention to look deeper into myself and what held me bound - my past! I found myself looking back into my past and how everything may have contributed to me being here in this prison, and could I have done something to stop it. Or was this my destiny? When I read about Joseph and how he came to be in a pit and found himself in prison and then the second in command to the Pharaoh, could he have stopped it? Could Joseph have walked into the destiny of God for him some other way, or did it have to be this way? His love for God was true. God had even given him a dream that showed Joseph how he would be used by God, and Joseph was right where God said he would be in the dream, in a place that he could and would save a nation. But Joseph had to go through something to prepare him for a day such as this. This was all going through my mind as I read my Bible. I was reading my Bible from cover to cover for the first time in my life. I did not know what to study or read about in the midst of my pain, so I started from the beginning and kept reading. This was when I found so many Scriptures that fed me and gave me strength. I could not believe the hunger and understanding that I had for the Word of God; I could not put it down. In reading about Joseph and all he had to go through to get to where God had called him, I could not help myself from thinking was this happening to me? Was there more to my situation than met the eye? What was it that God was really doing? God was going to reveal it all to me through His Word.

This was the tool that God was going to use to bring me full circle, His Word. Many of us don't read God's Word like we should. Yes, we go to church on Sunday and even attend the night that Bible study is on, but do we read the Word on our own? The real surgery takes place in us in reading God's Word, when it is you and God all alone - at least that is how it happened in me. I had studied the Word extensively, but never cover to cover. I was in amazement in all that I had missed. My heart was also at a place to receive whatever the Word of God showed me. This makes a big difference in us, being teachable. We have to be at a place with God willing to receive whatever it is that God is trying to show us. Many times in reading God's Word we censor what we allow in from God. We tell God "that hurts too much. We can't go there Lord, that is my protected place let's not look behind that door, Lord." We keep it closed up inside of us and don't let God in to help us heal and forgive. These places in us cause us a lot of pain and keep us bound. Most of us are not even aware of the power it holds over us. This is a trick of the enemy. He wants to keep you bound and locked up and not free in the victory that Jesus gives you.

The enemy would love us to sit in a corner and have a pity party, meditating on how we did things and wish we had done them better, but we can't change the past, and living in the past will keep you from the present and your future. God will take us through our past, not to have self pity but to learn, and we must surrender to God and allow Him to walk us through our past to learn from it. Then we can realize what we did wrong and what we need to change in order to do things better. Then we need to move on back to the present. But if we are not careful the enemy will keep us in the past in self pity, and we will not do as God wants us to do - meditate on His Word, not our past - learn from it, yes, but not live in it. Yes, I had many things to learn from my past and things I needed to let go. I could only do this by looking at my past with God's help, facing it and realizing what I could have done differently and learn from it and move on. Many things in my past, I needed to forgive others. It was not all my decisions that hurt me, but others and most of them were adults. But so often we stay in our past and allow it to be our excuse for not living in the present and striving for the future that God has planned for us.

My childhood was a hard one. My mother was an alcoholic and was not home most of the time to raise me and my brothers. Even at nine years of age, I would be left with my two brothers, seven and eight, for days at a time to tend to their needs and mine. Yes, my mom had tried many babysitters but, they would only eat all of our food and have friends over who would also eat our food, and we did not have a lot to share, and the worst part of it was that most of the babysitters that my mom found would also beat my little brother, so in our minds it was better to be by ourselves. We would wash our clothes in the bath tub and eat peanut butter and jelly sandwiches a lot. Sometimes the neighbors would even take us in and feed us. God watched over my brothers and me in many ways. We would get ourselves off to school and even try to help each other with our homework. I was never good in school. Spelling was hard for me and I seemed to not fit in anywhere. I did not have many friends, so I played with my brothers and their friends most of the time. My favorite time as a child was the summers when my brothers and I would be allowed to spend them with our grandparents or our father. It was like a fairy tale when we were with them. I thought many times to myself, if I could only live with either of them all year, but that never happened.

When I was about fourteen and a half, my mother and I had a terrible fight. My mom was not happy with me in how fast I was putting some of the parts together for her from her job. My mother was allowed to bring parts home from her work and assemble them and take them back to work to get credit for them in order to make some extra money. My mother worked for a typewriter factory, and she did not make much money. It was hard for us to survive on what she made; we needed the extra money she could make from home assembling parts together. My brothers and I helped our mom often putting the parts together. We understood how poor we were and we were happy to help our mom in any way we could to earn extra money. Mom taught my brothers and me how to do the work, and we were all pretty good at putting the parts together without much supervision. The parts had to be put together correctly for our mom to receive the extra credit when she turned them in to work. Because of this, we were careful to make sure they were done correctly. In the past we had assembled some parts for our mother and when she took them to work to receive her extra credit, they were incorrect, and because of this, she was not given anything for the parts we had done. We did not want this to happen again, so my brothers and I were careful in the work we were doing.

My brothers and I were putting together parts like we always did on weekends when my mom was allowed to bring parts home. The extra work was not always available to my mom, so she grabbed it anytime it was offered. It had to be done the weekend that it was given or you would not receive the extra credit. This particular weekend, my mom seemed to be upset about something; she was in a terrible mood. My brothers and I were sitting around a long coffee table on the floor assembling parts as fast as we could, making sure they were put together correctly, when all of a sudden my mother started yelling at me that I was not going fast enough. To my surprise and my brothers', my mother reached across the table that I was working at and stabbed me in my hand with one of the tools we were all using. I yelled and started to cry. I then got up from the table, holding my bleeding hand, asking my mom "why did you stab me?" My mom ran after me and grabbed me by my hair and told me to get back to work. My brothers then started yelling at our mom to stop and to leave me alone. This was when my mom told me to get out of her house and never to come back unless I got back to work. I was so upset that my mother had stabbed me, that I could not think about anything other than my mother had stabbed me. I was bleeding and hurt; I was frightened of my mom and mad at her all at the same time. I could not understand why my mom had stabbed me to begin with, but I also had all the emotions to why did my mom treat me so badly all the time anyway. This was like the straw that broke the camel's back. To me it looked like my mother did not love me or even care that she had hurt me. All I could think about at the time was that I needed to get away from what was causing all the pain within me; and to me that was my mother.

I had had enough. I ran out the back door with my brothers yelling at me to not go and yelling at our mother to leave me alone. I was almost fifteen, and I had no idea to what all was ahead of me. All I knew, I was getting away from what looked to be the reason of all my pain - my mom. I found myself living on the street until I was almost sixteen. I am sure if I had gone back to my mother's house, she would have allowed me to come back home, but with her pride and mine, that did not happen. To this day, I don't know why I did not call my dad. I know we were not close back then but he loved my brothers and me. My mom did everything she could to convince my brothers and me that our father was not there for us and that he did not want us. I believe I did not call my dad or my grandparents because of the fear that they would only take me back to my mom's house and not take me home with them, and, at the time, I could not see myself going back home to my mom. Living on the street appeared to me to be my only choice to escape all the pain that my life seemed to be full of. I had no idea I was leaving one pain to step into other.

My brothers and I were on our own for the most part of our young lives, and because of this, we did not have much respect for any authority. I know now that this was the reason that I did not have any respect for my mother's authority over me or my brothers, and due to this, my mother and I did not get along with one another. In my mind, at the age of fourteen and a half, my mother did not have any right to tell me or my brothers what to do since she had not been around for a lot of the years previously. There was a lot of anger and frustration in me as a young girl. I had no idea at the time that I was a broken child screaming for help. It was hard for me to accept help when it did come, due to me not being able to trust or love anyone completely. I only knew how to survive. God was about to teach me how to forgive and heal from my past in order for me to learn how to trust and love as He does.

I lived under trees and under street overpasses. Some friends of mine would even let me live in their basements for a few days here and there, but I could not stay long due to explaining to their parents why I was there, so this was mostly on weekends that I would be allowed to stay with them. Staying in abandoned buildings would prove to be a useful means of shelter, and food was mostly stolen. After I had been living on the streets for about eight months, I did come across a younger woman with a young child that had a small one room apartment who was willing to allow me to stay with her. I helped her with her daughter, and she gave me a roof over my head. She, too, did not have much money, so food was still a problem. Either she or I would have to go into the stores and steal whatever we could in order to eat or get items needed for the baby.

One day when I went in to a store to pick up some item, steal them that is, some food and one item for the baby, I was caught for shoplifting. When the officers took me to the station and looked for my name on the missing persons report or the list for runaways, they were shocked to find my name was not on either list. When they saw my age was fifteen and a half and that I was not reported as a runaway or a missing person, they contacted my mom to look into the situation further. When they contacted my mom, they learned she did not want to have anything to do with me. She did not even come down to the station to see me. I had been a runaway in the past due to me and my mom's relationship and her abuse toward me, but this time was different. My mom had given up on me. I am so glad that God never leaves us or forsakes us. He never gives up on us, but I did not know or understand this at the time. As a young girl, I felt all alone, but I knew my Jesus and I was calling out to Him the entire time for Him to help me.

I had not made it easy for my mom. I was so bitter and hurt from all the years of her not being there, for me and my brothers; and I did not know how to be around her as a daughter. Because of my mom's attitude toward the situation, everything would have to go before a judge. When the judge heard the whole case, my mother lost her parental rights, and I was put into foster care as a ward of the court. I was really weak at the time when I was picked up for shoplifting. My weight was less than 100 lbs, and it was hard for me to even sit and eat a full meal. My foster mother was going to have to tend to the healing of my body and my spirit, because both were broken. Again I was provided for by God, even in foster care. My foster mother was a woman of God, and God was going to use her to help me heal in many ways.

I had been raped three times before I even turned seventeen. One time, I came real close to losing my life, and life, at that point, did not seem to be one worth living. I kept asking God, why is it so hard to be a kid? I believe I was on a self destructive mode for many years after, all the way up into my late twenties. It was God that was watching over me and had a better plan for me; and God never gave up on me even when I had given up on myself. I accepted Christ at a young age, due to a church bus picking up my two brothers and me every Sunday while we were young kids. It was something that both of my brothers and I looked forward to every Sunday. All the church activities and services were happy times for my brothers and me. We got to pretend in a strange way that we lived a normal life like all the other kids that were at church with us. But we always had to go home and face reality and our mom.

We even went to vacation Bible school when we were allowed to be with our dad on our summer breaks. Our dad always went to church with us on Sunday, from what I can remember. This was special to me. I was not used to going to church as a family, and my dad gave this to me and my brothers in the summers every Sunday when we were allowed to stay with him. We did not understand why we could not go to be with our dad every summer. We were only told from our dad that our mom would not let us; and our mom would say it was because of our dad. We kids only knew we were not allowed to be with our dad and it made us sad.

One summer when I was about ten, I came to a realization that I needed Jesus in my life. One Sunday morning before going to church while I was staying with my dad on one of our summer breaks, I went to my dad to ask him a question. I had been going to vacation Bible school during the week, and now it was Sunday, and we were all getting ready to go to church as a family. I loved to watch my dad shave his face, and he was in the bathroom getting ready for church. I went in and sat down on the toilet seat and began to watch my dad shave and talk

A Journey Behind Prison Walls

to him while he did. I told my dad that I had been learning in vacation Bible school that Jesus loves me, and I told my dad that I loved Him also. My dad turned and looked at me and said, "Honey, I am so proud of you that you have learned this. You are getting to be a big girl." I then told my dad, "I have been listening to my teacher and she was telling us how we have to ask Jesus into our heart and He then will becomes our Savior, and then He is with us everywhere we go. I want to do that today at church," I told my daddy, "accept Jesus as my Savior." My dad bent down and looked me in my eyes with joy and said, "Honey, that is so good, but I want you to wait a little longer until you are old enough to understand what you are doing." My daddy continued to tell me that he was proud of me, and it was good that I had come to understand who Jesus was and what He had done for us all. But my daddy told me that accepting Jesus was a big decision, and he wanted me to wait a little longer until I was a little older and could understand everything that I was doing. My daddy gave me a hug and told me he loved me. I loved my dad and I told him okay with a saddened heart.

We all went to church that day, and, as I sat in the pew with my family, I heard the altar call for Salvation. I wanted to go up front, but I was not going to disobey my dad, so I sat in the pew and I lowered my head and said these words:

"Jesus I know you love me. My teacher told me about you, and I believe you are who she said you are. My daddy said I am too young to walk down front and accept you as my Savior. I don't want to disobey my dad, but I want to ask you into my heart sitting here in my seat. Jesus I don't want to go home to my mommy alone.

<u>Would you go home with me, please, and protect me, and I will try my best to be good. Amen."</u>

The tears slowly stopped, and I felt a peace come over me. As a child, I could not understand it all, but it felt good, and I felt like I was not alone in a strange way. I remember my daddy asking me if I was okay, and I answered him, saying, "Yes, I am fine daddy, I was only praying to Jesus." My daddy gave me a smile and a hug.

In looking back over my past while I was sitting on my bunk after I had gotten back to my unit and my cell from the track and the chapel, tears started to come back to my eyes again. I cried to the Lord, "I know my past. What is it that you are trying to show me in looking at it all over again? It only hurts when I look at it all. What do you want me to do with these memories Lord?" This was when God spoke to me and the healing began. God said to me "I want you to heal and forgive, and not let it hold you captive any longer. Learn from it and help others once you have learned" I cried out to the Lord saying, Lord, I don't know how to do that." God responded to me by saying, "I know. I will show you." I then went to God and surrendered my past and all the pain that it represented. I cried out to the Lord by saying. "Okay Lord, show me what to do, I surrender". It looked like to me I was surrendering to the Lord every time I turned around, but what I was really doing was surrendering different areas of my life to God, one by one, as He revealed them to me.

When I did this, I had no idea what God was going to have to do to help me with all the hurt and pain from my past that still lived inside of me. It was not only my childhood that was hurtful that I needed to be healed from. There was also a lot of abuse that I had endured as a young adult, including my first marriage that almost killed me and my first child. I had to run for my life and hers, by leaving Springfield, MO in order to protect us both, but now God was going to take me down a road that would lead me to freedom. The good news was, freedom was available; and God was going to show me how I could acquire it. And then, in turn, I was going to be able to share it with others that needed to do the same. Look at your past right now. Has the enemy tricked you as he did me to live in your past and not heal and forgive so you can move on? If this is you, I encourage you to take the journey I did, the one of healing and forgiveness. You will never be the same.

This was going to take some time. It was not all going to happen in one day sitting on my bed waiting for count to be finished, but this was the beginning of the rest of my life, one that I was about to discover was worth living and living with a passion that I had never had before. God took me through His Word and fed me in a way I had never let the Word feed me before. The key to everything was I had to open up my heart to the will of God and not my will. I wanted God's purpose and all that came with it. This was how I was able to gain the peace and joy that God had for me, but I had to go through the fire first. As I read the Word of God, it helped see and understand where I did not line up, with His Word. But at the same time, God showed me what I needed to do to line up with the Word, and I made a decision to do what the Word showed me to do. I was ready to allow in what needed to be in, and allow God to remove what needed to be removed. God will not take out of us what needs to be removed, unless we give it up first. We have to surrender it and give it to God. I had many things in me that needed to be surrendered, and God helped me with each one of them. As I went through this process, I began to experience more freedom, and peace and joy followed.

Many times, we understand that we are living in pain, and we even think we have done what we need to do to overcome it by praying. Our pain may be from our past even our current situations that we find ourselves living in. Pain comes from many different aspects of life, but we are too often looking for a quick fix. We want to say a quick prayer and it all be done; we are renewed. In what God has to do in most of us takes time, and what I needed most of all was a deeper relationship with God. This all happened in me as I read God's Word, the Word of God is necessary for us all to heal. Prayer is good and needed also, but not intended to be used alone. Once you have others pray for you, and you have prayed for yourself, you then must dig into God's Word and allow Him to walk you through the healing processes. We play a big part in the renewing of our minds. We have to seek after God, and we will find Him and all that He has for us.

Learning to see

When I went to work for Mike, I did not do it at a drop of a dime. I thought about it for a long time. I even prayed for guidance, for about six months. I was not walking with the Lord as I was when I was arrested, but I was saved and going to church every Sunday. I prayed and I looked to myself as being a pretty good Christian, one that was trying to follow God, at least I thought I was.

I kept going over in my head and asking myself how could I have stopped this situation from happening, and I kept coming up with the same answer. I could not see where I could have stopped anything from taking place the way that it did. I had done everything that I knew to do at the time, and I still could not stop the outcome from being what it was. Even in our best of decisions, we have to admit, sometimes, we still mess up even when we think we have it all together. God knows all. He even knows the blunders we will make of things before we get it right, but God will work it all out for His good and ours if we would only be patient.

My life verse kept coming back to me over and over again throughout my journey behind prison walls.

Roman 8:28 *And we know that God causes all things to work together for good to those who love God, to those who are called according to His purpose. (NASB)*

I knew I loved God, and I was saved, so this verse was referring to me and all my life's situations. All things will work together for good no matter how it may look to us at the time. I had to remind myself of this on many occasions. This verse got me through many hard times when I was confused and lost with what was going on with my life, and it would help me in many more years to come like many other verses in the Bible do. That is what the Word will do for all of us if we would only let it, but it can't help us if we don't read it.

Once we allow God to transform us by the renewing of our minds, we are able to make better choices. I was doing the best I could at the time with all the baggage I was carrying around.

Romans 12:1-2 *Therefore I urge you brethren, by the mercies of God, to present your bodies a living and holy sacrifice, acceptable to God, which is your spiritual service of worship. 2) And do not be conformed to this world, but be transformed by the renewing of your mind, so that you may prove what the will of God is, that which is good and acceptable and perfect. (NASB)*

In Romans 12:1-2, it speaks on what we must do in order for our minds to be renewed. I needed to completely surrender myself to the Lord, and once I did this, only then would the will of God for my life work itself out through me. I would then be able to walk the path that God had for me, hearing and understanding God in a new light. I had no idea until then that I was walking by my might and not God's. My spiritual relationship with God was broken and my choices were not being led by Him. Because of this, I was not able to see things clearly and make good decisions when it came to working for Mike. It was bothering me why I did not see the kind of person that Mike was. Why could I not see it? God was showing me that I did not see it, because I was not allowing God to show me. I was looking with my eyes, not His. In realizing this, I could let it go. I could not change the past, but I could change my future, by surrendering myself to the Lord and allowing Him to guide me.

Many of us want to know everything, A-Z as you may say, and it drives us crazy, if we don't have a clear understanding of everything. I was this way in many things, but then I learned that when you have true faith in God, you are asked many times to walk by faith, even when you don't understand it all. This was clear to me when I read:

Deuteronomy 29:29: *"The secret things belong to the Lord our God, but the things revealed belong to us and to our sons forever, that we many observe all the words of this law."* (NASB)

When I read this verse it gave me great victory and knowledge that I would not understand everything, that I have to give it to God, and accept that there are many mysteries that I will not understand; and my faith has to be strong enough to trust God with it. My past was gone, and I was here in prison for what looked like to be three more years. Now it was time for me to get busy about what God had for me here, not only teaching and helping others, but what God had to teach me while I was here, and to help me to lighten the load that I was carrying around daily. It was time to get busy in doing God's will and not mine.

An unexpected blessing, from an unexpected person

There was one more person I had to see before I could be cleared for work, the psychologist. When I came into the prison system, my doctor had put me on Paxil during the court process. This is a medication to help with anxiety. Going through the court process stressed me out so badly that my blood pressure had gotten out of control. More medication was given to me in order to try to control my blood pressure, but it did not help. This was when my doctor put me on Paxil in the effort to try to control my blood pressure. Paxil did help and my blood pressure returned within normal numbers. With all the pressure that was on me going through the trial, I was also diagnosed with heart disease. I found myself in the hospital going through many tests during the trial process.

When I came into prison, they did not stop the medication even, though I requested to have it discontinued. The trial was over, and I wanted to see how I would do without it. I learned that this was not possible, until the prison doctors gave me permission. I had no control, even in the medication that I was taking. I had to take the medication, even if I did not want to. If I did not, I could get in trouble. Because I was on the medication, I had to visit with a psychologist to see how I was doing. This first meeting would determine how often we needed to meet.

When I walked into the office, I was asked to sit down in the chair that was located in front of the desk. The psychologist was a man, and he seemed to be quite cheerful. In prison you have to be careful with any staff member, in everything that you share with them. You have to keep in mind to where you are at all times - "prison." Everything you talk about is put into your record, and your team has access to everything. What you share can affect you in future requests with your unit team. I proceeded with the meeting carefully with this all in mind and was thankful for all that had been shared with me in how things were inside of prison. I had prayed before entering the meeting and asked God to guide me and help me, and He did.

The therapist introduced himself and explained to me what the purpose of the meeting was. "We meet with everyone when they first come to Coleman in order to determine if they may need help in the transition process coming into prison. We know this is not easy, and some need a little help getting used to being here." I did not know that everyone had to meet with him. I thought it was only because I was on the medicine I was on. This did make sense. It was hard to get your mind wrapped around being in prison and away from everything you loved and knew. I had only been able to bear the transition up to this point with the help of God; I don't know how others get through it without Him.

As we began to talk, he said something to me that brought forth a response that changed the direction of the meeting. I knew with all my heart that at that moment God had taken control of the meeting. It was all about God and His will for this meeting, not man's. The therapist proceeded to tell me if I would only come to the understanding with what I had done, and seek out forgiveness from those I had hurt and my family, and not do it again; I could still have a productive life. He continued on to say, this is not the end of your life; it can be a new beginning. He also told me if I would only do this, being in prison would be a lot easier, and he was here to help me. I looked at the therapist and took a deep breath and with God's help I responded.

I started by saying, "I know that most of the staff here do not want to hear what I am about to say to you, but I am going to say it anyway. My transition is a little different than most due to the fact that I am here doing time, as you may call it, for something I did not do. I understand that you are only doing your job, like the jury and the judge also felt like they were only doing what they believe to be their jobs. But it doesn't negate the fact that I am still innocent. I know that you can't help me with being here because you are trained to rehabilitate those who need to change their lives around. I do not expect you to believe that I am innocent, and because you are not able to believe this, you can't help me in my transition in being here, only God can. Your statement to me was that I only needed to not do this crime again, and I would not end up here again, but my stress is this, I did not do the crime to begin with, and I ended up here anyway. I have to ask God to help me to move on in His will and to not be frightened of the world that I live in, looking over my shoulder everyday thinking that something like this could happen to me again. This is what I am dealing with everyday."

I continued to share with the therapist in what I had learned since I had come into the system. "There is not a staff member at Coleman or anywhere within the system throughout that could help someone like me, not because they don't want to, but because no one within the system would ever want to entertain the fact that someone could actually be in prison that is innocent. If you did, then you and your fellow co-workers would have to realize, as I have, that our system is broken, and then it would be difficult for you to do your job everyday. This is why I had to realize that the only one that could help me get through this is God." I told the therapist that he would be the last staff member that I would express this to while I was in prison. "I am not here to fix this system, and I am also not here to be punished for a crime. But I am here to learn from God and have a deeper relationship with Him, and I have surrendered this all to Jesus, and God will get me through this no matter how long I am here."

The therapist then looked at me and said, "I, too, am a Christian, and I do understand what you are saying; and I agree. It appears to me that you have an understanding in what it is that you must to do to be able to deal with being here. You are seeking the right one, Jesus. I am not able to talk to everyone in reference to Jesus because of my job, but I see something different, in you and I feel like I can speak freely. Don't let this place get you down and don't forget who you are in Christ. Trust Him and He will get you through this. Whatever God has for you, this has to part of His plan to prepare you for it. Embrace it and learn all you can.

These words were familiar to me. I had heard them from the woman on the track and my son-in-law had spoken these words to me in the courthouse prior to sentencing. God was using many who I was coming in contact with to help me keep my head up and my eyes on Him. I looked at him and said thank you. I continued to share with the therapist that I was wrong by saying that none of the staff at Coleman could help me, because he had. The therapist smiled at me and said, "God did it, not me." He then said "you don't need to see me any more unless you want to. If you would like to talk, put in a request, and I will put your name on the schedule. From what I see, you have your eyes on the right one - Jesus."

I then asked him if I could get off the Paxil. He said, "I would not recommend it right now. I would suggest that you give it some time to completely adjust. Remember, you have not even started to work yet. After you are here for a while and we see how you are doing, and then let's try taking you off." I thanked him again, and told him, "God bless you," he responded, "He already has." As I walked out of the office, I went back to my room to think about what had happened. As I went to God and asked Him to show me everything that I was suppose to gain out of this meeting; this was what God showed me. God was going to use me with the staff also, not only my fellow inmates. I went into see this therapist with the wrong idea, that he could not help me and I could not be used by God to help him. This was so far from the truth. God used us both to minister to the each other. The mission field that I was in was a lot bigger than I realized - nothing was too big for God! God wanted to use me to minister to the staff also while I was in prison, but I had to let God work through me.

Chapter 12

Finally, going to work

Within a few days after speaking to the psychologist my name showed up on the list to go to work. I was going to work for Mr. Red, who was the officer in charge of the plumbing crew. When you went to work at Coleman, most of us were required to wear our green uniforms and work boots. My boots were new and not broken in yet. I was told by a fellow inmate to put them in the shower and get them good and wet and let them dry - this would help break them in. I did this, but they still hurt my feet. I would still have to wear them with some discomfort before they would be comfortable. This also meant I was going to have to bear with some blisters until the boots were broken in - this took about a month.

When I arrived at Coleman, I had to go to the laundry and pick up all my clothing, including linen, towels, and under garments. I was also given work boots, and uniforms. My uniforms were old, but in pretty good condition. My boots and all my under garments were brand new. My laundry bag was given to me with my name on it. I could then drop off my dirty laundry to be washed on my laundry day. The only thing about dropping off your laundry to be washed was, your laundry was washed and dried within the laundry bag. When you picked up your laundry it would be wrinkled, and, most of the time tangled up in a knot. If you had the money to wash it yourself by using the washers and dryers within your unit, it was better. But if you did not have the money to wash your laundry on your own, at least the camp provided a way for you to have all your laundry washed at no charge to you.

I had to be up at 5AM in order to get dressed and have breakfast before going out to meet the truck that would pick me up for work. I would be working off the camp everyday. This was one of the benefits working on Mr. Red's crew. Everyday from 7AM until 4:30 PM, I would be off the compound. I would only have to come back on the compound for lunch.

When I went to the pickup spot that I had been told about by my friend, I found four other women waiting to be picked up for the same crew I would be on, including my friend who had told me about the job. I was nervous and did not have any idea in what to expect working inside of prison. All the women that I was going to be working with put me at ease pretty quickly with humor and watching them how they interacted with one another as we all waited to be picked up by Mr. Red. I felt a peace coming over me. I thanked God in my spirit as I stood and waited for the truck - "God you have done it again, protected me and have given me peace in the midst of this storm; thank you my Lord Jesus."

My first day at work was different than I had expected. All the women who worked on this crew actually had fun while they worked. We laughed and worked together, and, even the officer over the plumbing crew was friendly, but professional. He was willing to teach anyone who was willing to learn. I was interested in learning anything I could. I wanted to make the best of my time while I was in prison. I wanted to keep my mind busy and active.

Our office for our crew was located within a powerhouse. Within the powerhouse, there were two crews who met there. The crew I was working on, plumbing, and also the heating and air-conditioning crew. Mr. Chris was the officer in charge of the heating and air-conditioning crew. I did not understand it at the time, but God had brought me to this place so I could meet Mr. Chris and his crew. We would all become close, and God had work for me to do here that had nothing to do with plumbing or air-conditioning.

I was still amazed in how God guided me to the crew. I did not know anything about the system in prison, I only trusted God and when I was asked did I want to join the crew, I walked through the door that God had opened. I know many times this is hard for us to do, and, trust me; I don't always go through the doors that God opens for me. So often we are too busy trying to pry doors open that have been locked. I was learning to trust God in a new way. It was more complete. My everyday peace had come to depend on it due to the situation I was in. God knew everything, where I was and what was ahead of me. He also knew the heart of all that were around me, and by me trusting in Him, God kept me from a lot of nonsense.

The longer I was at Coleman the better I got at listening to God. This did not happen overnight. I am sure you are like me. We want things to happen right now. But we must be patient with God and go through the transforming process. I am so thankful that He is patient with us all. I was asking God everyday to guide me and show me all that I was around through His eyes. I know with all my heart this was what helped me to deal with all the different personalities that I had to deal with everyday. There were so many women that were from all different walks of life, different religions and backgrounds. I had to be careful to not offend anyone. This meant that every word that came out of my mouth had to be thought about and cleared through God.

This was something I was learning to perfect with God already, before I even came into prison, but now it was something that had to be done every second of the day. Yes, this is something that we all need to learn to do all the time in our everyday life. God now had allowed me to be put into a situation that this became a priority for me. God has to allow situations in our lives sometimes to get our attention in an area of weakness that we may need to work on, God is trying to help us, but we are not always letting Him have full rein. And this is because we don't take it as seriously as God wants us to, so He will allow us to be placed in a situation that will bring it to the surface, and then we see it for the importance that God intends it to have, as He sees it. I was even asked sometimes, "Lanette, why do you pause so often before you answer when you are asked a question?" I would answer; "I want to make sure I am giving you what God would have me say to you, and not me."

This changed my life in how I communicated with others. So often we want to say something to someone about something they are doing or not doing, but they are not ready to listen. But we go and tell them anyway. This can cause a wedge a lot of times between you and them, preventing you from being able to tell them anything. God asked me one day, "Who is this helping? Are you saying what you are saying for them or yourself?" When I thought about it, it was clear - for myself. If the person is not ready to hear what you are telling them and you say it anyway, it is for you satisfaction not for their good. God showed me it was better to pray for the person and wait on God to prepare them to hear what they need to hear. Then to wait on God for Him to release us when the time is right to go to the person and tell them only what God has released us to share. Some people have to receive things in small pieces and others can hear it all at one time. God is the only one that knows what someone is ready to hear or not hear and by praying and waiting on Him the wedge will not form. Then the message is received and healing and correction can take place.

I watched God work this out in my life one person after another while I was in prison. It amazed me to how much people were willing to listen to what God had to say to their situation when I waited and only shared with them when God released me to do so. I do this still to this day; it has blessed me and saved many relationships in my life from being hindered. God's ways are not our ways. We are never going to do everything like God would, but we don't have to. We are not God's. All we have to do is listen to God, and He will direct our path.

I worked on the plumbing crew for about three months, and we worked hard. We did all the plumbing on the compound and even outside of it. We were responsible for all the washers and dryers and even the ice machines. Every unit had an ice machine, and the kitchen, of course, had a two large ice machines. All of the ice machines had to be cleaned once a mouth, and this was one of the first things I was taught. I did not mind it. It was actually interesting to learn how things worked. Working off the compound was interesting. It gave you a small since of freedom. We were allowed to drive ourselves around from job to job. We had access to all the units and all buildings, unsupervised by an officer. It was a good feeling to be able to move around on our own, but I was still not home, and, sometimes, this freedom made me miss home even more.

Trusting God and staying close to Him was so important for me on a daily basis, it was needed for survival. When I was outside of these prison walls, I thought I was close to God and trusting Him daily, but I was learning this on a whole new level. There was so much to learn. I could not let my mind wander for even a minute. If I did, the enemy was right there to pounce on me and I would then lose my joy and hope. The situation I was in kept me closer to God. I found myself talking about the goodness and grace to my fellow workers on Mr. Red's crew as we worked. I did not plan it that way - it came natural. What else would I talk about, but Jesus? He was my way of life. It even amazed me to how much Jesus was in my every thought. I did not even think about how it would look, or what would they think, or would they even listen to me. It did not matter. My mouth opened, and I was talking about Jesus. Now this was different from what I said before in telling someone something that they may not be ready to listen to. That was referencing something on more of a personal matter to that individual. Jesus was a topic for all to hear.

So often we do not even talk to others about Jesus because we have reasoned it out in our own minds. Is this the right place, the right time? The excuses can go on and on. But I was in a place that I had totally surrendered to God's will and His plan and purpose, and things were happening without a long thought-out plan. God can do the most in us and through us, when we get out of the way, and let Him do all the planning. Now, yes, we do have to have some kind of plan of action for our lives. If we fail to plan, we plan to fail. But that is not what I am referring to. When it comes to the things of God, many of us need to learn to let go and let God. This was exactly what I was learning. I was not the one who was directing my daily activities, and because I was not, happiness filled my days, and the Gospel of Jesus was being proclaimed.

I worked with many women that did not believe in Jesus. Many had other religions and a few believed there was no God. But as we worked together, I was blessed to watch Jesus present Himself to them all. This was when God reinforced the importance in not getting upset or even disappointed if I did not see them come to Christ. God may be only using me to plant the seed. So often we push Jesus down people's throats because we want to witness them surrender to Jesus Christ. Yes this is a great blessing to witness, but we have to be okay if we are only the planter; planting the seed of Jesus or watering a seed that has already been planted. Whatever part we play is a blessing. We are all important within the body of Christ, and we need to have peace in whatever God uses us for.

Mowing the Grass, not work but a blessing

We never knew what our assignment may be from day to day on Mr. Red's crew; we would be told once at work. Mr. Red liked to keep us guessing. It was a technique used by many officers to reinforce they were the ones in charge. One morning, once we were all done with our safety briefing given by Mr. Red, I was given an assignment that concerned me at first. I was to mow the grass around the powerhouse. This was a concern due to my asthma. I had been told by my doctor at home to never mow grass because it could cause me to have an asthma attack. When I first heard the assignment, I was tempted to speak up and present the issue to Mr. Red that this could cause me harm; but I felt in my spirit that I was to keep the assignment, and I did

I was left at the powerhouse all alone while everyone else on the crew went with Mr. Red to do another job on the camp. I put on ear protection and a ball cap to protect me from the sun, and proceeded to mow the grass. As I mowed, I prayed to God and opened up my mind and spirit for whatever God wanted to speak to me about. God moved in my heart and spirit in a big way that day. I had been troubled by being in prison for charges that I had not done, but even more I had been asking, "God, how did something like this happen to me? Why did I not notice what the owner of the company was doing? God, why did I not see the signs that he was doing something he was not supposed to do, as it was stated in the courtroom at trial?"

Even though the trial was over, there was a statement at trial that was still bothering me. The prosecutor came to agree with my lawyer that I had not gone to work for Mike knowing he was committing fraud in one of his companies. But his statement that followed was what had been bothering me ever since. He continued with, "Mrs. Black should have figured out what Mike was doing and called the FBI." This was what I had been asking God since I had come into prison. Why did I not figure it out and call the FBI, why was I so blind?

When we seek God with all our heart and mind, He will come to us and speak to us, if we let Him; but we must listen. Even in my work assignment for the day, God had allowed me to be in a place with no distraction in order for me to hear Him clearly. I had to surrender to what I felt God showing me in my spirit, even though I did not understand it at the time. I could have missed a blessing if I had done what looked to be the best thing to do at first and not take the assignment, but I listened to my spirit. I needed to trust God even in this.

God spoke and I listened; *"my child this all goes back to your past. You are gullible and naive because of all the hurt you have experienced. You want others to like you and approve of you so much you allow yourself to be blinded to how things really are sometimes; things are not always what they seem to be. Remember when you came in to prison, I revealed to you the need for a closet when you were frightened was still there. I told you even then, we will work on this. Your past still has a hold on you, due to you not forgiving and releasing all who have hurt you. Yes, you have made some progress in this area, but it is time to work on the deep roots. It is not enough to only deal with what is on the surface, but what is also hidden below."*

As God spoke to me and showed me why I had not seen things as they were; tears began to flow down my face. I had to stop the lawn mower and go inside to the restroom to wash my face and try to get myself together. Once inside the cool restroom and all alone, I went to my knees and asked God to forgive me for being so blind. "Oh Lord I did not know that I was still so broken when it came to my past. How can I overcome this in my life once and for all?" Peace came over me and God continued to speak to me.

"You have taken the first step in this being out of your life, seeing it for what it is and bringing it to Me. Now we will start the process of removing it from you permanently. You must be patient and trust Me. I will walk you through the process step by step. You can be free from the need of the closet and all the other bondages that hold you bound, but you have to trust Me, and do as I show you."

I surrendered it all to the Lord, again but this time it was referring to the deeper things within me that I did not know were there - everything concerning my past. I asked God to show me the deeper things that I may not have seen yet, in order for me to be freed from them also. I cried out to the Lord, "Please show me everything that is getting in the way of me being closer to you and being within your will for my life. I want to remove anything that is not of you, Lord." I had no idea what kind of journey I was going to be on in order for God to remove this all from me. My intentions were true. I did not want anything that was not of God in me, and this was what God needed from me; to surrender even the things that I did not understand, the things that were so deep that I did not know they were there.

I thought I had already done this before I went into ministry, as many of us think we have. So often we only deal with the surface of issues and not the root. If we do not deal with the roots, they will spring up when we least expect it. What else would happen since we don't even know they are there? God had my undivided attention, and I had been stripped of everything that could have gotten in the way of me seeing and hearing Him. This is why I was able to learn this. How about you? Is your current situation similar to mine? Things have been stripped from you, and you, too, are asking why am I going through this? I had to want to see the thing that I had not seen previously, before God would show them to me, but it took the current storm that I was in to even want to dig deep.

I encourage you to look to God and see what is it that He may be trying to show you. We have many things in our lives that comfort us in such a way that God is unable to get our attention. He then has to allow them to be removed, sometimes for our own good and our growth in Him. Many of us need to look deep, but from our knees. Only then will we find the help we need. In the forgiveness that Jesus gives, and His grace that will guide us through the many levels we must go through to heal. The longer I was at Coleman, the more I realized it was not for a crime that I had been accused of and found guilty of, but because God was answering my prayer to be in His will, and for Him to finish the good work in me that He had started.

As I resumed mowing the grass, all I could do was give thanks to the Lord for what He had done for me. I understood I had a lot of work to do, but God had also given me peace that He was going to walk me through the healing process. I still did not want to be at Coleman away from my family, but it was okay; God was with me, and this was for His purpose in my life. Yes, I did not like where I was, but I was yielded completely to God, I trusted Him and I had peace that God was doing what was necessary in my life to bring me full circle to be in His will. This was what I had asked God to do for me before I had even started the journey behind prison walls. Part of the healing process is learning what is within us that are in need of healing. I did not know that my past still kept me captive. Now that I knew, I was going to be able to work through all the memories one by one and forgive whom I needed to forgive. This was going to take a while, but I worked on it every day as I went into God's Word. I asked God to show me how to heal and forgive, and He did.

Room Assignment by restroom, blessing or annoying

I came in from work one day and found my Bunkie all excited. She had received news from the counselor that I could move into another room and her mom could move into my bunk. I only had to go to the counselor and confirm that is was okay with me and the move would take place once Donna Ray's mom had arrived at Coleman. After I had gone to the counselor and told him it was okay with me, I returned to my Bunkie and informed her all was set. Even though we had planned ahead, and done all that was asked of us, this did not mean all would go smooth. I had been trying to minister to Donna Ray the importance in trusting in God and not man; this was about to be tested.

Once Donna Ray's mom arrived at the camp, we went into action to try to get me moved to my new bunk. We could not do the move ahead of time, because the bunk could be filled before her mom arrived. For her mom to be assigned to my bunk, it needed to be empty once she arrived. If it was not, the front office would give Donna Ray's mom another room. This was exactly what happened. We were not able to find our counselor for him to make the move in time. We would have to try again the following day. When I noticed how upset my Bunkie was, I told her to not worry, everything happens for a reason, and to trust God with this, not man. When my Bunkie's mom came to the unit and my Bunkie introduced us, we were friends from the start. As we talked we both realized that we both had a deep love for God and many things in common, including praying for her daughter to come closer to Christ.

We both agreed that God was at work even in our room situation. We don't always understand what it is that God is doing, but we both agreed to give it to God, and it would work out in His timing. The next day, my Bunkie's mom came to me to give me a praise report in reference to how God had used her the night before with her new Bunkie. My Bunkie's mom's name was also Donna; we called her Donna and her daughter Donna Ray. Donna proceeded to tell me about her roommate and how God used her to comfort her. My Bunkie's mom's first night was one that God used to comfort another. Only God could have set this up. We both used this to show her daughter what God can do if we would only let Him. She was still upset in how everything had happened. Donna and I kept praying for Donna Ray, but Donna was not upset at all that she had not been put in her daughter's room. She was in the same unit as her daughter and she was appreciative for this. If she was to room with her daughter, God would work it all out.

The next day, we found our counselor, and put into motion all the necessary paperwork for the both of us to move. But the move did not happen quickly. It took about three to four days before we both received our room assignments. With it taking as long as it did, my Bunkie's mom was able to spend some time with her new Bunkie when she arrived. Her new Bunkie needed someone to talk to, but not just anyone - a woman of God; and that was what God gave her. Donna was able to give her reassurance that God, was with her and to trust Him during the short time they spent together. We both had peace that God would work our room assignments out in His timing, and that is exactly what God did.

When we heard our counselor calling our names over the loudspeaker to come to his office, we knew it had to be for our new room assignments, and it was. My Bunkie's mom was going to be allowed to move in with her daughter and I was moving to a room right in front of the restroom. I was not too excited about my new room, but it was the only bottom bunk available. I gathered my things together and both Donna and Donna Ray helped me move my things to my new room. My new Bunkie was a young woman about twenty. She knew of me and was happy that I was going to be her new Bunkie. When you have a room to yourself in prison, you are always waiting to see who your Bunkie may be. Not everyone is easy to get along with, and some go out of their way to cause trouble. Most of the women in prison only want to do their time and go home without any issues, but many come into prison with a lot of pain and anger, and it is normally taken out on the Bunkie they bunk with.

As I unpacked all of my things my new Bunkie started to ask me questions about all the books I had and what did I use them for. I had been blessed by my church family in them sending me all of the reference books I asked for to help me study the Word. Half of my locker was filled with books. I started to explain to her that I used all the books to gain a deeper understanding of the Bible. She seemed puzzled, so I pulled out a book, and gave her an example. Using my "With the Word," my chapter-by-chapter Bible Handbook by Warren W. Wiersbe, I asked her to give me a part of the Bible she knew or would like to know more about. Once she did, I opened the book and showed her how it outlined the chapter in the Bible, and even how it gave us other Scriptures to look up in order to understand better what was being said. We went through this process together, and she thought it was cool. She then asked me if she could study with me sometimes. I answered, "I would like that a lot." God was already bringing me and my new Bunkie together, even though I was directly in front of the restroom. God had done it again, and put me right where I needed to be.

After work and dinner I would go out to the track and walk five miles. Some days it was harder than others, but it was my goal. I found the track to be a place of peace for me - and God. Even when others were on the track, it still felt like it was only me and God. The track became my prayer closet many days. One day after dinner, I went to the track to walk as I normally did, but this day was different. I felt real down and alone. I cried out to God, "God, it is all gone, the money, the ministry, even my reputation is gone. I am not even sure if I will have any friends or family once I get home. I am not even sure if I will have a husband when I get home. I have lost my faith in my country and the judicial system. It is all gone Lord." Then God said to me, *"now we can talk."* With tears rolling down my face, the Lord started to comfort me, telling me, that He was the one I was to depend on and no other.

I knew that God was with me and teaching me. God was so good to me. Everything that had happened up to this point was all God, working and intervening in my life. But I still had my weak moments. Whenever I would get down, and everything looked to be too much for me, God would always bring me back to looking at things through His eyes. When I walked back to my room, I had been renewed again. This was the enemy attacking me, but as I would cry out to God, he would always come to my rescue. I made a decision that I was going to make the best of things. God had not made a mistake. It was time to listen and learn from the Master, God. This happened often to me. I would get down and out about my situation, and I would go to God again and again and He would help me. At first I got frustrated with myself that I had to keep doing something over and over again. God taught me that this was to be expected, and I was exercising my faith every time I made a choice to come to Him and not believe the enemy and his lies. I did notice that I started getting stronger, and I would go a longer period of time between meltdowns. I was growing stronger with God and the fruit could be seen by many that were around me. I still had no idea to how many were watching me. God was going to bless me much later on in my journey behind prisons walls, to how my walk with Jesus Christ was blessing many that were watching.

A Journey Behind Prison Walls

Tried to start a Bible study, it was not time

As I learned that so many around me were not believers, I prayed about starting a Bible study group. As I prayed and asked God if this was His will, I could not understand that it would not be; I really did not wait for an answer. Being in prison, there were a lot of rules that you had to go by. I, being new to the system, did not know them all. There were also protocols that I was unaware of that were not written in the rule book. These were protocols made by the inmates of the prison. Just the same, they, too, had to be followed if you wanted to accomplish anything within prison. I started to ask around if anyone wanted to join me in studying the Word. We were going to start with the book of Ruth. One of the women at work suggested that we put up a notice on the bulletin board. She was also new to Coleman. It sounded like a great idea, so I made a notice to where we would be meeting, and what we would be studying, and to please join us at 6:30 out on the compound by the softball field. The notice was not up but a few hours when a woman from one of the units came to me with our notice in hand, and informed me that I could not post a notice up on any bulletin board without it going through our unit team or the chaplain. I was not aware of this, and I did not want to get in trouble. I thanked her for telling me, and I would remove them all immediately.

She informed me that she had already removed them all. She was an elderly woman - one that I had seen in church. She was involved with a lot of things in the church, and she was upset with me, and it was not only for me posting up a notice without permission. She then asked me a question that took me by surprise, and it was asked in a deep, mean tone also. "Who do you think you are to teach a Bible study? We have the chaplain to do that and other women that have been here a lot longer than you that are teaching Bible studies. Why should we come to your Bible study? We don't know you from Adam." I was left speechless for a moment and all I could say was I was sorry; I did not mean to offend anyone. The woman then told me if I wanted to teach a Bible study, and put up any notices I would need to have the chaplain's permission. She informed me to have the chaplain sign all my notices, and then I could post them up in all the units. I thanked her again for telling me, and I apologized again if I had upset her. It was not my intention.

I made an appointment to meet with the chaplain, and, on the day I was to meet with him, I did not understand why I felt out of sorts. I had met with pastors of big churches on the outside often, and I never felt nervous or out of sorts before; but there was something different going on within me. I did not understand what it was. I had no idea that God was teaching me something again, even in this. I was broken inside and I still had so much to heal from and learn from God. But since I had not yet been able to overcome all the areas that God was showing me, I was still doing things like I used to. I had been so busy on the outside with family and ministry that God had not been able to get my attention with some of the deep things in me that needed to be addressed. I knew this now. God wanted my undivided attention in everything and everything was a lesson from this point on. It was time for me to heal, and I needed to learn to listen to God first in everything. Remember, I did not wait for

God to answer me about starting a Bible study. I assumed it was the right thing to do and the time had to be right.

As I walked to the chaplain's office full of nerves inside, I did not understand it but I prayed for God to help me. As I arrived at the chaplain's office, I was asked to have a seat by the clerk, who was also an inmate. She asked me if I was new to Coleman and I told her yes. She continued to inform me of some of the things going on within the church that I could get involved in or attend. The chaplain then came out of his office and asked me to come in. Once in his office, he asked me what he could help me with. I informed him that I was one, who on the outside teaches many Bible studies, and I would like to do the same here at Coleman. But I had been informed that I needed to have his permission. This was when he looked me in the eye and said "you don't need my permission, but God's. If God has asked you to teach a Bible study here at Coleman, all you have to do, is do it." I responded that I was told that I could not put up a notice unless he signed them giving me his permission. I asked, "Is this true?" The chaplain then said "Lanette, you don't have to put up any notices. All you have to do is start teaching, and, if God has called you to teach the women in the camp, they will see you and they will come. You don't need anything from me; everything you need is from God."

God was speaking through the chaplain loudly, but I was not hearing what God was saying yet. I then asked the chaplain to confirm something that I had been told. "Is it true if two or more of us gather together for a Bible study, we can get in trouble for forming a riot?" Again, the chaplain said to me, "you don't have to worry about that. You are allowed to gather together for religious purposes. But understand this; here at Coleman or any other prison, for that matter, the women are not going to come to hear you teach because you did it on the outside. God is the only One that can bring them into your study. You need to know, Lanette, most women in prison keep themselves at a distance from newcomers at first. You will have to allow God to bring down the barriers that have been put in place over a long period of time." The chaplain wished me the best, and encouraged me to come to service on Sunday, and get involved in everything that I felt God was leading me to be involved in. As I was about to leave the chaplain's office, he stopped me and added, "Lanette, remember, God has a reason for everything He allows in our lives. God cares about you and what needs to take place in you. Don't miss what God has for you here. This is your time to heal and be prepared for what is ahead. Don't be afraid to take the time you need first to work on you; there will always be time to do Bible studies."

Again God was trying to tell me something, but I still did not listen. I was still functioning the way I had always done. As I left the chaplain's office, I started to put into action within my mind what I needed to do to start the Bible study. I started informing everyone of the day and time that we would all meet. My best friend, Donna, helped me put the word out. I sat down and prepared for the first night we all would be coming together. We were going to study the book of Ruth. As I sat in my room, I prayed for God to use me and bring out the ladies to hear His Word. Now, I had still not been given the go ahead from God to do this Bible study. I could not see still that God would not want me to do this. God wants us to teach His Word, correct? I had so much to learn still in following God and His ways and His timing. As I left my unit to go to the table out by the softball field, my friend, Donna, joined me. As we walked, we talked about our day and what was going on with the both of us. We both had not been at Coleman long, and Donna's daughter was still at Coleman with her, and they were both still sharing a room together, and it was difficult for Donna to watch her daughter not follow God.

As we arrived at the table, we were met with only two other women. They were the women I worked with on Mr. Red's crew; both of them were not believers. We all sat down, and I opened with prayer, and we all opened our Bibles and started to study God's Word. This was when a woman that I had seen around the camp joined us. I knew she was one of the women at the camp that had been in for quite some time. I was happy to see her joining us. As she approached the table, she asked us if she could join us; we all answered "of course." As she sat and listened, she started to challenge a lot of things we were talking about. We weathered through it, but I could feel the tension in the air for the two women who were not believers. We closed in prayer and prayed for everyone's families and cases and for God's protection over us all.

As I walked back to the unit alone due to Donna having something else to do, the woman who joined us at the Bible study came up to me to challenge me again. It did not go on for long, because I asked her to show me in the Bible where it said what she was trying to convince me of. She did not know off hand where it was in the Bible, but she knew it was in there. I asked her to come and find me once she had found in the Bible what she was trying to convince me of. I encouraged her that I was always willing to learn something new of the Word, and that I did not know everything, and I had plenty to learn. I don't remember what she was trying to argue about, but I did remind her that the Word of God says in 2 Timothy 2:23-26 to not be quarrelsome. This caused her to stop, and we parted on good terms. She assured me she would be looking for me the following day to show me what she was talking about, but she never showed me in the Word what she was trying to argue. I did this often in prison. I found many wanting to argue what the Word said or did not say. Every time this happened to me, I would first ask them to show it to me in the Bible, and then I would lead them to 2 Timothy; after all this, I was always left alone.

As I went to work the next day, the two women that I worked with that had come to the Bible study the night before expressed how uncomfortable they were with the woman that had joined us and how she was trying to argue with me. "You have to be careful in prison," they said. "You can lose your camp status and be moved to a higher security prison for fighting." We did not know this woman who joined us, all we knew about her was that she had been in prison a long time and this time was not her first. Both of my co-workers told me they would not be coming back to the Bible study because it made them too nervous. I assured them that I understood and encouraged them to not feel bad. They said they did feel bad, because they wanted to support me. I assured them it was okay, and we went on with our work that day joking and laughing like we did every day.

The next night that the Bible study was scheduled to start, Donna and I went out to the table to see if anyone else had shown up, and it turned out to be only her and me. We sat down at the table and studied the Word together and prayed. Donna could see that God was showing me something, but she did not want to say anything. Once we left the table and started to walk back to the room, Donna said something to me that got my attention. Donna said to me, "You know, Lanette, God may not want you to do this study yet. Maybe you should spend some time with Him and ask Him what He wants you to do." She was my best friend and everything she did was in love. I heard what she was saying and God opened my heart and ears to hear. I agreed with her and we hugged and we both went to our own rooms.

Once in my room I sat down on my bed and started to pray, pouring out my heart and asking God to guide me and show me His will. This was when God showed me I was not doing His will but my own. God showed me that He had not given me the go ahead to teach a Bible study yet. Yes, I was used in Miami FDC, but here at Coleman, God had not told me to lead a Bible study yet. God showed me that I was looking to do what I had done on the outside and at Miami, but that was not what God wanted me do at this time. God showed me that I had a lot of things to work on in me; yes, I was going to reach out and minister to others, but now it would be one-on-one. As I worked on myself one on one with God, I was also going to learn the importance of one-on-one ministry. It was time for me to sit in the presence of God and study His Word, not for the purpose of a study for others, but for my own growth and healing.

This was a place in my life I was weak. I spent a lot of time in God's Word, and I was blessed and fed by it. But God had some personal things that He needed to show me, and I did not need to be distracted. I had come to a place that I needed to deal with something that I had not dealt with. This was important for my own spiritual health and relationship with God, but it was also needed so I could be effective with helping others. I needed to receive the help first, so I could show others how to receive the same help from our Lord.

I believe that many of us that are servants of the Lord, and have answered the call to serve, have fallen into this trap, or will soon fall into this trap. We forget to have that private time with the Lord for our own spiritual growth. We become dry and worn out, not able to go on in ministry, because we do not keep ourselves before the Lord in regard to the things in our own lives that God may be trying to help us with. That is why it is so important for us to be open to the many men and women of God that He will place in our path to speak to us. God was trying to speak to me through the chaplain, but I was too focused on my will and my understanding in what God would want me to do. Many of us get ourselves so tied up and busy with things that God did not ask us to do or call us to do. The devil is busy in trying to keep the people of God tied up with busy work. Not to say the things we see ourselves doing is not needed, but it may not be us that God is calling to do it; or the timing may not be right.

That was my case; it was not the time to teach a Bible study. I would find out much later that I would be asked by God to lead a Bible study, and the outcome would be much different than what it was this time. I had gone out on my own and did what I thought I needed to do for God instead of waiting for God to show me His will. This was an eye-opener for me. I did not want to go out on my own and do anything. When we do this, it is not protected by God or led by God. That was what happened with our Bible study group. I asked God to forgive me and to please help me to understand Him and hear Him. It was time for me to sit down and listen and learn, and learn I did.

Chapter 13

Kiss from God

As God talked and I listened, I had no idea to how much healing I had to go through. There was so much in my past to deal with. God took it one by one encouraging me all the way. As I forgave and let go of the ones who had hurt me in my past, I did begin to feel better. I was able to maintain my peace for longer periods of time. One night, as I was going to bed, I felt restless. I could not sleep. It was hard for me to sleep in prison most of the time anyway, due to all the lights and noise. Being by the restrooms made that more difficult. You had all the noise that came from the restrooms and the lights shining in your face, but this night was different. I was not sleeping because of a battle that was going on inside of me. I was missing my family again; I could not stop myself from thinking about them and all I was missing. I wanted to be home so badly, and this night it was getting to me.

All I could do was cry out to God and ask Him how much longer would I have to be in prison? "Oh Lord, please let me go home. I can't do three and a half years away from my family. My grandkids will be so grown up and I will have missed it all." I rolled up in a ball and cried out to the Lord. Now at this time, I still had the desire to hide inside of a closet and to appease this need, I was still hanging up all my green uniforms from the top bunk. Doing this, they would hang down over my bed and made a makeshift curtain. This appeased my hunger for a closet, and also kept the lights out of my eyes. I did not realize how long I had been crying and calling out to God when something amazing happened to me.

Curled up behind my uniforms, crying and not able to sleep, I felt a warm and moist kiss on my forehead. I sat up on the edge of my bed looking around to see if anyone was in my room. I could see no one. I looked at the uniforms that were hanging from my bed, and they were still, and not moving. If someone had kissed me from the room, they would have had to lean through the uniforms to reach my forehead. This could not have happened since my uniforms were not moving. I continued to investigate. I stood up and looked at my Bunkie in the top bunk, and she was covered with blankets completely over her head sound asleep. I sat back down on the edge of my bed, and the Holy Spirit overwhelmed me with the presence of God.

I put my hand on my forehead, and it still felt warm and moist. Tears started to roll down my face. God came to me and said, "You are not here alone. I am with you. Don't be afraid, trust Me." I could not stop feeling my forehead and thanking God for His kiss. All I could do was lay back down on the bed, behind my uniforms, and thank Him for what He had done for me. I do not even remember going to sleep, only waking up in the morning feeling refreshed and ready for work with joy and peace in my heart.

God knew I needed a touch from Him, and He came to me in a very special way. It was personal. The kiss that He gave me that night did not only minister to me then, but many more nights to come. Whenever I felt alone and needed His touch, I would remember His kiss. My hand would go directly to my forehead, and I would feel like I did the night I received the kiss. It would bring me right into relationship with God and in His presence. This is what God wants with us all - a personal relationship. My relationship was growing with God; this was needed for God to help me with everything I was dealing with. When we are in despair, and can't see our way through something, God will come and minister to us if we call on Him. God may not help us in the way we expect, so often we put God in a box and limit what He can do for us. I was coming out of my box, and in this I was also not limiting God in what He could do for me and in me.

Learning to Crochet with Grandma Billy

Only a few rooms down from mine was a women that everyone called Grandma Billy. She was almost eighty and had been at Coleman for several years. She was not able to read or write, but she could crochet with the best of them. Grandma Billy did not crochet using patterns; she created her own pattern in her head as she crocheted. She had this amazing memory and could crochet anything you wanted. All you had to do was show her a picture and she would create it one stitch at a time. I had tried to learn to crochet from many others, but could not perfect it. This was when Grandma Billy told me to come to her and she would help me. I had no idea to what God was doing, and how Grandma Billy and I would become such close friends. But there was going to be even more to this relationship; God was going to use us both in an amazing way for His purpose.

In sitting with Grandma Billy, I was surprised to how quickly I learned to crochet. I started off easy, and even began to learn how to read patterns from others. I needed to get the basics and believed I could do it, and this was what Grandma Billy taught me. She would always tell me, "If I can do this, and I can't even read, you can learn this, and even be better than me." She told me, "Stop thinking you can't, and just do it" She was correct. When I stopped saying I can't and said I can, I learned. Of course, I had to practice and it took many weeks for me to be able to get the first stitch correctly. I would practice and take it to Grandma Billy for inspection. I remember thinking what I had finished was good, and I was ready to move on to the next step and make something. To my surprise, when I took it to Grandma Billy, she would undo all that I had done and tell me, "start over, you can do better." This went on for weeks; I would think that I was finally going to get to move on to the next row of stitches and when I would take it to Grandma Billy, again, she would take it apart and say, "do it again. You can do better." She did not let me get by with anything. If it was not what it should be, I had to redo it.

Because I respected my elders, I listened and did as I was told, even when I was frustrated. God taught me a lot even in this exercise. In change, we don't always take to it right away. We have to be patient and give it time. In learning to crochet, it was not all about crocheting. I was not used to sitting down and relaxing. Freeing my mind of the to-do list was hard for me. When I sat down and crocheted, I could not think of anything but what I was doing, or I would do it wrong, and Grandma Billy would take it all apart, and I would have to start over. God was revealing to me that I was unable to relax and free my mind. Downloading was difficult for me on all levels. I did not understand that I was always in survival mode, and this kept me overwhelmed, and God wanted more for me, and for that to happen, I needed to learn to rest.

God started to show me how this was effecting my everyday life and the stress it caused, but even more importantly, how it affected my relationship with God. When I would go into my prayer closet, God needed me to free my mind and listen to Him. This was hard for me. I was always thinking about something or saying something to God - listening was difficult. I needed to learn how to sit still and clear my mind; listen to whatever God had for me. As I crocheted, God revealed to me how hard it was for me to sit still. I was tempted all the time to stop the project I was working on and finish it later; but later would never come.

God used Grandma Billy to be my accountability partner. She would come to me and ask to see my projects. At first, she would tease me that I did not want to show my project to her because she may take them apart, but she caught on quickly that was not the reason; I was not working on them. As Grandma Billy would come to me and ask to see the projects, it would make me look at why I was not working on them. I wanted to make both of my daughters a blanket, and I was frustrated with myself in my low productivity. This was when I realized it was because I could not relax and get away from my to-do list. God had brought this to my attention for a reason. I needed to pay more attention to what it would take for me to relax and clear my mind. As I started to deal with this, with God's help, I learned to enjoy crocheting. I even noticed a difference in my prayer closet. I was able to hear God better. I did not struggle to sit and rest in His presence as much as before. In this lesson alone, I was able to grow more with God and maintain my peace and joy, by resting in Him.

The enemy keeps us bound in so many ways, in areas of our lives that we are not even aware of. God used something so simple to show me that I needed to pay some attention to this area of my life. It was causing me health problems with stress and even getting the rest that I needed. But as so many things in our lives, they are not only causing pain or a problem in us, but our relationship with God. This is something that I have to stay focused on; it can and will sneak in on me if I am not careful. We have to remember the devil will not give up on distracting us from God and our relationship with Him. It is so important, when we go into our prayer closet with God, that we are able, to hear what God is saying to us. The enemy doesn't want us to hear. We all need to look deep inside ourselves and see what it is that is keeping us from hearing our Lord.

God speaks to us in so many ways, His Word, in situations, even through others, but if we are so distracted, we will miss God in many areas of our lives. It was clear to me that I had to be diligent in my everyday relationship with God. He was trying to guide me in so many things; but I was not listening. I asked God to help me in this area of my life. I did not want to miss a word of guidance that God had for me. Being inside of prison caused all of my senses to be on alert. I needed God's guidance even more. Things were not always what they seemed to be. God knew all things. If I would listen to Him, my stay in prison would and could be uneventful, but full of God stories.

I was thankful to God that he taught me this lesson early in my journey behind prison walls. If I had not learned this, I am convinced that my journey would have been much different. Isn't this what God does with us all in our everyday life? We don't listen; we miss His guidance because we are not yielded to His voice. Is God trying to speak to you? You may be crying out show me Lord, and He is trying, but you have made up your mind how God will answer you. Remember that God's ways, our not our ways. Most of us have put God into a box, and limited how He can come to us. God is all knowing and almighty, the beginning and the end. Most of us need to free our minds in order for God to do what He does best, be God!

Remember, I had asked God to help me grow closer to Him and learn more of His Word before I even started this journey behind prison walls. I had no idea this was how God would answer my prayer, but it was for the best. God knew I had too much to work on inside of me to do it any other way. I know with all my heart, if God could have taught me what all I needed to learn in any other way, God would have done it. God loves us and wants good for us, but my heart wanted more of God, and God was giving me my heart desires. We have to be completely yielded to God and His will for our lives. When we do this, we can, and will, see the hidden thing that the devil doesn't want us to see. And the hidden things are the areas that are keeping us from God and His will for us. I encourage you to ask God to help you see, and He will. This was what God was doing for me, and God was using everything in my life to teach me all that I needed to learn; even the simple thing of crocheting had a lesson in it from God. My eyes were now more open than they had ever been before. God could, and would, use anything to help me heal and forgive and to grow closer to Him in our relationship, but there was a lot more to this than I thought.

Window room, a blessing or a lesson

Living in the cell across from the bathroom had its ups and downs; not far to walk in the middle of the night when the facilities were needed. But the noise and lights made it hard to sleep. I was waiting for a window room to come open, and I was going to put in a request. They were given out based on seniority. I did not depend on this, and I had made up my mind to make the best of the situation while I was in the room across from the restrooms.

After dinner and walking on the track, I would come back to my room and pull out all my reference books and sit on the floor in front of my locker and study the Word of God. I had this thing about sitting on the floor. Many did not understand how I could do this, since the floors were concrete. I had an extra blanket that I used for this purpose, and God also used it to minister too many. Since I was in front of the restrooms, many would see me sitting on the floor studying.

I would pull out my blanket and lay it out on the floor, and then I would pull all my reference books out of my locker and place them all around me on my blanket. Then sitting on the floor with a tablet, I would study God's Word. Many nights I would be sitting there for hours, not even noticing what was going on around me. Then it started. One night I looked up and one of the women from the unit was standing in my doorway not saying anything. I then asked her, "Can I help you?" She proceeded to tell me that she did not want to disturb me, but she had been noticing me sitting on my floor every night, and she was curious in what was I doing. "Are you in school?" She asked. I explained to her, "You could say that. I am in God's school."

She then asked about all the different books I had in front of me on the blanket. "How do they help you?" She asked. I answered, "I am glad you asked. Let me show you." As I showed her one book at a time, I could see her face light up with interest. I asked her to have a seat, and she joined me for about an hour. This started happening to me on a regular basis, with different women within the unit. Many came back night after night asking me more questions. Many even asked me for the names of all the books that I was using so they could have their families mail them to them. What God had done with me being placed in front of this restroom was something that I could not have worked out even if I had tried. I was being seen, by everyone who passed by daily, sitting on the floor studying. Remember, this was not common to see anyone sitting on the floor in prison. From what I can remember I was the only one in my unit that did this. God used this to draw the attention of others to ask me what I was doing. This was all it took to open a door for me to be able to share the goodness of Jesus, or encourage those who knew Jesus how they could grow closer to Jesus through God's Word. God is faithful and His Word tells us if we seek Him we will find Him. These ladies who were coming to me were seeking God, even if they did not know they were. When they asked a question, and I showed them how they could find it within the Word, this ignited a deeper hunger in them for the Word of God, and they wanted more. Now everyone that stopped by my room were not all Christians; many were Muslims and many other faiths. We had many intense conversations about the difference of our religions; all because I

A Journey Behind Prison Walls

had a room in front of the restroom, sitting on the floor studying God's Word. What others would have thought was the worst room in the unit, turned out to be the best room I could have ever been in.

I was in amazement in how God was using the simple thing of me sitting on the floor studying His Word to reach out to so many. I was beginning to enjoy my room by the restroom and had decided to not put in for a transfer when a window room came open. But again, God's ways are not my ways. He had other plans. God had shown me that He was going to teach me the importance of one-on-one ministry; and that was exactly what God was doing with me sitting on the floor studying His Word. Remember, I was not teaching a Bible study at this time. I was studying God's Word for my own growth, and God brought women to me seeking Him, one by one. I also did not notice, at the same time when God was bringing so many different women to me one by one asking questions to why I was sitting on the floor or what was I studying, That God was also bringing down many walls around me in me being a newcomer.

One night after work, I came into the unit to get ready for count, and was approached by a woman named Tommie. She informed me that we were going to be Bunkie's, and she would be happy to help me move. I was surprised. I had not requested a room change. She was also in a window room. She could tell that I was confused to how this all happened and she began to explain, "You are by the restroom, and my Bunkie needs to be close to the restroom due to the problem she has. This is why Mr. Seed has switched you both. We have to move you quickly. He has told us that we have to have you both moved before count."

As I got closer to my room, I noticed all of Tommie's Bunkie's stuff in the hallway outside of my room waiting for me to move my things so she could move in, but she did not look too happy. There was more to this than met the eye. Tommie was one of the women in the unit known to be a troublemaker. She was one that you knew to watch out for. And now I was going to be her Bunkie. "Okay God, what are you up to now?" went through my head, as I moved my things. My Bunkie was not happy, and I told her quickly this was not any of my idea, and I had no idea to what was really going on. I could tell this made her feel better that I had not requested to be moved. My Bunkie was like a daughter to me. We got along real well, and I was even making some progress in her studying God's Word. But I also learned by this time that I was not in control, that God was, and I needed to wait and see what God had for me in being Tommie's Bunkie.

Women from all over the unit came to help me move my things into my new cell so we could get it done before count time. I did not have to have all my things put away, only in the cell with me standing at my new cell's doorway for count. We barely got everything into the cell, when we heard count time called over the loud speaker. My new Bunkie was so happy, it made me uncomfortable, but I could not put my finger on why. God would reveal it all to me soon enough.

Once count was over, Tommie was going on and on about how happy she was to have me as her new Bunkie. She explained that her last Bunkie had a problem with holding her urine. She had a lot of accidents within the cell and this caused the cell to smell. She said she could not take it any longer, and Tommie had gone to Mr. Seed and complained, and this was why we were both being moved. Tommie offered to help me unpack, but I told her that would not be necessary. As I put my things away, she explained to me how she liked to do things within the room. I was not overly concerned with the things that she was explaining to me, because I was one that also liked to keep my room clean; but I was about to find out that Tommie was difficult to live with.

The first few nights were not bad. Tommie was nice and did not get upset with me about anything. The main thing that Tommie complained about was me moving around in the bed at night. It would wake her up. I would try not to move, but it did not take much to make the bed move. Even getting up to go to the rest room would bother Tommie. This became a real issue with Tommie. She began to show her true colors. Tommie started making my life miserable, going on and on about her not being able to sleep due to my moving. I tried to explain to Tommie if I was sleeping I had no control over me moving around in my bed; I was asleep. I explained to her that I was also entitled to sleep at night. She was not the only one that had to go to work early. Tommie worked at UNICOR, and she felt that since, she had to get up thirty minutes earlier than I; I needed to make the sacrifice for her to be able to sleep. The sacrifice would be me staying up and not sleeping. I could not do this. God was again teaching me something. I was not a doormat, and I had to stand up for myself, not in a mean and hateful way, but in love.

Tommie also did not like visitors in the room. This was a problem due to all the visitors I was used to having, and many came to me for prayer and guidance. I had to make other arrangements in reference to this. This was her room also, and I needed to respect that. But then I noticed that the rules of no visitors were only for me. She had visitors all the time. Even my closest friends could not come into my room and stay. They could only come to the doorway, and then I would have to leave the room with them, and we would then have to go somewhere else to talk. I kept asking God to show me why He allowed me to be moved into such a room. I cried out to God saying, "Lord I have no freedom in this room to reach out to others like I did in the room by the restroom. I don't understand why you would move me here, Lord help me. I need you to show me, Lord, what I am to do about this situation?"

I tried everything, praying for Tommie; even encouraging her to study the Word with me. She did not even like me sitting on the floor to study. This was the one area that I did not stop no matter how much she complained; it was my room also. But it did make her mad, and everyday it was something. My peace was leaving me. I cried out to God to help me but it felt like He did not answer. God was teaching me something. I did not understand what it was. I was so used to hearing God clearly and feeling His presence all around me, and, for some reason, God felt so far away from me. My friends were praying for me all the time. They would comment daily in how the toll of living with Tommie was stressing me out, and how I did not even reflect the joy and peace that I normally did. I had even gone to Mr. Seed and asked him if I could move to another room. He told me there was no other room for me to move to at the time, but if I was being harassed, I needed to report it, so they could deal with Tommie.

A Journey Behind Prison Walls

I knew there was still more to this situation with Tommie and me being put into her room, but I could not put my finger on it. Mr. Seed reinforced to me if I had anything to report on my Bunkie that she may be doing that was not allowed by the camp rules, that I needed to report it, and he would kept me anonymous. I then felt like I had been planted in this room for a bigger purpose by the staff. What was it that Tommie was into? I did find out later by a staff member that I needed to watch my back. Tommie was under investigation. Oh great, "okay Lord what is this all about?" but still no answer. I started watching everything that Tommie did. I did not want to get caught up in something and lose my camp status by being in the wrong place at the wrong time. Remember my charges were that I supposedly knew something was going on that should not have been, and my crime was that I did not report it. All I could do was watch and pray.

Being a snitch in prison can be very dangerous. I had no intention in being labeled this during my stay, but I had to keep my eyes open for my own wellbeing. Tommie came to me one day and asked me if I would keep some of her things in my locker. She said she had noticed that I had some room in my lockers. First of all, I thought to myself, "When was she looking in my lockers." This made me nervous. In prison you are only allowed so many of one item in your locker. If you have more than what you are allowed, it can be taken from you and you can also be written up for having contraband. She assured me that she was not asking me to keep anything that we were not allowed to have. Her lockers were full and she only needed someplace to keep a few items.

I thought to myself, the nerve in her even asking me to put her things in my locker. She was never nice to me.

She did everything in her power to make me miserable. I politely declined Tommie in putting any of her items in my locker. This did not please her, and she made it perfectly clear that I was not on her good side. "What else was new?" I thought to myself. The tension in our room had gotten so bad that I had a hard time sleeping at night. I was only getting about three hours of sleep a night. The weekends were the only time that I could catch up on my sleep, and this was only because Tommie was normally out of the room or sleeping herself, but this was interfering with everything I was trying to do. It had to stop.

As I spent time in prayer, I, waited for God to answer me and give me some kind of guidance in what was going on and what to do. I was learning that I could not trust in what I felt, but what I believed. God gives us all promises in His Word, and this was what I needed to hold on to. That He promised to never leave me or forsake me, that God wanted well for me, that God would finish the good work in me until the day of Jesus Christ. I began to look at my situation differently, and then, and only then, did I hear God's voice again. I was beginning to depend on what I felt of God and not what I knew of Him. My emotions would fool me if I let them, but God's Word never would.

God was allowing me to not feel His presence so I would come to a place in my faith that I knew that He was there even when I did not feel Him. God was teaching me to trust in His Word and the promises that it gave me, even if my situation did not look like He was at work, He was. This is what God showed me; He reminded me of the game of peek-a-boo. Peek-a-boo is game played mainly with small children; but it is not only a game. In the game Peek-a-boo, you are teaching the child even when they don't see you that you are still there. This is what God was doing with me. I could not feel Him, but He was still with me all the time. I felt a great peace come over me. I was free from my emotions and I had learned to not lean on them, but God. I had no idea to how valuable this lesson would prove to be. God is so wise and patient with us all.

Remember one of the areas that God had revealed to me that I needed to work on was me being gullible and naive; also wanting everyone to like me. I was a people pleaser. God was using the situation with Tommie to teach me that I was no longer that person. I was not bound by that behavior anymore. I was really changing. As I realized in amazement in everything that God was doing in me, all I could do was give thanks to God in everything that He was accomplishing in me. Again, what looked bad to me, God used for His purpose. I had only been at Coleman for about six to eight months, and, in this short time, God had already done so much in me. I was not the same person who had come into prison. I was excited to what else God had for me in the years ahead.

The old Lanette would have told Tommie yes when she asked me to put some of her items in my locker, not thinking of what the consequences could have been to me. I would have been blinded by my own intentions in trying to keep the peace and befriend her. I would do this even if it had made me feel uncomfortable. This was how much I was in bondage in trying to be a people pleaser. I was only able to see that I had overcome this bondage in my life because of what God had allowed in Tommie and me becoming roommates. God knows us better than we know ourselves, and many times, He has to show us what we are capable of in order for us to walk boldly and with full confidence in Him. God needed me to see what He had accomplished in me, and by doing this I did walk more boldly in Him, and I even looked deeper into myself in what else God had changed, and I was surprised in what I discovered.

I noticed that everything around me looked different. The skies looked bluer; the birds sounded differently, sweeter to my ears. My life did not have that dark cloud that lingered over it as before. I was even beginning to love myself. I liked who I was, and I was beginning to believe that I was important. It was like I had left one universe and I was now in a completely new universe that I had never seen before. And because of this, I did not have to be confirmed by others any more. That is what a people pleaser needs, others to confirm them. All I needed now was God, and He was the one that would confirm me in everything. This again was a life-changing lesson, one that I needed to learn. It changed the direction of my life and how I looked at everything. God only accomplished this in me because I spent time in His Word and with Him one on one. I cannot express enough the importance in spending time with God. He has so much to teach us. We have to give God our attention or we will miss so much that He has for us. God was reiterating to me again that there is a lesson in everything, if we would only be willing to learn it, but before we are able to learn everything that God has to teach us, we have to first accept that there is a lesson to learn. So often in life we become know-it-alls. We are not teachable. I prayed for God to help me to have a teachable spirit, and that I would not miss anything that He had to teach me no matter how big or small it may be. I encourage you to pray this for yourself, for God to help you to have a teachable spirit. You will never regret it. God has so much to teach us all. Don't miss it!

Chapter 14

Looking deep, did not like what I saw

One day on Mr. Red's crew, we had to dig a trench to install some new piping-PCP pipes. We had to do most of the work by hand; this meant a lot of work with a shovel. The sun was hot. We were given sunscreen and the work began. As the day went on, we all tried to make the best of things. The sun was hot and we all were miserable. As we finished the trench for the piping, it was about time to stop working for the day. All of us could not have been happier; we were all full of dirt and sweat and ready for a shower.

Before calling it a day and going into the camp for count, we all had to turn in all our tools. This meant returning our shovels to the landscaping trailer. I went around and collected all the tools that needed to go back to landscaping, so others could load the truck, so we all could return to the powerhouse in order for us to be released for the day. If we all hurried, we would get back to the unit in time to take a shower before count time. In climbing the stairs to the trailer, I noticed two women sitting on the steps. They were also waiting to be released from work to go back to the camp; they both worked in landscaping. When I reached the door and proceeded to go inside, one of the women on the step reminded me that I needed to clean off the shovels before I returned them to the tool cage inside.

I closed the door and went to the edge of the porch and started to hit the shovels on the side of the deck to knock off all the dirt that was on them. Then I heard one of the women yell at me, "stop making all that noise and take the shovels over to the hose and wash them off." The hose was on the other side of the trailer and I was exhausted. As I looked at them both, I noticed that both of the women were smiling and giggling at me. This caused me to respond to them by yelling "it is not quiet time."

I was so frustrated. I was hot, sweaty and tired. It had been a long hard day, and I was not in the mood for any silliness. I thought to myself, "would it kill them to help me? I have three shovels in my hands and they were all full of dirt." This was like the straw that broke the camel's back. As soon as the words left my lips, I felt ashamed. The two women sitting on the steps were right. The shovels did need to be washed off before they were turned into the tool cage. It was not their fault I was exhausted and dirty. I went over to where the water hose was and cleaned all three shovels. I then walked back up the stairs and proceeded to go inside to the tool cage to return the shovels. The woman, who worked inside the cage, was a woman that I knew from the camp. I had been blessed to minister to her and even pray with her on many occasions.

The Holy Spirit overwhelmed me in remembering what had happened with the two women sitting outside on the steps. Both of the women who were sitting outside on the steps were not Christians. When the women on the steps told me to be quiet and for me to wash the shovels off with some water before turning them into the tool cage, my response to them was not a good witness when I yelled at them that it was not quiet time. The woman behind the cage noticed that I was bothered by something and asked me if I was okay. I responded that I had been working in the sun all day and was tired. This was true. I was exhausted, but that was not the reason for my look at the moment; my spirit was sad. I returned to the truck with the rest of my crew in order for us to all return to the powerhouse to put all of the other tools away. Once this was all done, Mr. Red could take us back to camp and release us for the day. We were all hoping that we would get back to the camp in time to take a shower before count time.

Once inside the unit, it was entirely too late to take a shower before count. I walked over to my bunk and sat down, dirty and all. "Oh Lord," I cried out, "I am so disappointed in me. What is wrong with me?" I asked God. "Why did I act that way?" About this time, I heard over the intercom, "count time count time." This meant stop whatever you were doing and step to the doorway of your cell and wait to be counted, not speaking a word. All I could do was lower my head and keep asking myself the same question over and over again, "why did I act that way Lord?" Before I even realized it, the officers were walking down our unit and counting us. I then heard the all clear.

I gathered up my things to take a shower, and I was off to the showers before everyone else would get to them. I felt terrible inside and out. I was not sure at the time what it was going to take for me to feel better in my spirit, but I could do something about the outside; and that was take a shower. As I arrived at the showers, I found one opened and I grabbed it quickly. I stepped into the shower and started to remove all my work clothes that were full of sweat and dirt. I turned on the shower, and I stood under the water and let it run down all over me. From way down deep inside of me came a cry that was so hurtful, I could not control it. I was happy that I was in the shower room, with all the other showers on, because I could not be heard by anyone.

I cried out to God, "I am ashamed of my behavior. How can you use me to help others look to you with me acting like that? Lord, please forgive me and help me to change." This was when God came to me and showed me what really had happened. This was what God showed me.

When a glass is full of water and you walk across a room and someone runes into you what spills out? Water. Whatever is inside of us is what will come out of us, when we are pushed. God showed me that I needed to see what was inside of me when I was pushed in order for me to be able to work on it. God showed me that He allowed me to be pushed to the max in order for me to see what was within me; to see what would spill out. God continued to show me that, in normal conditions, this may have not happened, but when we are pushed to the max in being tired and frustrated, we are able to see how we would respond if pushed or challenged. This can happen when we least expect it. If we don't get it under control, it can happen at a time that could cause someone to stumble; and God knew I did not want that to happen. God told me that it made Him happy that it upset me in what I saw that was inside of me, and I asked God to help me to change. God let me know that we would be working on this together.

Here we went again, another area in me that needed to be refined by God. Trust me; we all are under construction our whole lives while we are on this planet. Everyday we should have the expectation to be a little better than the day before. If we have this mind set, God will be faithful and show us all the areas that we need to work on. What I learned by facing all the areas in my life that needed to be transformed by God was when I allowed God to transform them, I received more peace and joy as I changed. I was the one that was extremely blessed by all that I was allowing God to do in me; and then, in turn, God could use me to bless others.

As I stood in the shower with the water running over me, I understood what God was showing me. Many things in us are so deep that we don't even know they are there. God was still showing me the hidden things that were within me that I did not know were there. God has to allow situations in our lives to allow the hidden things to come to the surface so we have knowledge of them. God knows they are there, but we do not always. If we don't acknowledge the deep things in us that need changing, God is not able to help us change. We must acknowledge them first and give them to God, and then God can help us with them. Most of us have many deep things that we are able to subdue on a daily basis, and I had subdued many things over many years. But when our buttons are pushed, and, at a time when we least expect, these areas will show themselves. This was what happened to me. Now it was my responsibility to let God help me deal with what had been shown to me that was within me, and let God help me remove it from my life.

One of the women on the step at the landscaping trailer lived directly across from me. She was not happy with me, and she let that be known during count time with all of the dirty looks she directed toward me during count. Up until this point, I had never had anyone have an attitude with me other than Tommie, my Bunkie, and this woman was known for getting into trouble or making others' lives miserable. I prayed for her and asked God to help me reach her with His love and help me to make amends in what had happened between us at the landscaping trailer. When I walked back to my cell from taking a shower, she was in her cell across from me. Her body language let me know she was not open to any conversation. I left her alone for that moment due her not looking to be receptive and asked God to soften her heart and protect me from any further altercations.

In prison if you have an altercation with anyone, both parties are in trouble, no matter who starts it. You can lose privileges or even your camp status and be moved to a higher security prison. I did not want that for either one of us. I continued to pray for her and my protection, but the night continued and came to a close without me having any opportunity to talk to her. I felt heaviness on me that night as I went to bed. I was still disappointed with myself and my behavior earlier that day at the landscaping trailer. I thought to myself that I would not even be going through this if I had not spoken in anger to both of the ladies at the trailer, but this was my consequences for my behavior, and, again, even in this, I was learning a valuable lesson.

So often when we do realize that we have done wrong, and have even asked God for forgiveness, we feel that we should not have any consequences due to the sin. Forgiveness from God doesn't mean any consequences for our sin. God can, and does, give mercy on occasions and can limit the consequences we endure, but that is for God to determine, not for us to expect. I was living my consequences, and I had to embrace them and trust God to help me learn what I needed to learn as I walked through them. Remember the woman across from my cell was not a believer of Jesus. I was still praying that God could turn this situation around and open a door for me to minister to her about Jesus.

I never got the chance to present the Gospel to the woman across the hall. The next day while I was at work, a call came over Mr. Red's radio. Two women had been found in a landscaping truck being quite personal with one another; and because of this, all inmates were being called back to the camp for count. Once we were all back in our units and in our cells, the officers came through and counted us. After being counted, we were all told to stay in the unit until further notice. None of us were allowed to go back to work until after lunch, and the two women caught in the landscaping truck were being shipped out to a higher security level prison. They never came back to the unit. The woman across from my cell was one of the women being shipped out. I did not have joy in this. All I could think about was I had missed a chance to share Jesus with her. Opportunities to share the good news of Jesus Christ are valuable, and we should not waste them. I have never forgotten this lesson. It broke my heart that I had missed a chance to share Jesus with someone; and now the opportunity was gone. I can't say that I would have had a chance even if I had not done what I had done the day before at the landscaping trailer, but it did not help or put me in position to share the Gospel with her. I did not want this to ever happen to me again. This reminded me that we always need be careful in what we do and how we act with others. The devil is always looking for an opportunity to put a wedge between us and others in order for us not to be able to reach them for Jesus.

I continued to pray for her, even after she left Coleman camp, that God would bring someone into her life that she would listen to that could share the good news about Jesus Christ. God did show me that she was not ready to listen to the Gospel yet, and God was only protecting me, because her intentions for me were not good. God showed me that He was only answering my prayer that He would protect me from any harm that may be plotted against me. Many things are not what they seem. God knows all and I was learning to trust Him in all things. I was learning to listen to God in when to speak and when to be quiet. This was a hard one for me; I always had something to say.

God had already been teaching me this while I was in my prayer closet I needed to sit and listen more, and not always be so talkative. This was not only for the prayer closet but everyday life.

A Marriage broken

Having Tommie as a Bunkie, made me look forward to the weekends even more than I had before. I used my weekend to catch up on my sleep, but even more important than catching up on sleep was getting to see my family. My daughters were coming to see me and I was excited to see them. My husband had not been coming to see me as much as he did in the beginning, and I knew in my heart that something was wrong. Anthony had told me one weekend that he was coming to see me but never showed. When you know you are having a visit, you get up extra early to do you hair and makeup and you even pay special attention in ironing your uniform in the effort to look great. I waited all day and Anthony never showed.

When Anthony did not show, I even called our daughters to see if they knew where Anthony was or had they spoken to him, and I was told by them that he had left early that morning around 4:30 to come and see me. Visitation opened at 8 A.M and Anthony should have been at visitation on time if he had left at 4:30 A.M. that morning. Everyone at home was calling his cell phone, but he did not answer. I also had been trying to reach him on his cell phone with no luck. This is when we all thought he may have gotten into a car accident. Highway patrol was called and all the hospitals. Anthony could not be found anywhere. I was beside myself with concern and worry. Women all over the camp were praying for Anthony that he was okay and safe.

The day came and went with no news to where Anthony was. It was not until the next day that I found out from my daughters that Anthony had driven all the way to Coleman Florida to see me, but could not bring himself to come to visitation. Anthony told the girls that he had gotten a hotel room and stayed overnight and went back in the morning. When asked why he did not answer his phone, he said he had too much on his mind to talk to anyone. Everyone was upset with Anthony including his mother. All had worried all night that he had been hurt or a victim of a crime, and he was resting in a hotel room, at least this was what Anthony had told us all.

My calls to Anthony went unanswered even after I had been told where he was and that he was okay. Anthony did not want to talk to me at all. I knew in my heart that Anthony was seeing someone else, but he had never admitted it to me. His actions were getting worse. In the beginning, he would come with the girls to visit me every other weekend, and then he stopped. I was given many excuses by Anthony, that he had to work or he was too tired. Anthony was not living in our house anymore. When I was taken into prison, Anthony and our oldest daughter Keasha and her family moved into the house together. This was to help both families to make ends meet since my income had been taken from the household budget. With both living together, it was intended to help both pay all the bills and save. It did not work out that way. Anthony had moved out with a cousin of his within six months of me leaving. Anthony had told me that they all could not live together, but I was about to learn the real reason that he had moved out.

The following weekend, both of my daughters were coming to see me; only the two of them. I was looking forward to a girls' day. My daughters and I would have a girls' day together often when I was at home, going to the movies and out to eat. This would not be the same but we would have to make the best of it. Sunday had arrived and I was up early and getting ready for the visit. The camp was busy due to a special event that was going on. The camp was decorated with cartoon characters and even picnic tables were outside of visitation, available for all to use with their visitors.

Once visitation had started, the officer in charge of visitation would call your name over the loudspeaker for you to come to the visiting room once your visitors where signed in. Once I heard my name, off I went. I was excited to be able to spend the day with my girls. Visitation was different at Coleman camp. We did not have to go through strip searches going in or coming out of visiting, and the officers were a lot nicer to me and my family. When I walked into visiting, I gave each of my daughters a hug and we went outside to find a place to sit.

It was a beautiful day and it would be a nice change to sit outside at a picnic table instead of the concrete tables we normally had to sit at.

As we sat down, I could tell my daughters had something on their minds. They looked sad. I looked at them both and asked if they were okay. They both looked at me with no response. I asked my daughters if we could pray before we started and maybe that would help us in what we needed to talk about. Once we finished I looked at them both and said, "Whatever it is let's get it off your chest so we can enjoy the rest of our visit." My youngest, Faleasha started, "Mom, you know that Anthony did not come to see you last week, and we know why."

My heart started to beat faster and my palms started to sweat. I was not sure if I was ready to hear what they were about to tell me. I had not been inside even a year yet. I thought to myself, "Have I lost my husband already?" Faleasha continued. She said to me, "Mom we have been following Anthony, and we have caught him in the act in messing around on you with another woman." I looked at them both and said I had suspected it already but that doesn't make it any easier to hear; as tears started to come into my eyes. I tried to be strong and keep the tears from coming but that was when I heard Faleasha say, "There is more. We found out that Anthony is not living with his cousin, but with a woman, and she may be pregnant."

My heart dropped to my stomach. The girls knew that this was a tender place for me. I had always wanted to give Anthony a child, but could not. Anthony was my daughters' step-father, and had been since they were six and eight. The girls looked to Anthony as a real father because he was the one that was there for them most of their lives. Now they were hurt by his actions, but they were not only being hurt by what Anthony was doing, now they had to break the news to me. I could tell it was not easy for them. We were not allowed to hug in visitation other than the hug given upon greeting each other when the visit started. I lowered my head and placed it on the table and cried. I could not hold it back any longer. My girls tried to comfort me the best they could without being allowed to touch me. I was crying uncontrollably. I felt like my insides had been yanked out of me.

When I rose up my head from the table, all I could see in my daughters' eyes was hurtfulness and anger. As I looked at them with tears running down my face, all I could say to them was that I was sorry for them being put in the middle of this. I also told them "If I was not in here, you would not be put in this position. I am so sorry Anthony is putting you both through this." Both my daughters tried to assure me that they were both okay. They were worried about me. They continued to tell me that they had known what Anthony was doing for months. They did not want to tell me because they did not want me to have to deal with the fact that Anthony was messing around on me from inside prison. Both of my daughters shared with me that, after Anthony's actions the week before by not coming to visit me, after he had told me that he was coming, they knew they needed to tell me what was going on. My girls told me that it broke their hearts to see how worried I was the week before, and they did not want me to go through that again. They believed that Anthony had not come to Coleman at all, but was with his new girlfriend with whom he lived, and the only reason he did not answer his phone was because he did not want to be confronted by anyone and made to explain why he was not coming to see me.

I did everything I could to pull myself together for my daughters. I did not want Anthony's actions to control our whole visit. It was hard, but we all tried to put it out of our minds and talk about happy things. As the day came to an end, we said our goodbye and one last hug and off they went to drive the three and half hour drive home. I could tell by the look in their eyes they were still worried about me. My daughters were always good at seeing through my smiles that I would try to put on. I did not pull it off this time. My daughters were in the middle of everything, no matter what it was. It was out of my control being in prison. I could not handle any of my affairs on my own. I needed them to do everything on my behalf. I was used to being in charge and taking care of everything, and now I was dependent on my daughters to do everything, and I did not like that they had to do so much for me. I should have been able to trust and depend on my husband, but that was not the case.

Anthony should have been there for not only me, but for our daughters also. They needed him to be strong, but, in turn, he made things harder for them, not easier. It frustrated me because I couldn't do anything. I could pray and that was what I did - a lot! I kept seeing the importance of a man being the head of his house. If he is not, the family will struggle. I prayed that God would show Anthony where he was failing his family and that he would wake up and take his role, of head-of-house, but Anthony never did. My youngest daughter, Faleasha, was the one who took on the challenge of being the head of the family while I was in prison, and it took a toll on her.

I see that it is still something that she is healing from to this day.

When I walked back to the unit, I felt numb, like I was walking in a daze. As I entered the unit many tried to say hi to me, but I walked right past them. Once in my room, even my Bunkie tried to greet me, and I had nothing to say. As I sat down on my bed waiting to hear the call for count, the tears started to roll down my face. I could not stop them any longer. About this time, I looked up, and standing in my doorway was one of my best friends Donna. She ran over to me and gave me a hug. She did not let go until she heard the call for count. As she left she said, "I will be back after count."

I stepped to the doorway of our room for count, but I could not stop the tears from flowing. Tommie, my Bunkie, knew this was not a time to bother me. She did not even comment about Donna coming into our room before count time to comfort me, like she normally would have. As I stood at count with my head lowered in the effort to keep others from seeing that I was crying. My visit with my daughters, and the news they had to share with me, kept running through my head. I cried out to the Lord to help me with the pain I was feeling inside and the pain that my daughters also had to feel while they drove home. The pain was intense, more than I thought it would have been. I thought I had prepared myself for the news that I had received from my daughters, but it was clear that I had not. Months ago I had pretty much figured out that Anthony was seeing someone else due to his actions. I was still confused and could only ask the Lord; why did I feel the way I did; why was I hurting so much?

When the officers came to do count, one of them knew me well. She stopped by my room and asked me if I was okay, I could only reply, "I received some bad news in visitation today and I am trying to deal with it." The officer told me, "Okay, but let me know if you need me to do anything to help you." It made me feel good that she cared enough to stop and ask and not just count me and walk past, but the tears kept flowing. Once count was over, I sat down on my bed and that was when my friend, Donna, came back into my room and sat next to me. Again Tommie was quiet. She did not complain about Donna being in our room, and I could tell that Donna did not care even if she did.

I shared with Donna what I had learned in visitation from my daughters about Anthony. She hugged me even harder than before. I cried even more, and now Donna was crying with me. After a few minutes we both looked up and started to talk about how God did not give us more than we could bear; that I needed to draw from God's strength, and He would get me through this. As we prayed, I began to feel better. I was still sad, but I was able to control my tears. We decided to get ready for dinner and go up front with everybody else and wait for our unit to be called for dinner. As I walked up front, I passed many women that were my friends. They all gave me hugs and told me they were there for me if I needed to talk. They did not know what was wrong at the time, but were willing to help in any way they could.

Up until this point, no one at the camp had ever seen me cry. My crying was done in the wee hours of the morning in my bunk with only me and God. Women from all over the unit were reaching out to me with kindness and love; eager to help. Many of the women that

A Journey Behind Prison Walls   277

came to me I did not know well, but I had prayed with them or helped them in some kind of way since they had been at Coleman. Now they wanted to return the favor. The kindness did make me feel better. It helped me look at all of the women in my unit in a different light. We were all a family, different races and nationalities and even different religions, but we were still a family. In the midst of my pain God was helping me to look around and see what He was doing in my unit and not be consumed by my situation. He was bringing us all together, and, because of that, the goodness of God was going to be told. So many women, once they came into prison, closed out everyone; they didn't want to be included in anything inside of prison. This caused them pain and depression and it was hard to reach them even with the news of Jesus Christ; because of how they kept themselves separated from everyone. But God was breaking down the walls, and He was using my pain to bring some of them to my side. God is so amazing in how He uses everything in our lives to further the Kingdom of God, if we only let Him.

I could have pushed away the women who came to me and withdrew into a shell and had a pity party, but that was not what God wanted of me. Here I was again in the midst of my pain in my situation, and the help I needed was found in stepping out of my pain and helping someone else. As soon as I did this, I began to feel better. I was able to minister to so many women I had not been able to before this. We now had even more in common. I learned that so many had gone through, or was going through, what I was experiencing. Their husbands leaving them for another while they were in prison. Everybody was looking to me to see how I was going to deal with my husband leaving me. "What do we do?" they asked. I did not have all the answers right then, but I told them that we all would learn together. The Word of God was going to be what guided me through the pain, and the cool thing about this was many of the women looking for guidance were of different religions, but they needed answers, and their religion was not giving them any.

As the days went on, the sadness did fade some, but God was teaching me how to live with what others do to me and not allow it to get in the way of my joy. I had no control over what Anthony was doing, but I did have control over how it affected me, and I was not willing to give up my joy, so I didn't.

Everything in life is a lesson, but we have to recognize that it is to learn what we must learn. Many things in my life I had missed out on what it was that God was trying to teach me; I did not want to miss anything else that God had for me to learn. This is not easy, because most of the lessons that we must learn are in the midst of bad situations, and this is when we don't feel like learning anything. But this is a trick of the enemy. He doesn't want us to learn what God has for us. We must push through and seek out God in every situation. This is what I learned, and it changed my life in how I look at things to this day.

Chapter 15

The Need of Sandpaper in Our Lives

Working on Mr. Red's crew, the plumbers, was hard work and I was not making much money at all. I was only a level three and this meant about $23.00 a month. I noticed an opening in the Heating and Air conditioning crew. Mr. Chris was the officer in charge and his grade one was leaving; going home. Our crew's grade one had been on the crew for seven years and was not going home for almost five more. This meant no one else was going to be able to gain the level one position until she went home. Each crew had one grade one working on it. Level one meant more money, and I needed to make as much as I could to help out my children who sent money to me every month. The more I made, the less they would have to send.

To my surprise, the grade one from Mr. Chris's crew approached me asking me if I would be interested in applying for her position; the grade one. She told me that Mr. Chris had noticed what a hard worker I was and that I got along with everyone and that I was not a troublemaker. Both our crews meet in the same powerhouse every day. Mr. Red and Mr. Chris had offices next to each other. Our crews intermingled everyday; this was how we all knew each other. I told Kelly, Mr. Chris's grade one that I would think about it and let her know. Kelly was leaving in about two months, but they needed someone on the crew before she left in order for her to train the new grade one. This meant I would have to accept a grade three position for about a month while I was being trained, and then, once Kelly left, I would be given the grade one position.

After praying about it and meeting with Mr. Chris, I decided to accept the position. Mr. Chris and I hit it off from the first meeting. He treated me with respect, not like an inmate. I would also be allowed to enter the apprenticeship program for Heating and Air-conditioning, giving me more skills when I went home. It took a few weeks for all the paperwork to go through, but once it was all done, my name would show up on what they called the "call out." It would show the day I was to report to my new crew. Mr. Red was disappointed that I was leaving his crew, but he understood. My fellow inmates were also disappointed, but they, too, understood that we all need to do what we must do to get by while we are in prison.

I was close friends with several of the women who worked on Mr. Red's crew. We all did many things together; we did not only work together. I assured them that I leaving the crew would not change our friendships, and I reminded them that we all would still work out of the same powerhouse and see each other every day.

I was unaware at the time that Mr. Chris's crew would be moving to a new location within about six months, but we all had plenty of time to adjust to the changes. It was a bittersweet change for me, leaving my friends and getting used to new co-workers and a new boss. I had been told before I accepted the potion that working for Mr. Chris could be an emotional rollercoaster some days depending on his mood when he came into work. I had witnessed a few of Mr. Chris's bad moods while we were all in the powerhouse together. This had caused me to pray for him and his crew on many occasions already. It had come to my attention that Mr. Chris was also an atheist. I was now praying for Mr. Chris and for myself to be used by God to show him Jesus. I had no idea to how God would do such a thing with me being an inmate and him an officer; I left that all in God's hands.

My first day on Mr. Chris's crew was uneventful. I spent most of the day sitting in the break room reading all the safety regulations on all the equipment I would be working with. I was told by Mr. Chris he prefers for us to read them all at once instead of daily. We never know what equipment we would be working, on and he wanted us to be aware of all the safety concerns. This actually made me feel good that safety was a priority with Mr. Chris. I did not have to worry about not being prepared for the work that I was going to be learning to do.

Sitting in the break room I was able to watch my old crew come in and out throughout the whole day. It did feel strange watching them do work that I normally would have been doing with them. We all joked around and made the best of things as they came in and out throughout the day. Once I had finished reading all the safety regulations, I was allowed to go out with Mr. Chris's crew and start learning what we as a crew was responsible for.

Coleman was the location for not only the federal prison camp for women that I stayed at, but also the location for two penitentiaries, one low and one medium security prisons for men. I learned that Coleman, Florida was the largest federal prison institution in the US. Each prison had its own powerhouse that maintained the cooling towers and chillers that cooled the prison it was connected to. Also, within the cooling tower building was a generator room for each prison.

In each generator room was a generator big enough to run the prison it was connected to in case of a power outage. Each prison also had its own lift station. This was the system that processed all the waste from the prison - the sewer system. Mr. Chris's crew was responsible for it all, preventive maintenance and repairs when things broke down. I was about to go on an interesting journey of learning, one that would teach me a lot more than how to take care of equipment.

As I learned how to work on chillers and lift stations and preformed the maintenance on the generators, I also was being used by God to minister to Mr. Chris and the other women on the crew. But they were not the only ones being taught something; God was also ministering to me and teaching me more everyday about leaning on Him. When I started on Mr. Chris's crew we only had four employees. We needed to recruit some additional workers. This responsibility was going to fall on me to search out some whom would be interested in working on the crew. In doing this, you always want to look for workers that would get along with everyone and do their work and not cause trouble. You also want women who have a few years if possible. This way you have time to train them and they would be around to do the job.

As I put the word out that we were in need of new workers on Mr. Chris's crew, we grew to about six. One of the women that I had recommended to join our crew to do all the paperwork and the logs brought total disruption to the crew. She was an x-judge that had been convicted of a crime and was doing her time at Coleman Camp along with the rest of us.

When she heard that we were looking for workers, she approached me in reference to the job. She was looking for a laid back job that she could do and still be able to do all the other things she was involved in while she was at the camp. It sounded like a good fit, so I recommended her to Mr. Chris. From what I understood, she had about five years left - much longer than me and she would be able to be on the crew for a while. It looked like she met all the requirements.

We will call the x-judge Cathy. I had no idea that I was in for a long journey with her joining our crew. If I had known this ahead of time, I would not have brought her to the crew. But this is exactly how God works; His ways are not our ways.

Cathy was unpleasant about everything. There was nothing about the crew that she liked, and she did not like the fact that I was the grade one; I was over her. Looking back on it now, I realize that Cathy was mad at the world and terribly unhappy, and she also was on the crew for a purpose. God was trying to reach her in her dark and unhappy place. She caused Mr. Chris to have many bad days, and he looked to me for suggestions since I was the one who recommended bringing her on our crew, and she was beginning to get on my nerves also. She pushed me to my limit often.

Every day I had to pray specifically for God to give me strength to deal with Cathy and for God to help me to not show anger, but love toward her. Cathy also lived in my unit and she also sang with me on the church choir. I could not get away from Cathy. She was everywhere I went. Now prior to being on the same work crew, Cathy and I had never had a disagreement.

This was one of the reasons I had suggested for her to come to the crew in the beginning. After her coming to the crew, it did not take long before she was causing a disruption for everybody on the crew. Every day I had to face the irritation that she was causing not only for me but Mr. Chris and the rest of the women; Mr. Chris kept looking to me for the solution; I was looking to God for the help. God had a plan in the midst of all of this, and it was not only for me.

God always has a lesson in everything He allows in our lives. Often we miss what God is trying to teach us, and I was missing this one for a while due to my frustration with Cathy, or, at least to me, it looked like I was. Then one day when Cathy and I were in the unit together because we did not have to work that day, she and I had a confrontation that changed my attitude toward her and others like her. We were off work this particular day for some reason. I don't remember why.

That morning I was praying and pouring out my heart to God in what was going on with Cathy and me, pleading for His help. God showed up and spoke wisdom into my life through this situation. God told me that Cathy was my sandpaper. God reminded me that I had asked Him to round my edges. "Finish the good work in me, Lord, and remove anything that is not of you. Sand and smooth me for your purpose, Lord," is what I had prayed. God showed me that many will come into my life for the sole purpose to sand my edges. This was what He was using Cathy for in my life currently, but she would not be the last.

As I sat on my bunk and listened to God showing me how the current situation with Cathy was pushing me to the limit every day, and because of this, I was being forced to choose not anger, but to love. I remembered a time prior to this that I did not do well.

A Journey Behind Prison Walls

The memories all came back to me of the situation that happened when I was still working on Mr. Red's crew digging a ditch. I lost my temper with the women at the landscaping trailer when I was turning in the shovels that we were using that day. Remember, when I was in the shower, I was broken and so disappointed in myself in how I responded in anger to the women sitting on the step. I asked God in the shower that day to please help me to not ever act in anger again, but in love. I asked God, help me love the unlovable.

This was what God was doing in this situation. It is not easy to love the unlovable, but God loved us first, even when we were not so lovable. Not that we are that lovable everyday even now knowing Jesus as our Savior. We do have our days that we have to admit, we don't have it together, but God never gives up on us. God was answering my prayer, but it took me almost four months to notice it was Him.

Later that same day after I had spent such an enlightening time with God and that Cathy was only my sandpaper, I ran into Cathy in the hallway. She was not nice to me this day either like always, but, this day; it did not affect me the same way. As she yelled at me saying a lot of things that were hurtful and embarrassing, I can't remember all the details, other than it was all about how my husband was leaving me for another woman. But this time, I smiled as I prayed to God under my breath where she could not hear me. I let her talk and as she came to a close, I asked her, "Are you finished?" She answered me, yes; and my response to her was, "thank you, Cathy, for being my sandpaper. You have helped me to be a better person polished by God." Cathy looked at me with a puzzled look on her face, she was speechless - Cathy was never speechless!

Many women in the unit were looking on, and, even some came up to me and asked me what did I mean by that, and I shared with them also what God had taught me in the perspective of people coming into our lives to be used by Him as our sandpaper to smooth our edges. I was amazed to how many were going through the same thing I was, and they needed to hear what I had heard from God that morning.

This changed my life not only with Cathy, but also in how I would deal with other like her in the future. After learning this lesson about sandpaper, I noticed quickly all who were being used for this purpose in my life. I was then able to gain what God was trying to teach me quicker. I was learning with every lesson that God was making it easier for me to keep my peace and joy, not to mention how it was opening doors for me to help others also. Cathy left our crew within a few weeks of this encounter, and she and I were able to converse with one another on a casual basis. I prayed for Cathy often. She had such sadness about her. She was used to being in charge, and, being in prison, she was like the rest of us. She was having a hard time with this. I could not help her with this hardship, but God could, but she had to let God in. God was answering my prayer on many levels with this situation with Cathy. I would not see all the fruit from this until much later, but it would prove to be well worth the four months it took weathering this storm with Cathy and Mr. Chris's crew.

I continued to work on Mr. Chris's crew and learn all that was needed in order to be the grade one. I was soon able to be the emergency person on call, after about six

A Journey Behind Prison Walls 287

months. This meant if something went down and was not working after hours, the officers would come and get me to fix it. If I was unable to get the equipment running again, they would then have to call my boss, Mr. Chris. Due to all the training I was always able to get whatever it was back up and running without calling Mr. Chris in. It was kind of cool that I was the one called when the lift station would go down in the penitentiary and waste was overflowing into the cells. I was the one who knew how to fix the problem. At first it was intimidating, but I would remember my training and all that Mr. Chris had taught me, and, before I would know it. I would have it all back up and running.

It normally happened on weekends or late at night, about one or two in the morning. The officer would come into my unit and ask me if I was Lanette Black, and then inform me which unit was down and did I feel comfortable to look at it. I was also allowed to wake up one of my fellow teammates to help me, and, some jobs, I would need to wake up two fellow co-workers. This was my call. All I had to do was tell the officer what I needed, and they would get it for me. In prison, we didn't have much control over anything. In a strange way God had given me some of my freedom back. I was in charge in this small area and it felt good.

I had to have confidence in my training or I would have never even gotten out of my bunk and told the officer, yes, I can take care of the situation. The Word of God and what it teaches us is much the same way. Until we put action with our faith, we may not be doing much of anything with what God is teaching us in His Word. We study, pray and wait, but when it is time to get up and go, do we? Like when the officers would come and wake me up and ask if I felt confident enough to try to look at the problem or should they call my boss, Mr. Chris, at first I wanted to say no; call Mr. Chris. But I had to make a choice. Was I going to trust my training and take a step of faith? This is what so many of us need to do in our relationship with God, and what He is calling to us to do, take a step of faith.

I learned if I would take the first step of faith, God was there to help me no matter what. Many of the things that God was doing in me and through me while I was on this Journey Behind prison Walls had already been sowed into me many years before I arrived at prison. I still had many things to learn and will have until I leave this earth and find myself in heaven with my Lord, but so often we are sitting and waiting after God has called us from our perch. I encourage you to take a step of faith and trust what all God has taught you. Your training is good and you can depend on it. God is with you every step of the way, and God will not let you down. And the joy that is to come once you step out is beyond explanation. Make a choice today to take that step of faith, and let God do the rest.

Cancer, Fear or Faith

While I was at Miami FDC, I was sent outside of the prison to get a mammogram. Due to my age, they needed to have a mammogram done for me and in my file. It had been almost a year since I had gone out and taken the mammogram, and now I was being called to medical to receive the results. I had forgotten all about the mammogram, but I was going to be reminded about it this particular day. As I went to medical, I thought I was going to receive some blood test results, but that was not the case. I signed into medical and waited for my name to be called. Once I was called, I was led into an empty room to wait for the doctor assistant to come and go over my results. Once the doctor assistant entered the room, she had a seat and started explaining to me that they had received the mammogram results from Miami FDC. She explained that she did not understand why it took them so long to forward the results to Coleman, but now with the results in, she needed to schedule other mammogram.

She explained to me that the x-ray showed a small lump in my left breast, and they needed to look at it again and see if it had grown any since the last mammogram. We then started to go over my medical history and all the breast cancer within my family. My mother, grandmother and my aunt on my mother's side all had breast cancer.

My grandfather on my mother's side had also had breast cancer, which is rare for men to have. I already knew I was a high risk for breast cancer. I had already had a lump removed when I was twenty two on my left breast, which was not cancerous. Fear was now running through my body. The fear was not only because of the news I was receiving but also dealing with where I was. I knew I could not run out and have this taken care of. It had already been one year since the last mammogram. Due to my family history, the last time a lump was found in my breast, I was in surgery having a biopsy within a week of the test results. It had been a year, and I had no idea to how long it would take for me to have other mammogram.

The assistant explained to me that she was going to put a rush on me being scheduled for a new mammogram, but she also explained to me that it was out of her hands to how long it could take. I confirmed that I understood, and the appointment came to an end.

As I left medical, I was numb. I walked back to my unit before going back to work. Once in my room, I pulled out my Bible and read all the Scriptures that came to me in reference to healing. I put myself on the altar of God and asked God to heal me. I prayed for a few minutes longer, and then stood up and went outside to find an officer to call my boss on the radio to inform him I was ready to return to work.

Once Mr. Chris came to pick me up, he could see I was concerned with something. He asked if there was anything he could do. I told him about the medical appointment and the news that I was given. He told me he was sorry, and, if too much time went by without an appointment, to let him know and he would see what he could do.

Mr. Chris was not a Christian, but he knew I was. I thanked him for being so caring, and I would take him up on his offer if it was needed. I told him that I was trusting in God to heal me and to provide for me whatever was needed inside of these prison walls.

I told Mr. Chris, "God may use you to do that."

Mr. Chris laughed and said, "Okay Lanette, you look at it your way, and I will look at it my way, but if you need me I am here." I grinned and said thank you again. Mr. Chris and I had a lot of short conversations about God. They never lasted long, but they were having a big impact on Mr. Chris more than I knew at the time.

Over the next year or so, I spent a lot of time going back and forth to medical for mammograms' and ultrasounds. All the testing confirmed the lump was still there, and it had not grown in size. This was good news 'Thank you Jesus.' I kept asking for a biopsy to be done, but one was never scheduled. I had to go as far as writing the Warden of the prison to complain in how this situation was being handled, and with my medical history, time was not on my side.

I even took Mr. Chris up on his offer, and he, too, made some calls on my behalf. Then out of the blue with no warning, my name showed up on the medical call out for me to be seen by a surgeon. Fear went through my body again. I quickly went to my room and sat down on my bed and pulled out all the healing Scriptures that I had been reading and praying over the last year. I asked God to give me peace and to guide me in what to do when I met the surgeon. One of the many Scriptures that gave me peace during this time was:

Psalm 103:2-5 *Bless the Lord, O my soul, And forget not all His benefits; 3) Who forgives all your iniquities, Who heals all your diseases, 4) Who redeems your life from the pit, Who crowns you with loving kindness and compassion, 5) Who satisfies your years with good things, So that your youth is renewed like the eagle.(NASB)*

It was important for me to not forget all the benefits that the Lord had for me and was giving to me everyday. The devil wanted me to again look at my situation and not what God was able to do for me and through me. This situation had gone on for a long time and because of that, there were a lot of people involved. This meant whatever the outcome was going to be, many were watching. God could use the system and the doctors to heal me, or He could heal me with no help from anyone; it was all up to God. I had to defer myself to God's timing and not mine. I needed to stay focused on God's Word and allow Him to do things His way and not mine.

God loved me and I needed to stand strong and receive the loving kindness and tender mercies that God was giving me. I needed my youth to be renewed to me, and I was going to see soon what that meant to be renewed like the eagles. I did not realize it at the time how God was working in my situation all for His glory.

I had already witnessed God do that on many other occasions, but again I was not focused on the entire things of God and what He can and will do in our situations. You would think after this had happened to me as many times as it had, I would have gotten it by now. I am so glad our Lord in heaven is so patient with us all.

As the day came for me to go to medical, I was a bunch of nerves. I had women all over the camp praying for me and even staff. As I went to the appointment, I did like I always did, signed in and waited to be seen. I waited for hours before I was seen.

For a moment, I thought I was going to be rescheduled due to the time. It was almost lunch time. Then they called my name to come to the back. I was placed into an examining room and asked to be seated and the doctor would be with me in a moment. It was not long and the doctor walked into the room.

He was a tall, slender man with a stern look on his face; he did not have much of a personality, no bed side manner as you may say.

He sat down in the chair next to me and pulled out my file and began to read. This was when a nurse came into the room to assist the doctor. She asked me to step up on the examining table and that was when the doctor interrupted and said that would not be necessary. The nurse looked at me as I looked at her, and I could tell she was as confused as I was.

The doctor stood up and looked down on me and said, "I was reading you family history and you have a strong history of breast cancer in your family. You have also had one lump removed while you were in you twenties, correct?"

I answered him, "yes that is correct."

He then proceeded to give me his recommendations. "Since the family history is so strong, there is only one thing that I would be willing to do for you and that is a double mastectomy."

My heart dropped to my feet. I could not even think. I had to take in a deep breath and get my thoughts together before I could even respond. I said a quick prayer and yelled in my spirit, "I Need You, Lord. Please give me what to say to this doctor."

And God did.

I looked at the doctor in the eyes and asked, "Are you telling me that you are not willing to do a biopsy, and my only choice is to allow you to perform a double mastectomy on me?"

The doctor responded to me, "You are correct." He then explained why this was his recommendation. "I do not see any reason in wasting the money on a biopsy procedure when my recommendation to you would be the same no matter the outcome of the biopsy."

I then reiterated to him what I had understood him to say. "Excuse me, doctor, for one moment please, are you telling me that it doesn't matter to you if the lump is cancerous or not? That you believe the only course of action is to remove both of my breasts?"

The doctor quickly responded to me, "Yes, that is what I am saying to you."

My response to him did not even take a minute. With God's help, this was my response to the surgeon. I stood to my feet so we were both eye to eye and I looked at the doctor with all confidence and said, "I am sorry that I cannot take your recommendation due to the fact your course of action doesn't give my Jesus much credit." I thanked him for his time and told him that I would not need his services.

As I stepped out of the examining room, Miss B, one of the doctor assistants was waiting for me. She looked at me and asked, "Well, what happened?"

I looked at her and told her that the doctor wanted to perform a double mastectomy and no biopsy. Her response was immediate, "and what did you say?"

My response to Miss B was the exact response that I gave the doctor; "that I will not need his services because his recommendation does not give my Jesus much credit." Miss B smiled at me and said, "that a girl."

As I left medical and walked across the compound, I came in contact with many women who had been praying for me and were eager to hear what had happened. Once

I had shared with them all that had taken place, they were all in shock and immediately they all became concerned for me. Many of the women inquiring had experienced breast cancer while they were on the outside of prison, and they all knew what was involved in fighting this cancer and were concerned for me if I was going to get the necessary treatment inside of prison.

I had also spoken to a few women who had breast cancer while they were in prison, and they expressed to me the difficulty in getting treated. Everyone that I came in contact with I encouraged them to continue to pray for me and I let them all know that I had decided to trust God with this. If I had been given a report that cancer had been found, and the best course of action for me in order to have a long life was to have a double mastectomy, I would have done it in a minute. I had a lot to live for, but to have both of my breasts removed when nothing had been found that was cancerous I could not do what the surgeon had recommended.

Once back to my room, I pulled out my Bible and read again the healing Scriptures that I had been reading now over a year. Every time I felt myself getting frightened with all that was going on I would pull the Scriptures out and read them and pray. But now I found myself led to read:

Isaiah 40:28-31 *Do you not know? Have you not heard? The Everlasting God, the Lord, the Creator of the ends of the earth does not become weary or tired. His understanding is inscrutable. 29) He gives strength to the weary, and to him who lacks might He increases power. 30) Though youth grow weary and tired, and vigorous young men stumble badly. 31) Yet those who wait for the Lord will gain new strength; they will mount up with wings like* *eagles. They will run and not get tired, they will walk and not become weary. (NASB)*

I heard God loud and clear, I needed to not forget who He was, God almighty. He was still on the throne and this was not over. God was going to help me through this and I needed to trust Him. This scripture was taking Psalm 103:2-5 to the next level, at least for me it was. In Psalm 103:5 is says; *So that your youth is renewed like the eagle's*. I was about to mount up with wings like eagles. All I had to do was wait for the Lord and His timing, and this situation was going to turn around for His glory and purpose.

I was not sure at the time what that meant, if I would get the biopsy or be healed; whatever God's will was, I was okay with it. I am not going to try to pretend that I did not get frightened in what was going to happen to me. Breast cancer is a serious illness; one you don't play with. If I had not been in prison, this whole situation would have played out differently. As soon as the mammogram report came back, a doctor would have set me up for a biopsy and we would have taken it from there. But I was not on the outside. I was in prison and I had to trust God on a whole new level, more than I had ever done before; and I knew in my heart this was all about my growth in my relationship with God and learning to trust Him more than I had ever done before. But I also knew that God was going to somehow use this situation to minister to others and give them hope.

It was not even a month later, I was walking across the compound to the commissary that I felt a hot burning sensation throughout my entire left breast. It hurt so bad that it stopped me in my tracks and caused me to grab my left breast in pain. It lasted for about three minutes or so, and then it stopped as quickly as it had started. I stood there for a minute and got myself together and then went on to the commissary to turn in my order for supplies.

As I sat and waited for my order to be filled (this normally took about an hour), I thought about what may have happened to me. At first, I got scared thinking that something may have burst inside of me and poison may have been running throughout my system. Then God tapped me on my shoulder, as you may say, and said, "No, that was Me; you are healed." The devil was trying to distract me and at first I was listening, but then God spoke and He had my undivided attention. I started thanking God right then and there. Tears started to fall down my face with joy.

A woman that I knew came over to me and asked me if I was okay. I responded, "oh yes, having a God moment." She smiled and agreed by saying amen and walked away. I continued to thank God as I waited, and I almost missed my name being called by the clerk in the commissary. Some of the women sitting around me had to get my attention and tell me, "Lanette, they are calling your name." If you are at the commissary and they call your name three times and you do not respond, you will miss your turn and you will not be able to shop again and get your supplies until the following week. I stood up and retrieved my items and off to my unit I went. I could not wait to get back to my room and sit down and try to take in what had happened to me. I was so overwhelmed with excitement; I wanted to yell it from the mountain top.

But I did not have any proof. Was anyone going to believe me? I did not know if I was going to have any more tests done on my breast since I had denied the recommendations of the doctor. This is when the devil tried to come in and rob me of what God has spoken and done on my behalf. I did not have any evidence to what had happened; only what I felt God had told me in my spirit.

On my journey through prison walls, God was also teaching me how to listen to Him and have confidence in what He was saying and showing me. God spoke to my spirit often, but I kept it to myself in fear of what others would say. Would they believe me, or think I was crazy or that I was full of myself?

Everything that I was experiencing on this journey would not only minister to me and teach me, but also minister to others. God spoke to me in many ways - His Word, through others, and even through my situations. God had been helping me grow in each of these areas and now He was going to help me achieve confidence in how I was hearing Him in my spirit. This was an area in my life that God knew I needed to gain confidence in, and this cancer scare was going to help me in this area, but I did not know that at the time.

So often we put God in a box and we are not able to hear Him because of our own expectation in what God can and will do for us, in us and through us. We see in God's Word that we should be dependent on hearing our Father's voice, but most of us live our daily lives without even hearing a word from our Father in heaven. This is one of the reasons why we make so many wrong decisions. Hearing our Father's voice is the only way we can choose the right path that God has for us. If we don't learn to listen and have confidence in what we hear is from God, we will go astray.

What a ploy of the enemy to convince us that we can't hear our Father's voice, or that hearing God's voice is only for others and not us. As I spent time in the Word and in prayer with God, God showed me in His Word the importance in being able to hear Him and understand that it was Him that I was listening to. I would like to share a few of the Scriptures that God led me too.

Jesus is at the door, if you hear my voice
Rev 3:20-22 *Behold, I stand at the door and Knock; if anyone hears My voice and opens the door, I will come in to him and will dine with him, and he with Me. 21) He who overcomes, I will grant to him to sit down with Me on My throne, as I also overcame and sat down with My Father on His throne. 22) He who has an ear, let him hear what the Spirit says to the churches. (NASB)*

If you will listen
Psalm 81:8 *Hear, O My people, and I will admonish you! O Israel, if you will listen to Me! (NASB)*

Listen to me my children
Proverbs 8:32-34 *Now therefore, listen to me, my children, for blessed are those who keep my ways, 33) Hear instruction, and be wise, And do not neglect it. 34) Blessed is the man who listens to me, Watching daily at my gates, Waiting at my doorposts. (NASB)*

If you will hear His voice
Hebrews 3:7 *Therefore, as the Holy Spirit says; Today, if you will hear His voice, (NASB)*

My sheep hear my voice

John 10:27 *My sheep hear My voice, and I know them, and they follow Me. (NASB)*

<u>If anyone has ears to hear, let him hear</u>
Mark 4:22-23 *For nothing is hidden, except to be revealed, nor has anything been secret, but that it would come to light. 23) If anyone has ears to hear, let him hear. (NASB)*

As I studied the Word of God, and opened my heart and spirit to what God was saying to me, my life was changed permanently. I finally got it. God wanted to have a relationship with me, and it included us having conversations. Now grant you, most of the time, I was doing all the listening while God spoke, but this changed my life for the better.

Now God speaks to us all differently through His Word, others and even in our situations. God was helping me in all these areas on my Journey behind Prison walls, but this particular season was more directed to me gaining the confidence in hearing God as He spoke to me in my spirit. Everything I did and how I did it changed almost overnight. The heavy load that I was carrying around on my shoulders was removed.

It was not mine to carry to begin with. My responsibility was to listen to God and be obedient. I found myself with more joy and peace than I had ever experienced in my life, and this was while I was still living in prison. Yes it took a few months to perfect, but I worked hard on listening to God everyday and not carrying the burden of deciding what to do. All I needed to do was go to the Lord and let Him guide me. This became a way of life for me and it still is to this day. I encourage you to read the Word and spend time in prayer with God and ask Him to speak clearly to you. Then, sit back and be quiet, and listen to what God has to say to you. It will change your life forever.

Most of us don't hear God because we are not still enough. We expect God to come to us like He did Moses in the burning bush, or a loud deep voice is what we want. Knock me over God. Yell at me if you have to. But that is not how God works most of the time. Even Elijah in 1 Kings 19:11-12 was looking for God in the wind, earthquake and even the fire, but after the fire, a sound of a gentle blowing came; and this was when Elijah heard God. We are no different.

We have put God in a box in our own expectations in how God will or can approach us. Because of this, we miss God often. This is why it is so important that we spend time with God. When we spend time in His Word, participate in small groups with other believers or worship the Lord with others in the house of God, the list could go on and on. But as we grow closer to God, we also learn how to listen to our Father in heaven, and this is when we notice our lives change for the better.

We make better decisions. We even treat others differently, all because we trust our Lord to give us daily guidance in how to handle the things of this world - doing things His way and not our way. I would like to encourage you right now, whatever it is that is keeping you from growing closer to the Lord, decide today to made a conscious choice to spend more time with God, and watch your joy and peace either grow or even return to you.

Within a few days of me expressing how God had spoken to me and told me that I was healed, I had many women come to me and ask me how could I tell it was

God speaking to me and not the devil trying to fool me? I told everyone who asked that God would never say anything to you that did not line up with His Word. If you are ever being told something that is not in the Word, it is not of God. The devil will try to fool you, make you think he is God; the devil is the master of lies. I went through this also, and God showed me a simple test to do in determining who was speaking to me. God is love; the devil is not capable of showing love or giving it. In everything that God shows us, the root will be in love. As I used the test of love on all my conversations, to test who I was having a conversation with, it proved to be effective.

For example, have you ever done something wrong and before you can even get yourself together, the devil comes in to beat you up about it, telling you that you will never be anything, and that you have failed again, and you can't keep expecting to be forgiven over and over again if you can't get yourself together. The words may not be exactly the same, but I am sure you can relate. This particular conversation would not pass the test of love or God's Word.

Whenever God convicts any of us in what we may be doing is wrong – sin, God always comes to us in love, showing us that what we are doing is wrong. At the same time, God reassures us that He is a forgiving God, and that we can do better if we would only repent, trust God and allow Him to help us. That is when God helps us back up on our feet and encourages us to try again, but this time with His help.

I do this with every conversation I have to this day, and if it doesn't pass the test of God's Word and being done in love, it is not God. Many women came back to me over the years that I was in prison and shared with me how this test had set them free from being tossed to and fro by the devil. God can do that for you also. Put everything that is said to you through this test. Limit how the devil can fool you and enjoy a lot more freedom because of it. I know I do.

God had told me that He had healed me, and now I had confidence in what He had told me, and I took Him for His Word; I was healed. I had many that did not believe me, but that was okay. Everyone that asked me about my situation, my response was the same, I am healed and I know I am, because Jesus told me so. The responses were different from person to person, but it did not stop me from telling everyone I could tell.

Even when I went back to work, and Mr. Chris asked me what happened, I told him the same thing. His response was somewhat amusing. "Okay, Lanette, now how do you know that? Is that what the doctor told you?" "No," I responded, "Jesus told me I was healed." Mr. Chris did not argue with me. He only laughed at me and gave me a crazy look like I was the crazy one. I knew in my heart that God would give the evidence needed for all the ones that doubted to believe. I did not need any evidence. God's voice was enough for me.

Chapter 16

Hurricane One

Working on Mr. Chris's crew had a lot of perks, but also it was a lot of hard work and responsibility. When things were working and running smooth, our crew had it pretty easy. But when things stated to break down, it looked like everything would break at the same time. Every morning Mr. Chris would pick us women up at the camp in a S150 Chevy truck.

Once at the powerhouse I would normally take the truck, along with a few other women from the crew, and make rounds to check all the equipment. Remember, we had five facilities to confirm all was well. I had the freedom to drive from facility to facility unsupervised. Again it was a piece of freedom while inside of prison. God gave me a lot of favor while I was in prison. I had it better than most, but it was still hard being away from my home and family.

As I would drive and perform my daily duties, I would often think about what was my family doing at that exact moment. In looking around in how my daily activities would be, it did not look like I was in prison, but I was. But this is how so many of us live our lives.

We walk through life in a daze, clueless to how much we are bound. I had to stay focused on God throughout my Journey behind Prison walls, and not only my situation. Many of us need to do this in our daily lives. Being in prison, I was beginning to realize I was freer than I had ever been. Yes, I did not have the freedom to come and go as I pleased, but my spirit was freer than it had ever been because of the time I was spending with God. I still to this day, try to keep that freedom now that I am at home, but I have to work hard at it every day.

Working on Mr. Chris's crew, and being the grade one, Mr. Chris made sure he enrolled me in all training that would come available. I learned how to drive every big piece of equipment on the compound; JLG's, CAT equipment and all the different kinds of forklifts. This meant anytime a person was needed to drive any of the equipment on the compound, my boss, Mr. Chris, may be called to borrow me. Mr. Chris was good to me and always asked me did I mind to go and help out the other crews. I never minded helping other crews. I loved the opportunity to drive the equipment, but, I did appreciate him asking me if I minded.

Every day that I spent with Mr. Chris, I would always refer to Jesus and how He saves; either to Mr. Chris directly or the other women on the crew. I had already been told that Mr. Chris was an atheist, and the music he played, while we were all in the truck, reflected his lack of relationship with any god, much less one with Christ. I had to be careful in how I approached Mr. Chris about God. He was the officer in charge, and I was an inmate. Most of the time, I would direct my comments and conversations to the other women on the crew, but always where he could hear them also. After a while, Mr. Chris started to ask me questions, sometimes with the other women around, and sometimes when it was only him and I.

One day when Mr. Chris and I were driving alone in the truck, he asked me a question; as he would most days. But this day, the question was different. Even the tone in his voice that he asked it in was sarcastic, like he had already made up his mind that I would not be able to answer it to his satisfaction to trick me. He looked at me and asked, "okay woman of God, I have a question for you. How do you explain the Trinity?" As I heard the question and the sarcasm in how it was asked, I prayed to myself and asked God to help me with the answer. God knew Mr. Chris better than I did, and I trusted God to answer the question in order to get Mr. Chris's attention, leading him closer to His son, Jesus.

I looked at Mr. Chris as he was driving with a smirk like look on his face waiting for me to answer. And this is what God gave me to tell him. "Mr. Chris it is like $1 \times 1 \times 1 = 1$." The truck went silent. Then Mr. Chris laughed and replied, "I have never had anyone answer that question that way in all the times I have asked it. I will have to get back to you on what I think of that answer." I laughed to myself as I thanked God for His perfect answer, because once God gave me the answer, it made all the sense in the world to why it was perfect for Mr. Chris.

Mr. Chris loved math. He was a wiz when it came to mathematical problems. When he would show us women how machines were put together, and explain how it all worked, his face would light up with joy. It blew my mind in how God, within a split minute before I could even really think how to answer the question, stepped in and gave Mr. Chris the perfect answer he needed. I could tell by looking at Mr. Chris, he was pondering deep and long on this response. I could not wait for the next question Mr. Chris would give God to answer.

We had many days like this - he asked and God answered! I kept looking for Mr. Chris to come to Jesus, but it did not happen. He was searching and I understood the

Word to say, if you seek for God you will find Him. I had to keep praying and be patient and let God do the work. Mr. Chris and I had a strange relationship. He would come to work many days mad and did not want to be bothered by anyone. In those days I was the only one who could communicate with him and get our orders for the day. It was like God had prepared both of us to be around each other. Mr. Chris gave me respect that was not normally given to an inmate in prison. I would learn much later why this was and what all God was really doing.

One day Mr. Chris called me into the office and told me that we all needed to prepare for a hurricane, Katrina. This was in 2005 in August, my first Hurricane inside of prison. My heart dropped as he spoke because my mind went directly to my family. Since I was able to drive all the big equipment on the compound, I would be used by the compound to bring in supplies to the camp. But I first needed to help Mr. Chris secure everything in and around all the cooling towers. We also had to go to each generator room and run checks on them to be sure they were all in operational order in case the power went out. We, as a crew, did many things in helping all five facilities to prepare for the hurricane. The men in the other facilities were not allowed to come out of their facilities to help. All work had to be done by us women.

As the hurricane got closer to Coleman, the staff called a town hall meeting in order to give us all instructions in how we all at Coleman would ride out the storm. I, myself, was happy the meeting was being called due to this being my first hurricane in prison. Many others were frustrated with it all. In the meeting, we were all informed that each unit would have their own unit team staying within their units until the storm passed. We were all told, when we slept in our bunks to keep on our shoes. This was in case we needed to seek cover quickly. We would be ready to move. Food would be brought into the units for each meal, and we would not be getting any hot meals but bagged meals - lots of sandwiches! These meals would be prepared by the men in the men's prisons. I found out, that the way the men's prison were structured they would still be able to use their kitchens, but we would not due to safety.

As long as we had power, there would not be much of an inconvenience. Each unit had two microwaves, and most of us had food within our lockers that had been bought off commissary. We all were allowed to buy items off commissary each week on our shopping days. You could only buy so much a month, and our lockers would only hold so much. You did have to have money in your account to buy. Many of us would share with others who had nothing. The whole week of shopping at the commissary before the storm was real busy, due to everyone stocking up on supplies for the storm. The women who had been in a while knew what was ahead; we would not be getting any hot food from the kitchen. If you wanted hot food, you would have to cook it yourself in the microwave.

I had plenty of food in my locker and plenty of batteries for my nightlight and radio. I was prepared for the long haul. I was going to use this extra time off from work to study the Word and be there for all the women within my unit that I had gotten close to. I was also asking God to open doors for me to speak to other women in my unit that I had not been able to approach for whatever reason. There are many cliques in prison, and you have to respect them or you may get hurt. Most knew me in the unit as a Christian and one that you could trust, but I had not been able to talk to everyone one-on-one. I had a lot of Christian tracts to pass out due to my friends from my church mailing them to me in all my letters. This was the perfect time to pass them out. I was praying for God to give me the opportunity to pass them all out.

Most of us were not frightened for ourselves, but our families. We could call and check on our families as long as the phones were on, and watch the news on the TV's as the storm would go through each of our homes, but we were not sure to how long the electricity would stay on. If the electricity went out for any reason, we would only be able to get updates on our radios. As the storm came closer, we all made our calls home and asked if they were prepared and ready. We informed them not to worry if they did not hear from us for a few days, because the phones may be down.

We each did make sure our families had all the phone numbers to reach Coleman staff in case there was an emergency. We could not receive calls as inmates, but our families could call the unit team or the chaplain's office to inquire if we were all okay. This was how most inmates would receive bad news from home, through the unit team or the chaplain's office. I had been called many times to go along with a friend as they received news that was not good. This was not a page you wanted to hear "please report to the chaplain's office." Every time I would hear this over the loud speaker, I would pray for whoever was being paged, in case it was to hear bad news from home.

In leaving work, I understood that Mr. Chris and Mr. Red would be staying in the powerhouse together. They also had to be on site in case of any emergency. I knew that if things did break down, I would not be called out to help until all clear had been called, meaning the storm had passed. But this did mean, due to the nature of my work, I would be out of the unit before most were. As I went into my unit I could see everyone was in from work, and were preparing for the storm. Most were getting themselves set up in the TV rooms to watch news and other programs to help the time go by. I did not spend much time in the TV rooms during my Journey behind Prison Walls, due to the activity that went on in the TV rooms. Because of this, I learned to not watch much TV, but listen to my radio.

At this time, I was still roommates with Tommie, but during this hurricane, she too was quiet and did not bother me much with her rules. God was blessing me with peace with living with her; but I had to really work at it and stay in prayer. As the storm came closer, she would make comments on how this was not all necessary, the staff being in the unit with us and how uncomfortable it made her. I would show her that I was listening intently to whatever she had to say, but I was careful in my response. It was time for me to listen to her and pray. The officers came through the unit often. I did not mind this, but others did. Many of the women did not follow the instruction to keep their shoes on while in their beds; the officers would call them out on it every time they did a walk through.

Many of the women were like my Bunkie. They did not like anything on their beds to get them dirty. You would never go into another's room and sit on their bed, unless you were invited to do so. Many would get offended, and would wash their bedding on the spot because you sat on it. This could even cause a fight if you did this. Remember, in prison you did not have much that was yours. Your bed was your personal space and you did not invade another's personal space without being invited. This was why many did not want to keep their shoes on while in their beds. I watched many women go into the shower room and wash their shoes, so they could put them on while they were in their beds as instructed by the officers. It did not bother me. I did as I was told. I did not spend much time in my bed. I loved to put a blanket out on the floor and pull out all my books and study the Word.

My Bunkie did not like that I would lay out my blanket and books on the floor to study, and I did try to do it most of the time when she was out of our room, but the current situation did not allow me to do that. I prayed before I laid out my blanket and asked God to give me favor that Tommie would not kick up a stink over my blanket and books on the floor, and God answered my prayer, because Tommie did not bother me at all.

It was hard for me to stay focused due to my concerns for my family, but I kept reading and studying, and it helped get me through. Many would walk by and ask me what was a studying, and I would share with them and even some would join me. I, again, did not know how my Bunkie would deal with this, but she did not complain. God was answering my prayers in an amazing way. Many would ask could they come in and sit down, and I would say of course and even let them sit on my bunk, while I would sit on the floor. Many would go and retrieve their own Bibles and come back to my room, and we would study together for hours. This did not only help them, but me also, get through the storm.

Is this not what the Word tells us, in the midst of the storm to stay focus on our Lord? This is what I was doing, and many others in our unit were doing the same. God was using us in the midst of the storm to help others. Many did not know what to do to get through this. They all felt so helpless due to the situation. We could not reach out to our families like we normally would if we were on the outside. We had to trust God on a whole new level, and, for many, this was their first time trusting God in this way. God's Word tells us that we are the light. God can use us to shine in a time of darkness, if we would only let Him. This was what God was doing with me while I was in prison. I had to keep reminding myself what God's Word said in order to not get discouraged and fall in to self pity. As we read in Matthew 5:14-16

***Matthew 5:14-16** You are the light of the world. A city that is set on a hill cannot be hidden. 15) Nor do they light a lamp and put it under a basket, but on a lampstand, and it gives light to all who are in the house. 16) Let your light so shine before men, that they may see your good works and glorify your Father in heaven. (NKJV)*

God had allowed me to be where I was in order to shine for Him. So many needed to see God's light, even though I did not feel like shining. It was time to let God shine through me and give hope to the ones who had none.

***Isaiah 60:1** Arise, shine; for your light has come, and the glory of the Lord is risen upon you. (NKJV)*

The thing that impressed Isaiah most here was the glory of God and the dawning of a new day for the nation. We have this everyday in our lives. Every day is a new day to shine for the Lord. We don't always recognize it. We often let our circumstances dictate our days and not Jesus.

Jesus tells us in John 8:12 that He is the light of the world, and whoever follows Him shall not walk in darkness, but have the light of life. We have to decide to receive this, and allow the light to shine. I was not in a place that I wanted to shine. I did not feel like it most of the time, but I was learning to shine for Jesus, even when I didn't feel like it. Most of us have to come to a place that we don't allow our emotions to dictate our actions, or what God can do through us or in us. I was beginning to understand what it meant to be in God's will and not my own. What I also learned was that, once I let go and let God, His will was what brought me the greatest joy. The enemy did not want me to discover this. We have to decide to believe God even when we can't see or understand the outcome.

***John 8:12** Then Jesus spoke to them again, saying, "I am the light of the world; he who follows Me shall not walk in darkness, but have the light of life." (NASB)*

I was not walking in darkness, but the devil wanted me to believe I was. The devil is a liar and we have to realize when the devil is attempting to talk to us and guide us and choose to not listen. When I stopped looking at the storm that was rolling in on us, I was then able to look around me and see what it was that Jesus wanted me to do - shine for Him! The storm did not stop, but this time was not about the hurricane that was approaching us, it was all about God having the undivided attention of many women in my unit. All I had to do is take a step of faith and God did the rest. God used me to minister to many women during that time and them to me.

It surprised me to how much I was not worried for my own family and the damage the storm might have brought. I watched many women come back to God that had fallen out of relationship with Him. On the other hand, I was able to plant many seeds with women of many different faiths. I did not understand at the time that God was opening a dialog between them and me in order for us to have many more conversations and even prayers together. This storm initiated many new relationships between me and other women within my unit. God was working. All I needed to do was to not look at my situation, but at Him.

God is trying to use us all right where we are, but most of us don't let Him use our situations for His Glory. The disciples, in Matthew 14:22-33, shows us how afraid the disciples were in the midst of a storm. They could not see anything good coming out of the storm; but when they looked a little closer, they could see Jesus was walking on the water toward them.

Even Peter in Matthew 14:28, NASB, said, "Lord, if it be You, command me to come to You on the water." When Peter took the step of faith and stepped out of the boat onto the water and walked toward Jesus, he did not sink until he took his eyes off of Jesus. This happens to us all the time. First we don't see anything good coming out of our storm.

We do not see Jesus approaching us in our storms, and, when we do see Jesus, we take our eyes off of Him and begin to sink because of what our circumstances look like. I would like to encourage you to remember what is says in 2 Corinthians 5:7, we do not walk by sight, but by faith. The enemy will try to confuse you. We have to fight against the lies of the devil.

2 Corinthians 5:7 for we walk by faith, not by sight. (NASB)

God was using me every day, but God wanted to do so much more through me and in me. I had to make a decision and stick to it daily, that I wanted God's will in my life and to trust Him in everything, even when it did not look good. As the storm ended and the all clear was called, I was called out with my crew and Mr. Chris like I knew I would be. The damage was limited. We did not have much to clean up, but the victory that was done inside of my unit was great, only because I yielded to God and His will. I looked into the storm and saw Jesus approaching me. I listened and did not look away. This is the only reason I did not sink.

How about you? Is Jesus approaching you in your storm but you have already decided that nothing good can come out of this storm you have found yourself in. Consider for a moment to what I am saying to you. Are you missing Jesus in your storm? Are you missing the true blessing of what God is trying to do with you and in you? Have you let Jesus into your boat? Notice in the Word when Jesus got into the boat with the disciples the storm was calm. I don't know about you, but I needed my storm to be calmed. And Jesus did this for me in the midst of it all and He wants to do that for you also, but you have to let Him in .Decide today. Look at your storm differently; look for Jesus; He is waiting on you to respond to Him.

John 16: 33 These things I have spoken to you, that in Me you may have peace. In the world you will have tribulation, but be of good cheer. I have overcome the world. (NKJV)

Jesus has already overcome your storm. Join with Him today in the victory of your current storm and the storms to come. If you will only trust in Jesus, your life will change for the better in ways you never thought were possible. He did it for me; He will do it for you.

Hurricane Two

Only two months later, in October 2005, we found ourselves preparing for another hurricane coming directly toward us. The staff at our prison had gotten together and decided there was a safer way for us all to ride out the storm. I was doing as I had done before in checking all the equipment to make sure it was all in good operating condition in case it was needed during the storm.

Then, as before, we were called in for a town hall meeting. We all gathered in the visitation room and waited for our instructions. As the warden stepped to the podium and began to inform us all how we would ride out the storm, we had no idea that he was going to say what he said.

There was a brand new penitentiary on the property that had not been used yet due to waiting for it to clear all the necessary inspections. The penitentiary was going to be called Pen 2. There was already one penitentiary on the compound. This would be the second one. It was not completely finished yet, but we women were going to be staying in it nevertheless to ride out the storm.

When the warden announced the plan for us to move to Pen 2 for the storm, women throughout the room were stirring and voicing their concerns and disapproval with the move. We had a lot of women at Coleman that had been inside for ten years or more, and they all had a lot of knowledge to what was allowed in housing inmates and so forth. Remember, we also had Cathy, who was a judge on the outside, and was also knowledgeable of what was allowed and what was not.

Inside of prison, you have to have access to a law library, and many of the women inside made it their business to learn as much about the law as they could while they were inside.

I did not know that we were not supposed to be housed in Pen 2, but they did. The warden knew this would be brought up, and he cleared this up quickly. As the warden gained control of the room, he informed us all he had already gotten special permission from the Federal Bureau of prison to house us in the penitentiary for the storm, for our own safety. All of us women at the camp were camp status, and had been for most of our time in prison.

This meant an open atmosphere and not locked doors. We did not have wire around our camp, and we only had, most of the time, one officer to watch over all four units - about 500 women. Going into the penitentiary for even a few days was something none of us were looking forward to. We all could remember the storm that we had gone through only two month prior, and we all had done well right where we were. Why did we have to go to the penitentiary? That was running through all of our minds. We all could not help ourselves from thinking, was there something they were not telling us?

In moving to Pen 2, we would not have any access to TV's or phones. We would be out of contact with all of our families, and the only updates we would be able to receive on the storm would be from staff or our radios. This was not sitting well with any of us, but what could we do? We were only inmates.

The decision had been made. We all were then given the instruction to what we could take and not take. Most crochet in the effort to pass the time. We were all informed that we could not take any crafts with us. We would have one microwave to share while at Pen 2. We could take a few items of food and some clothing and religious materials or a book to read. We were instructed to put all item in our laundry bag, and we would carry it with us on the bus when we were transported to Pen 2. Also, our mattresses would be moved to Pen 2 temporarily for us to sleep on while we were there. We also had to carry all our bed linen over with us on the bus.

Everyone worked hard together to get everything moved over to Pen 2. The factory called UNICOR, supplied the trucks to move the mattress and many women at the camp had acquired their CDL license while working at UNICOR, and they were used to drive the trucks to move everything that needed to be moved. UNICOR was a factory that inmates could volunteer to work at to earn money while inside of prison.

They did not make the same as you would if on the outside, but they did make more than any other jobs on the compound, and often learned a skill that could be used on the outside once they would go home. As we all worked together in loading the mattresses, it was interesting to watch how all the women were working together and having fun, even the ones who did not like each other. God uses so many different situations to bring us all together.

To get the mattresses on the trucks we all had to make a line from each cell to the truck and pass it from one woman to the other to get it loaded on the truck. Each woman was responsible to get their mattress to the truck themselves, but our unit and all the other units decided that was not the best way to get it done. We all needed to work together. We had many women who were not capable of loading their own mattress.

They needed help and everyone stepped in and helped. I watched many women who would have not normally done much for anyone, they even stepped in and helped load mattresses that were not their own. It was a blessing to watch and be a part of it all. As all the trucks were loaded, they were taken over to the Pen 2 to be unloaded. The crew was not as big to unload. Staff was also at Pen 2 to make sure all mattresses were put into the correct cells.

All the women left back at the camp and not unloading mattress at Pen 2 were preparing for the bus ride over to the Pen. I was personally not looking forward to the next few days. We would be locked up like the men, who would be staying within the Pen. Each unit was loaded on the busses, also driven by inmates.

As I sat down on the bus, I lowered my head and prayed. I asked God to help me with the next few days that I would not look at my surroundings but to Him. Tommie, my Bunkie, was not concerned at all. She had lived at a high security prison already; she worked herself up to Coleman camp by her good behavior. Tommie's train of thought was that this was going to be a time for her to catch up on some sleep; no work. She took as much food as she could carry, and tried to get me to do the same thing. I could not take as much food as she did due to my bag was loaded with my Bible and several other study books. I did take all my tracts and as many other handouts as I had, praying again that I would have a chance to hand some of them out.

As we loaded the bus and started the short bus ride to Pen 2, I tried to prepare myself as much as I could, but my emotions still got the best of me. When we approached Pen 2 and pulled up to the gate for an officer to open the gate so we could enter, tears started to flow down my cheeks. As the bus pulled through the gate, I looked up and all I could see was fencing and barbed wire. It sent chills down my back. This was the first time since I had been in that I could actually see the wire and fencing as I was being locked on the other side; it was emotional for me. A friend of mine sitting next to me noticed my tears and hugged me and reminded me that it was only for a few days. I looked at her and she smiled at me and I was able to gain my composure. The bus proceeded around Pen 2 and came to a stop. We were all instructed to get off the bus and follow the officers ahead for our room assignments.

As we walked inside, I could not help myself looking at how big Pen 2 was and cold. I would only be here a few days, but soon many men would be coming here, and they would be calling this place home for a long time if not life; this brought sadness to me for them. I could not get out of my mind how they would feel coming into a place like this with no hope of ever leaving.

Again I remembered I was only here for a few days, and this gave me peace. As I walked into Pen 2, I was instructed by one of the staff members to where my room assignment was I was also pointed in the right direction of my unit. As I walked through many doors, I felt some comfort in seeing that all the doors were propped open. I prayed that they would stay that way. My Bunkie was not far behind me, and we both found our room at the same time; and both of our mattresses were already laid out on the floor. We were not allowed to move our mattress; this was an assigned bed just like in our unit.

I put my things down on the top of my mattress. I then went back outside to find the rest of my friends. We were allowed to move around from unit to unit until everyone was brought over on the buses. I began to relax and be intrigued with the size of the prison. As I walked and investigated all the rooms within the prison, it came to me that while we were here we should all pray for all the men and staff members that would be located within this prison in a few months. The unit did not have much privacy, not even with the showers. They put up some sheets for us women to shower, but the men would not have any kind of curtain. Because of the security risk the men that would be housed here at this prison would have to be watched at all times, for the protection of themselves and others. It was an eye opener to how good we had it at the camp. Again God was showing me how much I should appreciate what I had; it could be worse.

Each unit had a microwave, and we were to be brought in some bottled water. The showers were not working yet, but they were working on them. The drinking fountains were not in yet and we were to be given several bottles of water a day to drink. The unit was cold and damp. We were the first ones to be housed in this prison. We had no idea what worked or did not work. We were all about to find out together. Tommie, my Bunkie, was being real nice. She explained everything to me in what I should expect and to not worry. We would all be fine due to us only being here for a few days. It looked like God was using her to comfort me; God is so cool to whom he will and can use.

After all the busses were unloaded, we were all instructed in what to do next over the intercom. All inmates were to go to their assigned rooms and prepare for count.

None of us knew what the process was going to be in this strange prison. Normally, in this kind of prison, an officer would be on post within the unit at all times due to the isolation from everything. We had no panic button like at the camp in case of an emergency, and we had no phones. As count was finished, we were informed that our unit team would be in to answer our questions and to prepare us for what would be happening over the next few days while we were housed in this prison. We waited for hours and no one showed up. Until around 6:00 PM from what I remember. I remember it being late because of all the complaining from all the women in the unit. Count had taken place around 2:00 PM and we all had been left alone with no instructions, food or water. We also did not have a staff member within our unit; I repeat we were all alone.

Our unit team finally came in around 6:00 PM, and they had a lot to contend with. The women in the unit were not happy. With no water and our showers not working and dinner had not been brought in yet, there was a lot of complaining. When the unit team came into the unit they asked all women to go to their cells and close their doors. This did not go over well with most of the women. I learned this later when I was out and about talking with the women in the unit what was bothering them. They shared with me that they were worried that the staff was going to lock the cell doors. They all told me that this was not allowed without an officer on post in the unit due to safety. None of the women trusted the staff because of how things were going; up until this point, things were not going well.

Everyone in the unit was concerned to how our next few days were going to be spent during the storm. We were camp status, meaning that we did not have barbed wire or locked doors to contend with normally. Many of the women were having a lot of anxiety due to the thought of the doors being locked. Nothing had been explained to any of us in what we all should expect over the next few days. We were being told a little at a time. I believed the staff themselves did not know exactly what they were going to do. It looked like they were figuring it out as they went, since this was the first time this had ever been done. My Bunkie, Tommie, was not upset at all. This was strange to me. She did not like things out of order. We ate some of our food out of our bags and waited things out. Tommie was a blessing in how she was handling everything.

When we were all asked to go into our rooms and close the doors, my Bunkie and I did as we were told. But we could hear all the complaining from all the other women in the unit. The officers were warning them if they did not behave, they would lock the doors. As everyone quieted down, the officers came around to each room with a book to verify who was in the cell.

They wanted to make sure everyone was where they had been assigned. Once this was done, we were told to open the door and stand in the door way, dinner had arrived and also some water. We were each given a sack dinner and one bottle of water. The sack contained a turkey sandwich with cheese and a juice and crackers and some cookies. We were all told that more water would be given out later in the night.

Once the staff left, everyone came out of their cells, to cook items in the microwave and to talk about all that was going on. We had Cathy with us also, her being an x-judge, everyone was going to her to understand what staff was allowed to do and not do. This had everyone even more upset. My Bunkie and I worked together to fix some dinner, taking some of her things and mine, and we made us a dinner that was not bad.

She went to the microwave to cook, and I walked around the unit to see how everyone was doing. I was able to pray with a few that were frightened and encourage others. This was frightening to me also, but I knew from the previous hurricane that there would be many women who would need to hear from God in this storm; so I put my fear away in God's hands and asked God to use me.

As all of the women in the unit were eating their meals, I again watched how many women were helping each other; sharing food and other items to make the stay easier. It was so refreshing to see everyone coming together and helping each other, even ones who did not like each other were working together. This was what everyone had done during the first storm. But everyone had returned to their everyday routines once the storm was over. Now we all found ourselves in a storm again. Isn't this how we do in our everyday trials and tribulations?

We learn something during a tribulation in our life, "a storm" and once the storm passes, we return to what we knew before the storm. This doesn't happen all the time, but often enough that we have to repeat storms in our lives more than once in order for us to learn what we need to learn and keep it.

God is so patient with us; He never gives up on any of us. I am so thankful to God that He never gives up on any of us. I, for one, have been blessed by God's patience and how He never gives up on us. It has taken me many storms to learn some of the things that I needed to learn from God.

But now that I have learned the lessons that God was trying to teach me, I am glad that God allowed the storms to come my way. I know that it is hard to take this approach during a storm. This is why I ask God before a storm ever hits to help me to stay focused on Him and to not miss whatever it is that God is trying to teach me in everyday. Once we get used to looking at everything through God's eyes in our everyday lives, when the tribulations do come in our lives we are better equipped to weather them and learn what it is that God has for us.

Many of the cells were leaking, and the women that were in them needed help in moving their things to keep them from getting wet. We did not get to the mattresses in time, they were already soaked. We did not have any means to call the staff. The door to our unit was not locked but we had been instructed to not leave the unit. One of the women opened the door and yelled out for someone, but no one came. Now, while all this commotions, was going on with the cells being wet, we also had a woman pass out and fall to the floor.

Our unit also had a doctor that had been convicted of Medicare fraud. She quickly went to the side of the woman who had collapsed. We all called her Doc, and she helped the best she could until help came. Again the same woman who had been yelling for help for the women, who had their cells wet, went back to the door to yell for help for the woman who had collapsed; still no one came. When the woman who had gone to the door did not see anyone coming, she decided to take the chance and leave the unit and go for help. She could have

A Journey Behind Prison Walls

gotten in trouble for leaving the unit, but she went anyway.

She returned with an officer and the officer yelled for all of us to go to our cells. Everyone dispersed but the ones tending to the woman who passed out. The officer called on the radio for medical and the unit team to come to our unit. Once everyone showed up, the woman was removed and taken to medical for evaluation, and then the unit team addressed why some of the women had their things out of their cells.

The unit team was led to the cells that were leaking and showed them their mattresses were all wet. The unit team told them to hold tight while they found them a dry room and a dry mattress. This took hours. As time passed by, and the unit team had not come back with a new room assignment or mattresses for the six women who had been flooded out of their room, we began to wonder if they would ever return.

Count time came, and still no one had come to address all the concerns and problems our unit was having, ten p.m., and count was called, and all were to go to their cells and close their cell doors. There were six women who could not, due to their cells being flooded. The officers did not want to hear why they were not in their cells, and told them to go to their cells right away.

They did what they were told and stood in three inches of water to be counted. Now they also had wet shoes. After count was completed, we all came out of our cells to check on the women who had to go into their cells that were flooded. Yes, the water was not going to cause them harm, but I was more concerned about their emotional status. When I approached them, many of them were crying and others were angry.

They did not know what to do for the night. It was already after ten PM and they still did not have a room or mattress to sleep on. It was not until an hour later about 11:00 p.m., that some staff came in to address all of the women that had been flooded out of their rooms. They now had new cells and mattresses for them to sleep on.

It was now almost 11:30 p.m., and I was finally going to bed. My Bunkie was already sleeping, and the events of the night had not concerned her at all. I remember, from the beginning this weekend for her meant catching up on her sleep; and that is what she was doing.

As I climbed into my bed and in between my sheets, I went to my Lord in prayer. I prayed that God would be with every woman in the prison and all the other inmates in the other facilities riding out the storm. This was different for us this time, no TV to watch the news and no phones to call home. I asked God to use this time for His purpose with every woman in the place. I also asked God to use the many of us that were Christians to reach out to the staff members also and shine for Jesus during this time. This was not easy for any of us including the staff. Again this had never been done before; we were all out of our comfort zones.

Up to this point being in prison, I had learned being out of my comfort zone was a way of life. It was when God moved or did His best work in all of us. This storm was going to be no different. It was up to each individual to what they would let God do.

God was definitely here to give peace and hope to all who would receive it. I prayed for all our family members and anyone in the path of the hurricane - it had been named Wilma. We found out later to how much damage this hurricane would do. Most of us had radios, and we could listen to the updates to where the storm was and where it was going.

The ones who did not have radios, we would update them as we would hear the updates. There was a women's camp that was in the direct path of the hurricane; we were all praying for them also. They did not have a facility like we did to go to. They would have to ride it out where they were. Most of the women did not look at the prison we were in as a blessing. But it was. We were all safe. We did not have the things we wanted or were used to, but we were safe and this, too, would pass.

The next morning, the officers came in to count, and then some staff followed them with breakfast. The prison was cold and damp, and it was beginning to get to me. My asthma was starting to act up. My Bunkie was the first one to respond quickly. She went to the microwave and made me a cup of coffee. All the women at the microwave let her go ahead of them once she told them what she was doing and why. I looked up to my Bunkie returning with a cup of coffee and several women with her including Doc to see if I was okay. I used my inhaler and sipped on the coffee and the attack got better. As I was drinking the coffee, many women were outside my room praying for me; this was what gave me the most peace.

Doc proceeded to tell me what I could do to help myself from not having so many attacks in the cold and damp place. My Bunkie listened intently. She did not want me to have other attack. My Bunkie was not normally a nice person, not someone you would want to be around, but I was seeing the other side of her. I kept praying for God to be able to reach her.

Doc told me to drink as much hot drinks as I could, try not to drink anything cold, and keep warm. One of the women praying for me outside the door, ran to get one of their extra blankets and gave it to me to use. She said, "Here use this and stay warm." I thanked her and thanked God for His provisions; God was working all around me; I was truly blessed to watch Him at work in so many.

The storm raged outside. We could hear it and see it through the small window in each room. This was also during a time that you could not smoke inside of prison; but you had to go outside to smoke. This was a real problem. The staff did not come around that often and all the women that smoked were going through withdrawals. Many did not wait. They smoked in their cells. This was causing me some problems also. I cannot deal with smoke at all; it will bring on an asthma attack whenever I am around it. Finally, the staff came up with a solution. A door from our unit went out to the yard. This door would be used for the men when they would be housed in this prison to go into the yard and get some exercise. The problem was the staff had to locate the key. We found out later, we were never in any danger of the cell doors being locked. They did not have the keys. Once security found a way to get the door open, and the rain had a break, the women were all allowed to go outside and have a smoke. This helped a lot with some of the tension in the unit.

Our second day at Pen 2 was not much better than the first day. The storm was still ranging outside. Yes, we were all safe inside, but the anxiety was high due to no one being able to call home and check on their loved ones. I spent most of my time with other women studying the Word and encouraging them. I had taken a lot of handouts with me, and I passed them all out to everyone that was interested in taking one. My intention was to not take any tracts back to the camp, and I did not.

The second night at Pen 2, we were all surprised with a hot meal. The men's prison was still able to cook in their kitchen. Due to this, the men cooked us women a hot meal and our staff brought it to us and served us. Remember the inmates do all the work at the camp, including preparing and serving all the meals. Due to where we were all being housed, we were not able to help the staff even in passing out the food. Our staff had to do all the work, and we were thankful to them all for everything that they were doing for us. They could have given us a sack lunch and not go to the extra effort. With everything we had been through, it was a nice surprise.

God was teaching me, at every turn, a new appreciation for the little things in life - hot food was one of them! As dinner came in, we also noticed that the woman that had passed out the first day that we were brought to Pen 2 was now back. We still did not know what had happened to her but it was good to see her, back to her normal self and with us again.

As we all sat down and ate our dinner, there was calmness over the entire unit. It amazes me in how the little things in life can bring such joy and peace, but we too often take them all for granted. As I finished my dinner and went to my room to wait for a shower, I sat on my bed and thought about where we were and who would be living here in these very cells later in the year once we women had gone back to the camp. I have to admit spending a small amount of time in Pen 2 gave me a bigger appreciation for the camp where I lived. The men that were to come into Pen 2 prison may never see freedom again. It was cold and dreary. I had been in other maximum security prison before coming to the camp, but none of those were quite like the experience at Pen 2.

My experience at Pen 2 was different from anywhere I had been up to this point, and I know with all my heart that God had allowed me to experience living at Pen 2 in order for me to learn something; and I did. Living at the camp was not easy, being away from my family and everything I knew was hard; I cried almost every night. It was like someone had pushed the pause button on my life, and I was unable to push the play button; someone else had the remote.

Everyone's life that I knew and loved was living and planning for their futures and putting all their dreams in place. Even dreaming was difficult for me being where I was. This was something that had been bothering me from the beginning when I was first loaded into the van at Fort Lauderdale after sentencing; and this feeling had not left me until now.

Through this experience living at Pen 2 I realized that "I was able to dream." I would be leaving this situation in due time, but so many others that would be living at Pen 2 Would not be able to dream. They would be looking at these walls for life at Pen 2. This was not true for me. I was going home to resume my life with my family and friends. God had a plan for me, and it was past time for me to look to the future and stop looking at what it could have been and look at what things would be, if I let God unfold His plan and vision for my life.

As I realized how good I did have it at the camp compared to how little others did have while they were in prison, I felt sad and overwhelmed all at the same time.

So often we all get settled into what we have and take it for granted. When I arrived at the camp, I was excited and happy to be at the camp finally. I had an appreciation for it due to where I had been. God was teaching me how easy it was to fall into a lack of appreciation in what we have; it had only been a year. It doesn't matter what we have, how much or how little, it is in our nature to take it for granted after a while.

We have to be mindful of this and keep a watchful eye on our comfort level and taking things for granted. As the night went on, I found peace in the Word of God and prayer. Again, God was teaching me valuable lesson while I was at Pen 2. Again, I had to stop and take a look inside to what needed to change in me to learn what God was trying to teach me. We must not allow ourselves to get too comfortable in anything of this world. This is when we can fall to the temptations of the devil.

The devil wants to gain a beachhead in each of us. It is up to us to stand guard and make sure he is not allowed to gain this in our lives. I was already falling back into my comfortable and non appreciative outlook, and I did not even know it until I came to Pen 2. Everything in our lives that God allows is a lesson. God was reaffirming this again to me at Pen 2.

God showed me that even most missionaries have less than I did, and they were appreciative in what they had, and happy to be able to be in the mission field being used by God. They were content. I knew I needed to be alert and watch myself that I would not take for granted anything that God allowed to come into my life. This way the devil would not be able to use any of these things against me.

It was our last night at Pen 2 and my outlook was a lot different from what it had been when I first arrived. I walked the halls and the common area talking and listening to the other women throughout the unit. Due to what God had taught me in my cell, I was much more able to help others with their own emotions. God showed me at Pen 2 how dislocated, from the reality of what He sees and understands, we can be if we get consumed with what is happening around us, and how we can get too comfortable and unappreciative in what we do have.

The Word tells us in James to count it all joy when you fall into various trials. Every time I read this in the Word in the past I knew what it meant; now I was living it. Isn't that how God teaches us? When we read God's Word, the Holy Spirit gives us understanding, and then God allows a storm to roll in for us to live it and put into action what we have learned. This is one of the ways that God can perfect in us what He has taught us - work out the kinks in us as you may say!

James 1:2-4 *My brethren, count it all joy when you fall into various trials, 3) knowing that the testing of your faith produces patience. 4) But let patience have its perfect work, that you may be perfect and complete, lacking nothing. (NKJV)*

The next morning, we all had to pack our things up and prepare to go back to the camp. It was good to be going home; yes, I said home. The camp was my home for the time being, and I was happy to be going back there. I, again, had an appreciation for what I had. All mattresses had to be loaded on the trucks, and we also had to clean our unit before we could leave. Then each unit was called to load the busses for the trip back to the camp. When our unit was called to load the busses I was overwhelmed with joy; my faith had produced patience in me. I was not worried with what was ahead me; I had great peace. As we all loaded the busses, and sat down for the ride home, there was a calmness and quietness that had not been on the bus on the ride to Pen 2. When we came to the barbed wire that had caused me to cry when we first arrived at Pen 2, this time I smiled as we rode through the gate. You know the joy you get when you take a real hard test in school and pass it; that was how I felt.

Once back at the camp, we all had to help unload our mattresses and then unpack our belongings and make sure the unit was in order. Once everyone had done what was required of them, the phones were then full and the lines were long. Everyone wanted to call home and check to see how their loved ones were doing. We would then have lunch at the cafeteria when our unit was called. Things were going to get back to normal, or at least we thought they were. We found out later in the day that there was other women's camp that had been destroyed during the hurricane, and they would be moving all of the women from that camp in with us. We had two women per room and now we were going to have three. My Bunkie was not happy about this at all. We had to move our lockers in order to make room for the mattress that would come into each cell. My friends and I all started to pray for the women that were coming to the camp. We even collected things to put on each bed to welcome them to our unit. We were told that they were not able to bring much with them. We wanted to give them some comforts that they may not have been able to bring. We were told that they would not be able to bring any food.

We collected as many food items that we could along with some other items and laid them on each bed. We noticed other women in the unit watching what we were doing, and they, too, started to prepare goodies for their soon-to-be new roommate.

As the busses started to show up with the women from the other camp they were kept in processing for hours. Even though they were in the system, they had to be processed into our camp like any newcomer would be; this took hours. Since there were so many it was after 12:00 midnight before they were allowed to come into the camp. Many of us, waiting for the women to be released from processing stayed up and greeted them when they were released to the unit. They were tired and weary from all they had been through. We all would be able to talk the following day. It was time for them to get a shower and go to bed for some well deserved rest. We were told that they had not been able to take a shower since the hurricane had started. This meant it had been at least three days, if not longer, since they had been able to take a shower, and most of us thought we had it bad being at Pen 2. Busses of women would be coming to our camp over the next thirty days. All the women could not be transported at once since there were not enough busses or staff to transport them all at one time. At least, this was what we all had been told.

The woman that was assigned to my cell was a Christian, and she was overwhelmed with joy by all the items that we had left for her on her bed. My Bunkie even contributed some things; she did not want to be left out. I showed her where the shower was and asked her if she needed anything, and she said, "not now, but may be tomorrow." Once she had a showered, we talked for a little while before she went to sleep.

This was when I found out that she was a Christian, and she had been praying that she would get a Christian for a Bunkie. I gave her some of the rules of the camp and prayed with her before we both went to sleep. I told her that I would be getting up early in the morning to go to work, but while I was gone if she wanted to lie on my bed, she could. Her mattress was on the floor, and I knew it was not that comfortable. I told her that I was not picky about my bed and to make herself at home.

Before going to sleep, I asked her if she wanted me to leave out my coffee for her in the morning before I went to work. She said that would be great. I remembered how much it meant to me to have a cup of hot coffee when I first came into prison. I wanted to do the same for her as it had been done to me. It does not take a lot to reach out to others. It is the little things that minister; we only have to be willing to give. As we both fell off to sleep, I was excited about what was ahead, but I also felt concerned about something too. I could not put my finger on it, but something was not right, and I felt like it had something to do with my Bunkie, Tommie. The next few days we would be receiving more women from the other camp and making room for them. We had to turn two of our TV rooms and our multipurpose room into rooms for the women who were coming. We called them fishbowls because of the windows around them. The women in these rooms did not have any privacy at all. These rooms were only to be used until a room within the unit was available; then they would be moved out of the fishbowl. The beds were also three-tiered in the fishbowl. I thought this was crazy. I could not understand how some of the women even slept in them, much a less climbed up in them.

I did not even know we had three tier beds. I found out that they were being made for Pen 2. The rooms we were in while at Pen 2 were not going to house two men, but three. My heart broke for them all over again. The rooms were smaller than what we women had at the camp, or at least they looked to be. It was tight for us women when we were only there for three days. I could not see how three men would be able to stay in those small rooms with all their belongings and lockers, some for life.

My appreciation for what I had was again renewed. After the women were with us a few weeks, the ones who could work were given jobs. Most were happy for this due to boredom. All the women, who were coming into the system directly from sentencing and not being transferred from the other camp, came to our camp also. We were getting crowded real fast. As time went on, my new Bunkie and I became good friends. I had put in, before she had come to the camp, for a new room due to how difficult it was to live with my current Bunkie, Tommie. I was concerned with leaving my new Bunkie and moving to a new room, but she assured me to not worry. She was not going to be at our camp long, and I needed to do what my spirit was leading me to do.

The day did come, not long after our conversation, that I was called into the counselor's office. My request for a new room had been granted. I was moving to a new room; one without a window. My counselor made sure that I understood that I may not be able to move into another window room, and was I sure I wanted to move. I assured him that I was positive. I returned to my room and informed both of my Bunkie's that I was moving, and Tommie appeared happy about the move.

My other Bunkie helped me pack and move my things to my new room. I knew my new Bunkie to that I was moving in with. We were already friends, and she, too, was a Christian. Not too many moved from a window room once they had one. Everyone was wondering why I had moved. My new Bunkie, Fiona, told everyone that we wanted to be Bunkie's and there was nothing more to it. This was true, but I also did not feel comfortable with Tommie as my Bunkie, and I still could not put my finger on why, but this, too, would become clear soon.

Chapter 17

The Favor of God

As I settled in with Fiona, I found myself sleeping better and able to focus more on my studies. I had no idea how much my old Bunkie was bothering me. I know we have to learn to not let others bother us, and I had gotten better, but it was still getting to me. I had only been in my new room about a week, when I came in from work one day, and the officers were in my old room and removing my old Bunkie, Tommie. No one knew what was going on, or they would not say. Later that night, I found out that Tommie was caught doing something she should not have been doing, and she had been under investigation for quite some time. She was going to be moved to Tallahassee, a higher security prison; she lost her camp status. Being at a camp was a privilege. You could lose this privilege if you did not keep all the rules and behave yourself. Everything made sense now. I knew something was not right in my spirit, but could not put my finger on it. I was learning how to listen to the Holy Spirit. Being inside of prison, you can't take anything for granted, but is this not true in everyday life no matter where you are? God was teaching me how to listen to Him and all of His warnings. I was truly in God's boot camp. The survival techniques that God was teaching me were not only needed in prison, but life. All these lessons would come in handy once I was home.

I was always trying to meet all the new women who came to the unit, trying to minister to them and help them settle in. One day, I noticed a younger woman in

A Journey Behind Prison Walls 341

the unit that I had not seen before, Denise. She did not look even old enough to be at the camp. You had to be 18. As I introduced myself, I learned that she was 18, and she was in great need of being comforted. She was frightened, and she also had problems with chronic anxiety attacks, and she was having one when I went to introduce myself. I began to talk to her and I found out she was a Christian. I started to pray for her quickly for her anxiety to stop; and it did. From that day forth, we were very close. Denise would come to my room every day. When she was having an anxiety attack the officer would send someone to find me so I could come to her and help her overcome it. One night she was having one that was so bad, the officers allowed her to sleep in my room, by putting her mattress on the floor next to my bed until the attack passed. I remember the night like it was yesterday. I would hold her hand and pray for her as her whole body would shake. I am not sure how long it took, but I do know it was until the wee hours of the morning before she finally went to sleep.

Denise and I spent a lot of time together studying the Word of God. A lot of her anxiety was due to things that she did not understand in the Bible. She understood that every time she sinned, she would lose her Salvation, and she would then go to hell and not heaven unless she asked for forgiveness and asked Jesus to save her all over again. Denise was asking for Jesus to save her every day for "Salvation." She even told me a story of a day that she could not get a hold of her father, and she thought the rapture had happened, and she had been left behind, because she had sinned earlier in that day and had not asked for forgiveness yet. God was showing me how the devil can cripple Christians by them not understanding

God's Word correctly. We have to be careful who we listen to. It is so important that we read the Word for ourselves and ask God to guide us in everything that is within it. Denise was saved because of what God had promised her in His Word, but she did not live a life that was full of victory due to her misunderstanding of many other Scriptures. I led her in the Word to many Scriptures that would lead her to peace in her Salvation that Jesus had provided for her. I gave her the following scripture to read and study every time she felt like she was not saved due to her sinning:

John 3:15-17
15) so that whoever believes will in Him have eternal life. 16) For God so loved the world, that He gave His only begotten Son, that whoever believes in Him shall not perish, but have eternal life. 17) For God did not send the son into the world to judge the world, but that the world might be saved through Him. (NASB)

Romans 3:23-24 *for all have sinned and fall short of the glory of God, 24) being justified as a gift by His grace through the redemption which is in Christ Jesus; (NASB)*

Ephesians 2:8-9 *For by grace you have been saved through faith, and that not of yourselves; it is the gift of God, 9) not as a result of works, so that no one may boast. (NASB)*

Titus 3:4-7 *But when the kindness of God our Savior and His love for mankind appeared, 5) He saved us, not on the basis of deeds which we have done in righteousness, but according to His mercy, by the washing of regeneration and renewing by the Holy Spirit, 6) whom He poured out upon us richly through Jesus Christ* *our Savior, 7) so that having being justified by His grace we would be made heirs according to the hope of eternal life. (NASB)*

John 5:24 *"Truly, truly, I say to you, he who hears My Word, and believes Him who sent Me, has eternal life, and does not come into judgment, but has passed out of death into life." (NASB)*

Acts 4:12 *"And there is Salvation in no one else; for there is no other name under heaven that has been given among men by which we must be saved." (NASB)*

1 John 1:9 *If we confess our sins, He is faithful and righteous to forgive us our sins and to cleanse us from all unrighteousness. (NASB)*

Ephesians 1:13 *In Him, you also, trusted, after listening to the message of truth, the gospel of you Salvation-having also believed, you were sealed in Him with the Holy Spirit of promise, (NASB)*

John 10:28 *And I give eternal life to them, and they will never perish; and no one will snatch them out of My hand. (NASB)*

Now that you have read these scriptures, and it may not even be the first time you have read them, but maybe the first time you have understood them, or, maybe it is the first time you have read them all together, whatever your situation is, I would like to encourage you to stop right here for a moment and look deep within yourself and give God this moment to minister to you. Maybe you are saved, but have not had victory in your Salvation like Denise. Somewhere down the line, someone or something has convinced you that you lost or lose your Salvation on a regular occasion. My prayer is that you receive victory from God's Word today just like Denise did, that you are saved, and Jesus has sealed you with the Holy Spirit, and no one can snatch you out of His hand. God wants you to believe in Him and His promises for you. God wants you to be victorious in the things of God, and you will not be able to do that if you don't have confidence in your own Salvation. You will not ever be effective in spreading the good news of the kingdom of God if you don't have confidence in your own Salvation., How can you help others to come to Christ if you are not confident in Jesus and the Salvation He gave to you. This is a trick of the enemy, and I pray that God brings truth to this lie of the enemy today in your life if you have been stumbling in this area. I pray victory over you today and that you become a soldier in the army of God, full of power and vigor to spread the Gospel to all who will listen.

Now maybe you are not saved at all. This could all be new to you. If this is true for you, I pray that you would right now stop and sit down and ask God to help you understand what it is He is saying to you in His Word. Are you in a place that you are sick and tired of doing life by yourself? You keep thinking that there must be more to life than what you see, but you have not been able to put your finger on it. I pray that you find yourself wanting to have God in your life and Jesus as your Savior. If that is you, and you would like to ask God into your heart, and Jesus to be your Savior, say the prayer below. It is words I give you, but the true Salvation comes from you saying them and meaning them. God wants to be in a relationship with you, and this is where it all begins. Believing that Jesus died for you on the cross and that you can't save yourself and you need Jesus to save you. We are all sinners and need a Savior, which is why Jesus came into this world to die for you and me. All you have to do is say the words below, and mean them, and you will be saved as it promises in John 3:16

Lord Jesus I am a sinner. Forgive me of my sins and wash me clean.

Come into my heart and be my Lord. I surrender. I am yours.

Deposit your Holy Spirit in me and guide me and help me to live for you.

In Jesus name I pray,
Amen!

If you said the prayer above, you are now my sister or brother in Christ. We would love to hear from you. You will find a web site on the back of this book. Please contact us and let us know you have received Jesus as your personal Savior. We want to pray for you and rejoice with you in your decision.

A prayer answered "with a strawberry pop-tart"

Denise did not have too long to be in prison, but the short time she was with me, she became like a daughter to me. One night, I was lying in my bed, and it had been a hard day for me for some reason or another, I don't remember why. But I was in my room, and I had been studying the Word, and I had put all my things away, and was sitting on my bed praying. As I was praying, I had a thought that it would be nice to have a strawberry pop-tart. Strawberry pop-tarts were sold in commissary, but I did not have any. I did not normally buy them, so I don't know what made me even want one, but I had a taste for one. I put it out of my mind and continued on with my prayers. As I finished praying I pulled out my journal in order for me to journal a little before bed. This was when I looked up and noticed Denise standing in my door way with a strawberry pop-tart. I looked at her puzzled and she said, "This strawberry pop-tart is for you." I know I looked puzzled still. I then asked her, "and what made you bring me a pop-tart." Denise proceeded to tell me what had happen in her room as she was getting ready for bed.

She told me, "Lanette, I was getting ready for bed. I had said all my prayers and was already up in my bed, and was pulling my covers over me, when God told me to get up and pull out my strawberry pop-tarts and heat one up for you." Denise said she told God, "I don't want a strawberry pop-tart," and God said, "But Lanette does." This was when Denise said she got out of bed and went into the microwave room and warmed me up a strawberry pop-tart. All I could do was smile at Denise. I then shared with her what had happened to me while I was praying. I shared with Denise, "when I was praying I got an urge for a strawberry pop-tart. I knew I did not have any so I put it out of my mind and continued to pray." Denise sat down on my bed and we both laughed how God had used her to bless me with something as simple as a strawberry pop-tart. I shared with Denise the importance in trusting God for everything. I told her, "See how God used you to give me this pop-tart. He will do things like this throughout the rest of our lives for the both of us, in and out of prison." I knew she was leaving soon. God used her to bless me, but it was more than that. God was showing Denise that He was talking to her, but also God was showing us both that He will provide for every need; all we have to do is trust Him.

Denise had gone back to her room, and, again, tried to go to sleep. She was awakened again by God. This time God gave her, a vision to who my husband was going to be. She again came to my room and looked at me with a smile on her face. I looked up at her and asked, "Did God show you something else?" She laughed and answered me, "yes." She said, "I was back in my bed and God gave me a vision to who your husband will be in the future." Again, I had been writing in my journal to what I wanted in a husband, and I was also praying for whoever this man may be that God would bring into my life. Denise again sat down on my bed and shared with me all the details that God had shown her. My husband was going to be older than me with gray hair and would wear glasses; he would also be much taller than me. Denise continued to tell me about what kind of relationship this husband-to-be would have with God. She told me that he would be a man of God; one that would be matured in His faith. He would also be a gentleman and would treat me in a way that I had never been treated before. He would love me as Christ Jesus loves the church, and I would find peace in submitting to him as he submitted to God. In closing she said, "I can't explain this part, but I see the letter C." Denise told me she thought his name may start with a C.

I was in amazement; I opened my journal and showed Denise everything that I had written before she had come into my room. All the things that I had asked God for in a husband were in the details that Denise had given me. We both laughed and thanked God for His guidance and for answering my prayers so quickly. But once Denise left, I went back to the Lord in prayer and thanked Him for what He had given me through Denise. This was when God asked me a question that made me look deep into myself in reference to an area that I had never looked at before. God asked me, "Will this man of God want you, can you submit?" I stopped and did not answer God quickly. I knew what the question was related to, submitting to a husband as the Word calls a wife to do. This was an area that I was weak in. I was an independent woman. Most of my life, I could not depend on anyone but myself. God had taught me how to depend on Him; but now I needed to learn how to trust a husband and submit to him as God would call me to. My answer to God was, "no; not how I am right now." I then asked God, "Will you teach me?" God answered me, "yes."

Over the next year or so, God took me through His Word and taught me the joy that can be gained by submitting to your husband as he follows Christ. We are then as wives submitting to the will of God. I had picked my husband before. Now God had showed me that He had a husband for me. And because I was willing, God taught me how I would be honoring Him, my Lord, in submitting to my husband. So many of us think this is a hard thing to do. I found it easy to learn because of my love for God and wanting God's will in my life. I loved God and wanted to please Him in everything. Once we align our relationship with God to where it needs to be, the things that God asks of us come easier. They can even bring us joy in doing them. I became excited in meeting this man that God had shown me. I prayed for the husband that God had shown me often. Many times I felt lead to pray for his finances, his health and even his peace of mind.

Now I had to wait and trust God in what He had shown me. I did meet the exact man that Denise described in her vision, once I was home. It did not happen quickly. I had to be patient. When I got home from prison, I started participating in small groups quickly. I found myself joining three. I wanted to stay focused on God, and not be distracted. I met my husband within six months of being home. We were best friends. His brother, Noel introduced us. The three of us would go out together often. We also attended several small groups together. One of our groups was called, "Gordon's." As my husband and I got to know each other and studied the Word of God together, our friendship grew stronger. One day my best friend, Cisco, notices the C, came to help me fix my kitchen. I did not make much money, and Cisco, being a cabinet maker, came to help me fix my kitchen that was in such bad shape. During this process, we became more than friends, and we went out on our first date, after being friends for almost three years. We continued to date, and became husband and wife on

February 19, 2011; sharing our first kiss on our wedding day.

One day, I pulled out my journals that I had kept while I was in prison, and went to where I had documented all my prayers for my husband-to-be. I shared with my husband all the dates and what I had prayed for him. I learned from my husband that during the times that I had been led to pray for him by God, was exactly what he needed. God was again showing how wise He is. He knows everything. I had not even met my husband yet, but God knew who he was and what he needed in prayer, and because I was willing, God used me to pray for him. This blessed me and my husband in how He had used me to pray for him before we had even met. We were both excited to what God was going to do with us both now as husband and wife.

Denise was able to come to my wedding and when she met Cisco her response was, "I have know you for a long time, Cisco." She shared with Cisco that God had shown her a vision of him when she and I were in prison, and she shared with Cisco that he was the man that she had seen in her vision. This gave Denise great joy again in how God had used her, and she was now witnessing what God had given her come to pass.

Denise left not too long after we had shared this great moment together while we were in prison. It was hard for me to watch her leave, but I was happy for her at the same time. She had so much ahead of her, and God was going to use her, and she was finally beginning to believe that she could be used by God. It was a true blessing for me to watch this frightened little girl come into prison and leave a powerful woman of God. The anxiety attacks did not have power over her anymore. She was leaving healed and not bound by the same things she was bound by when she came into prison. This was all because Denise had surrendered to the Word of God and let it have its perfect work in her. God wants this for us all. God's Word is so powerful, but as I said before, we have to read it for it to be able to do the perfect work in us it is intended to do. Denise only had to let go and let God. Will you do that today and let God have His way in your life?

God was not done with Denise and I being together. As I was blessed by her being at my wedding, I was also blessed by going to her wedding. Watching her marry a great man of God and seeing that she had continued on the path that God had put her on while she was in prison. She is busy, to this day, working in spreading the good news of Jesus Christ. She and her husband have a passion to serve God, and they live life to the fullest serving God everyday. I know with all my heart that was hard for her to do - go through prison. It was all for her ultimate good; and for God's will to unfold in her life. This can happen for us all in a storm. All we have to do is let God do what He does best - guide us and teach us His will!

Philippians 1:6 *being confident of this very thing, that He who has begun a good work in you will complete it until the day of Jesus Christ; (NKJV)*

Remember when you look in the mirror, God sees a child He loves, He wishes for you to see the same thing. God will help you open your eyes and see clearly. All you have to do is trust Him.

Don't ever forget God loves you
Just the way you are

"But"
He loves you too much
To leave you that way

News that could take me home

One night after I had gotten in from walking five miles on the camp track, I went to the phones to call my daughter, Faleasha. Once she was on the phone, I could tell she was excited about something. My daughter, Faleasha, had been trying to free me from prison since I had been taken from the courtroom after sentencing. Everything Faleasha tried fell through. She was so frustrated and for good reason. She spent a lot of time running back and forth to the courtroom, filing motions after motions on my behalf. I was concerned for her as her mother because it was consuming her. Faleasha knew more than anyone how innocent I was, because she worked with me in the same company. She knew that I was telling the truth and others were lying. One lie in the court that hurt me, other than the owner testifying that I knew he was committing fraud, was a woman testifying that she had seen me in Mike's building on several occasions. This was not true, and even in the courtroom, I could not see why she would lie. What benefit was there to her in lying?

My daughter was the one that took care of all my affairs from the day that they took me into prison at sentencing. On top of everything else, my daughter had to deal with the appeals attorney we hired and him not doing what he had promised he could and would do. I had not been at Coleman even a year, and my daughter had to dismiss the appeals attorney. The lawyer, that we had hired prior to going to sentencing, had made all kinds of promises to what he would do if I was taken into prison at sentencing. My family and I were of the understanding that, I would be allowed to self-surrender within about three months after sentencing. This did not happen. Due to this, all my affairs where not taken care of, and my daughter had to close up a lot of loose ends for me. The appeals attorney told us prior to sentencing, if I was taken into custody after sentencing, he would do a motion for me to be allowed to be out while my appeal was being done. This motion was never done.

When my family would call the law office to find out the status of the motion being filed, they were always asked for more money. My family and I had paid $5,000.00 to the appeals attorney, before we even went to sentencing. This would have covered most of the things that needed to be done within the first few months that would follow sentencing. We found out that was not true. In calling the law office, we also found out that the day after sentencing, our appeals lawyer went into the hospital for heart surgery, and would not be back to work for months. My family was assured that everything that needed be done, in the months that our lawyer would be out recovering, they could do, with him out of the office. But as the months came and went, nothing was done, and I sat in prison waiting. The only calls my family received from the law office were for more money. My family did not know what to do at first, so they paid more. After a few more months, and not being able to talk to the lawyer or get any satisfaction in any motions being filed on my behalf, my daughter had to terminate the relationship with the appeal attorney. All the money that had been paid to the law office was gone. It was never returned, and now we had to fight on our own. We did not know much about the system, but my daughters read a lot and asked a lot of questions to those who were supposed to know.

Now, Faleasha had news, news she thought may bring me home by overturning the case. She was so excited; it was hard for me to keep up with her as she told me all the details. I had to keep asking her to slow down. She began by asking me, "Mom, do you remember the woman who testified that you were in Mike's building on several occasions?" I answered, "yes." My daughter then said, "I spoke to John today, and he told me about an interesting conversation he had about a year ago, during the same time the trial was going on." John and Ron were the ones that took over the operation of Financial Freedom Christian Counseling. My daughter had been with him earlier that day, and John had shared with her what he had figured out recently after meeting her. I responded to my daughter, "okay." What was the conversation that you two had that would involve me and the woman who lied in court?" My daughter responded in saying, "The woman who lied knows John, and a year ago, when the trial was going on, she was going to John's church and had gotten saved. She came over to John's house one night to get his opinion on something she was being asked to do. She shared with John that since she had been saved, she did not feel good about what she was being told to testify in an ongoing court case that she was involved in. She told John that the prosecutor was asking her to lie. They wanted her to tell the court that a woman had been in a building that she had not been in. She expressed, if I lie, an innocent woman will go to jail; but if I tell the truth, I will go to jail and I will lose my child to the court system. If I lie, the prosecutor promised to not send me to jail or take my child away. John told her she needed to always tell the truth no matter what the consequences were to herself; that she needed to trust God to get her through whatever it was she was going through. John told her that sending an innocent woman to jail would not be what God would want her to do in any circumstances."

My heart fell to my feet. I knew she was lying in the courtroom, but I did not understand why; now I did. After getting my thoughts together, I asked Faleasha, "What can we do?" My daughter told me she was going to call the FBI the next day and see what could be done. "If nothing else, this is not legal," she said. "The prosecutor has broken the law himself. I will make calls to as many people as I can and see what our options are." An appeal had not been done yet at this time, since we had to terminate our relationship with the appeals attorney. This could even be something that could be used in an appeal. Now I had to wait and see what Faleasha could find out.

The wait went on for days. Faleasha called and left several messages for the FBI to call her in reference to what she had found out, and no one ever called her back. Faleasha called lawyers to try to find out what they could do to help her, nothing again. Everywhere Faleasha turned was a dead end. When my daughters came to visit me on a Sunday, we talked about this in great detail. I could tell that both of my daughters were frustrated; I could not get frustrated. I needed to be strong for my daughters. I explained to my daughters that they had done everything that they could do. It was time to let it go. This was not easy for anyone, because it meant that I would have to do the full three and a half years that was given to me in sentencing. I could tell that this was not easy for my daughters to hear, but it was needed. It was time to stop the madness and trust God only and not the system that put me in prison. It was hard for Faleasha. She had been fighting so hard for me, and it had become a way of life. Now I was asking her to stop. I could see she was relieved, but also she had to face the fact that I may have to stay in prison until 2007, that was the hard part. As long as we were fighting, we all had hope that I may go home soon, but now we all had to face that I would not. This was emotional for us all.

Faleasha was doing some other motions on my behalf that she felt would bring me home. We both agreed that she could finish what she was working on, but it was time for us to let it all go. She agreed. Once back in my room after visiting with my daughters, I broke down in the reality that I may have to do all the time that had been given to me at sentencing; I started to cry. My Bunkie asked if she could do anything for me, and all I could tell her was no. She asked if my girls were okay. She knew they had come to visit me earlier that day. I responded to her that they were both fine that I was upset about something else. She then said "okay" to me; "but I am here if you need me." I sat on my bed and prayed. I cried out to the Lord saying, "Lord, I know you are blessing me and I want to trust you, but I really thought I was going home soon, and it looks like I will not be going home anytime soon. Lord, you know my heart and all I want is to be in your will. If this is your will, I need you to help me find peace in being here in prison for such a long time. Lord, I miss my family and being a part of their lives." I reminded the Lord what I had heard Him say to me, that I would be going home soon and that the day had been appointed for me to go home, and for me to have peace in waiting for His timing.

This was when I heard the Lord come to me and say," Yes I did say that to you, but do you have peace that this day will come in its appointed time?" I realized in that moment that I had heard God correctly, but I was adding my understanding in what God had spoken to me, and I did not have peace. I was on my time frame still, not God's. This was another lesson teaching me how to listen to God. I had to be careful in what I was hearing God say to me and not add in my own interpretation. I would go home on the day that God had appointed. I needed to wait and have peace in waiting for God's will. It could be the exact day my sentencing said I would leave. Up until this day, I had not accepted that I may have to spend the full three and a half years in prison. Everyday I would get up out of bed thinking to myself that this day could be the day I would go home. I had not realized thinking this way was consuming me. I needed to stop and have faith in whatever God's will was for me. I prayed for God to help me receive whatever it was that He had for me. If I was to stay in prison for the full three and a half years, then so be it.

When I stood up, I had an overwhelming amount of peace, I was not crying any more. I was approached by many of my friends even, my Bunkie, in reference to if I was okay. I shared with them all what a great lesson that God had taught me. My prayer for them was that they would be blessed by what I had learned as I was. I stopped looking to go home everyday from that day forward. Because of this, I had a lot more peace and I slept better at night. I did not realize that every night, when I would go to bed, I was full of disappointment because another day had passed, and I had still not gone home. The devil had a hold on me in my expectations in going home, and God helped me to gain true perspective and trust Him. Due to God enlightening my mind, I was able to minister to others better and also receive from them what God had for me in them. I learn thing, best with visuals, and God used one in teaching me this lesson that helped me a lot. When we are in a storm, we must be careful that we do not only think about getting out of it. God has so much more for us while we are in the storm to learn. It is not for our destruction, but our perfection. God shows us clearly His intention for our tribulations in:

Romans 5:3-4 *And not only that, but we also glory in tribulations, knowing that tribulation produces <u>perseverance</u>; 4) and perseverance, <u>character</u>; and character, <u>hope</u> (NKJV)*

Perseverance: steady and continued action or belief, usually over a long period and especially despite difficulties or setbacks. (The perseverance is in seeking God and believing in God. You faith and dependency for God will grow during the storm. It is during this period that character is built).

Character: the set of qualities that make somebody or something <u>distinctive.</u>

Distinctive: different from others. You stand out. (Is this not what God is trying to do with all of us? Then He is able to use us to draw others to Him)

All this produces Hope

Hope: To wish for something with expectation. (This is what we do in prayer. Not a wish, but we have Faith with expectation. This happens when we spend time with God. In the midst of a storm this is what happens in us - hope.

God had a lot to teach me in this storm, A Journey behind Prison Walls, and up to this point, I was missing some of it. I did not realize that I had been focusing on going home so much that I was missing some of the things that God had for me. I was not willing to be distracted any more. Now God had my attention, and I was ready to learn. God knows me better than I know myself, and He knows I learn thing better with a visual example; a parable. God showed me a parable in, how we should weather the storms of today, using a locked door and the need of a key to open the door once reached. God used this parable in respect that the door represents the end of the storm, and we are trying to reach the door, but, when we reach the door, we will find the door to be locked. Once reaching the door, we will need a key to open the door in order to walk through it and reach the other side. In a storm, most of us are not paying too much attention in what is going on around us. All we can think about is the storm being over, reaching the door, and getting to the other side. But a key is needed to open the door once we reach it, and this key is acquired in the midst of the storm; on the journey through it.

Now in the beginning of the storm, I believe we are not allowed to see the door, so we will not focus on it and miss what we are to learn during the storm. God knows us. If we see the end of the storm, we will be distracted and be consumed in reaching the end. Because of this, we are not able to see the end, until it is time to focus on leaving the storm behind. This is what God did for me. God said the day had been appointed that I would leave, but He did not tell me the day. I had to trust God with that day. It was His timing and not mines. But too many of us spend entirely too much time looking for the door we can't see. What we are to be focused on is the moment we are in. In the storm, God has others we are to minister to and touch with His Word. In this, we also receive something from them; a key. The key represents the things we will learn in the storm, as in God's Word, perseverance, character and hope to mention only a few. So when we finally find ourselves in front of the door, "the end of the storm," we then have the key needed to unlock the door and reach the other side. This is when we move forward in our faith and our relationship with God, moving to the next level. So many of us miss the greatness that God has for us in our storms because we are too focused on the pain and despair they bring in our lives. God wants us to look beyond the storm and see what He has for us and others. In this our storms will carry a whole new meaning to us, not one to dread, but embrace.

Chapter 18

Health being attacked

Our chaplain at the camp was a woman, and her name was chaplain B. She put together a program called the Daughters of Esther. This was a group of four women, one from each unit. The women picked to be in this group would be called on by chaplain B to pray for women at the camp and even chaplain B, herself. I and three other women were chosen by chaplain B to be in this group. We were all called to the chaplain's office one day in order for chaplain B to explain to us what our roles were. Chaplain B had made up some business cards with all four of our names on them and our room number and unit number. Chaplain B explained to each of us that every new woman that came to the camp would be given this card regardless of religion. She informed us that she would be telling each new woman upon their arrival, if they needed anything in reference to prayer or someone to talk to, that they could come to anyone of us, and we could be trusted. She also informed us that she wanted us to be in all the new believer classes, so we could help the new believers understand what they had done by accepting Jesus into their lives. She wanted us to be mentors. All four of us were honored. This was strange in prison. Inmates were never given any responsibility like this. This was the favor of God. I enjoyed meeting all the new women that came to the unit, but now they would know who I was, and God was using this card for me to be able to reach women of all faiths and give me the opportunity to pray for them. But one night, I was the one who needed prayer.

One night, my friends and I went to dinner. I had a salad and a hamburger patty. I was trying to slim down and I did not want to have a heavy dinner. After eating, I felt sick within thirty minutes of eating. My friends and I always went to the track and walked five miles after eating dinner. This night, I felt like I needed to get to the rest room. Diarrhea was on its way quickly. I barely got to my unit and the restroom when the worst diarrhea I had ever had started. My stomach was rolling and making all kinds of sounds. Then the cramps started. Within an hour, I was throwing up violently. When I did not join my friends on the track, they all came to the unit to check on me. I could not get too far from the restroom, so I was not able to go and tell them how sick I was. When they came to my room, I was getting up to go back to the restroom again. I was already getting weak. I had been in the restroom about five times within thirty minutes. My friends went to their rooms to see what they may have to help me out. Some had crackers and some had tea. I tried to eat and drink what they brought, but I would only go directly to the restroom again. This went on for hours. My friends went to the office and told the officer on duty that I was real sick, and could they call medical. The officer came back later and told me and my friends that I would have to make it till morning. I told the officer, when he came in to count, I may be in the restroom, he told me no problem. He would wait until I was able to go back to my room.

When count was called, sure enough I was in the rest room. The officer did as he told me and waited for me to return to my room so they could clear count in my unit.

At any time that count was called you could get in trouble if you were not in your room. It was called interfering with count. This was why I told the officer before count time that I may be in the rest room, and I was. Count was at 10PM, and I had eaten around 5PM. This had been going on for hours. My Bunkie was beginning to get frightened now. She had some small packages of Gatorade that she gave to Donna so she could mix it for me to drink. Donna, my best friend, stayed with me the whole time along with another woman from the unit. It took the both of them to help me to get back and forth to the restroom. I was real weak, and I began to shake all over. This was why they wanted to give me the Gatorade to replace some of my electrolytes. As soon as I would drink any of the Gatorade, I would have to go directly to the restroom again. Now after the 10PM count, we were not allowed to be in each other's rooms, but the officers gave us an exception. The officers told us that they would also pass on to the next shift that I was sick, and I may have some women in my room helping me.

The officers were apologetic in regards to not being able to get me any help. I understood it was not their fault. I had to wait till morning. I needed God's help to get me through the night. I began to shake so badly that I was shaking the whole bed. This made my Bunkie even more frightened. It was getting real hard to walk to the restroom with all the shaking and the weakness. The two women helped me to the restroom again and now it was maybe about 11:30 PM. Once in the restroom, I asked one of the women to go and get Trevor. I can't explain it other than it was God, but I felt like she was the one that needed to come and pray for me. One of the girls said that she was sleeping, and I told them, "She would not mind if you wake her. Tell her that Lanette is sick and needs her." It was not but a few minutes when they came back with Trevor. I was still sitting in the restroom waiting for her. She had gone right to bed after dinner, and she had no idea to what all was going on. Once she was in the restroom, Trevor asked me, "What's wrong?" I told her that I had eaten something at dinner and I think I have food poisoning. She asked me did we tell the officers. We told her yes and the officers told us that we had to wait till morning. I told her I had been going to the restroom with diarrhea and vomiting since about 5:00 PM. I told Trevor that I was so weak and shaking, it was difficult to walk now. I told Trevor I had them wake her up so she could pray for me.

Trevor was happy to pray for me, but she wanted to also help me with a few things right in the restroom. She asked me how my bottom was, "is it sore yet?" "Oh yes," I responded, I told her it hurts a lot. She told me to hold on, and she went to get something from her locker that would help. She came back and gave me some Tucks pads. Trevor instructed me to keep them and use them as much as I needed to. We all went back to my room, and I was so weak now that the women were almost carrying me back to my room this time. Once I sat on my bunk, my shaking started to shake the whole bunk bed again. Now after 10PM it is also quiet time, and Trevor did not have a low voice, and when Trevor prays, she prays loud. Once I was seated on the bed, Trevor knelt in front of me and put her hands on my knees. Trevor began to pray. She prayed with power and she prayed for about five minutes. Then, all of a sudden, my legs started to stop shaking. Trevor noticed it and prayed even louder. Slowly my whole body stopped shacking; Trevor thanked

God for hearing our cry and healing my body. She asked for protection over me and to give me a peaceful night's sleep. It was clear now why God had me wake up Trevor. She did not care that is was after quiet time. She went boldly and loudly before the throne for me, and God answered her cry.

As Trevor left my room she told me it was an honor to pray for me. She said, "You pray for so many of us all the time at all hours of the day or night. It was now your turn that I prayed for you." She told me it did not matter the time during the night if I needed her to send someone to wake her up. She said she would come and check in on me in the morning. I told Donna and the other women to go to bed, and if I needed anything, I would send my Bunkie to get them. They both did not want to leave, but it was time for them to get some rest. I felt better. I was not shaking anymore, and once they all left, I did need to use the restroom, but I was able to walk on my own. The vomiting stopped and I only had the diarrhea two more times during the night. I know that God healed me when Trevor asked Him to. I now needed to recover. The next morning, I was still too weak to go to work, so I had to go to sick call in the medical building. Once I was there, I had to wait to be seen. They told me what I already knew. I had food poisoning and I would need to stay in my unit for a few days to recover. As I walked back to my unit, I thanked God for healing me and getting me through the night. God had taken care of me throughout the whole night. I did have a peaceful night of sleep like Trevor asked for me.

Trevor did as she promised and came to my room and checked on me often. She brought me soup and tea and crackers to eat and drink. Trevor tended to me throughout the whole day, making sure that I did not have a need for anything. After everyone was off work, many of them came to check on me, and they, too, prayed for me. Even during the work day, my boss came to my unit to check on me and make sure I was okay. I felt so much love with all the ones that God had put around me. Even in prison, God gave me a family that loved me and cared for me, and I loved them also. As they all came and went, I thanked God for all of them. We were a family inside of prison, but even better than that we were a body of Christ, and we were acting like the body serving each other in love.

Galatians 5:13: *For you, brethren, have been called to liberty; only do not use liberty as an opportunity for the flesh, but through love serve one another.(NKJV)*

Christian Freedom is not for selfish fulfillment,
but for serving others. Freedom brings with it the responsibility to serve.
Love motivates us to fulfill the law of God.

Matthew 22:36-40 *"Teacher, which is the great commandment in the law? 37) Jesus said to him, "You shall love the Lord your God with all your heart, with all your soul, and with all your mind." 38) This the first and great commandment 39) And the second is like it: "You shall love your neighbor as yourself." 40) On these two commandments hang all the Law and the Prophets (NKJV)*

Who could have ever thought that I could be blessed so much inside of prison walls? I was living everyday watching women grow in a relationship with God, and due to their relationship growing, I was blessed to watch them all come together and love one another in love. When I first arrived at Coleman, many were caring about no one but themselves. Most women stayed off to themselves and did not step out of their comfort zone. If they did, it was to serve their own personal purpose. Now, yes, there were a few cliques that would mingle with each other and help one another, but for the most part, everyone stayed to themselves. But now, through studying God's Word and fellowshipping together, God was doing a great work in all of us. And I was blessed to have a front row seat to witness it all. The women at the camp were learning what 1 Corinthians 13 was all about and even putting it into practice.

1 Corinthians 13:4-7 Love suffers long and is kind; love does not envy; love does not parade itself, is not puffed up; 5) does not behave rudely, does not seek its own, is not provoked, thinks no evil; 6) does not rejoice in iniquity, but rejoices in the truth; 7) bears all things, believes all things, hopes all things, endures all things. (NKJV)

In these verses, the fullness of love is described, in each case by what love does. Love is action, not abstraction. The women at the camp were practicing this for all to see. How about you, how do you love? Can you love better? I believe we all can learn to love better, but we must first acknowledge that we need to and God will teach us how to love. He is really the only one that can. God is Love!

As we women at the camp continued to grow in God's Word by fellowshipping together and studying together on Friday nights, it appeared that my health started to be attacked more. Not long after having food poisoning, the plantar wart that I had on my foot since coming into prison started causing me a lot of pain. I had gone to medical several times, and the nurse practitioner had done several treatments of freezing, but my foot was not getting any better. I had been walking up to five miles a day until my foot pain had made it impossible to continue. I was having a difficult time working and on my feet all day, much less trying to walk the track five miles a day. I enjoyed walking the track. It was my quiet time with the Lord. No one would bother me, and I was able to have long talks with the Lord uninterrupted. Maybe that was the whole plan of the devil, to interfere with the special times I was having with the Lord.

One day I went to medical to receive another freezing treatment. I was not encouraged with this process since it did not seem to be working, but it was my only option being inside of prison. It was not like I could seek out a second opinion. Once I was called back to the examiner room, I pulled off my work boot and laid face down on the examiner table like I had always done. The nurse practitioner started commenting on how she thought the area on my foot was not a plantar wart, but a mass or something since it had not gotten any better. I then asked her if I could see a foot doctor. She answered quickly that would not be possible. She started to poke on it like she had always done, asking if this hurt or that hurt; it all hurt. She then told me to hold still. She was going to do the freezing treatment and for me not to move. I hated the treatments, because they did hurt some, and left my foot sore for a day or so. I was told they should not hurt, but they did. That was when the nurse practitioner did something I did not expect.

As I lay on the table face down, after being told to not move, all of a sudden, I felt severe pain in the heel of my foot where the area was that was to receive the freezing treatment. I yelled out in pain to please stop, but she did not. The nurse practitioner instructed me to not move and hold on for a moment, which was exactly what I did. I grabbed a hold of the table I was lying on as tears rolled down my face. I was crying and asking her to please stop, but she still did not. I did not know what she was doing. All I knew was it hurt, and it was not a freezing treatment. What seemed to be forever, whatever it was that she was doing to my foot, she stopped. As an inmate in prison, you are not able to do what you may do on the outside. I was told to lie still, and that was what I had to do. As I tried to get myself together to ask her what she was doing, the nurse practitioner began to tell me what she was trying to do. She informed me that she thought the area that we had been freezing did not need to be frozen, but punctured. She had taken a large needle and pushed it into the heel of my foot as deep as she could without numbing it or warning me what she was doing, in the effort to puncture what she thought was an area that needed to be punctured.

She then informed me that she must have of been wrong, and there was nothing to puncture. She then, without warning, performed the freezing treatment on the heel of my foot in the exact place she had used the needle. Now, this sent a burning sensation throughout my foot that I had not felt before. The needle must have left a hole in my foot that gave an avenue for the freezing treatment to go deep into my foot. Normally the freezing treatment is done on the surface. This time the pain was a deep burning that would not stop. The tears began to flow all over again. I felt trapped. I was not being told what was going on, and I was not sure what was going to happen next. This made me cry even more. I was so relieved when I was told to get up from the table and put my boot back on. I would not be allowed to walk to my unit across the compound without my boot. Even this was not going to be easy due to the pain I was feeling in my foot.

I loosened my shoe laces as loose as I could get them, and slowly pushed my foot into my boot. This made the pain even worse. I was told I could leave, and I would be put on the call out in a few weeks to come to medical and receive another treatment. I could not think about that at the moment. All I wanted to do was get back to my room and remove my boot and sit down. As I walked across the compound to my unit, every step was more pain. I cried out to the Lord, "please, Lord, help me get to my room and ease the pain, Lord." As I walked, the tears began to come even stronger than before. I was not only crying from the pain of the foot, but the humiliation I felt by not being able to have any say in what had happened to me. I felt like a piece of meat. I had not been told what was going to happen or given a choice if I wanted it to happen. I had no say, and I felt like I had no value, at least to the ones in medical. I kept asking the Lord, "What kind of place is this? We are here in prison, but we are still human beings, Lord, oh Lord why do they treat us this way?" All I could do was cry and walk slowly to my unit.

Once at my unit, I walked slowly to my room. Some of my friends were in the unit, and came up behind me asking me what was wrong. As soon as I reached my room, I sat on the bed and proceeded to try to remove my boot. I was crying so hard, I could not answer any of the questions that were being proposed to me. My friends could tell I was not able to answer them due to how hard I was crying, so they stopped asking questions and proceeded to help me remove my boot. I grabbed my ankle and rocked in my bed trying to compose myself with what had happened to me. I was finally able to tell my friends it was my foot, it hurts. They instantly said, "Let's take you to medical" I cried no. Slowly, through my tears, I was able to tell them what had happened to me in medical and why my foot was hurting so bad. They were all instantly angry, and all encouraged me to write a copout and complain. Copouts were an internal document that inmates could use to request something or make a complaint. One of the women in the unit heard me crying that was not one of my close friends. She did not come to our fellowship groups or our Bible studies. She was one of the women that lived in the unit that everyone feared. I had been talking to her and trying to reach her with the gospel.

When she heard me crying, she ran into my room and asked me, "who hurt you, Lanette?" She continued to tell me that she would take care of it for me. "Tell me who it was that hurt you," she screamed. I looked at her and informed her that no one had hurt me. I told her I was crying because of what had happened to me in medical. I told her, "even if it was a fellow inmate, you know that I would not condone you doing anything to them." I reminded her that we had spoken about this recently. She smiled at me and said, "I know, but you are so good to everyone here and I don't want anyone hurting you and making you cry." She then said, "If you ever need me, all you have to do is ask." I told her all I needed her to do was pray for me! She smiled and said, "You know we are working on that, Lanette." The encounter with her did make me smile, and it did take my mind off the pain in my foot and the humiliation that I had experienced in medical. God works in mysterious ways.

Once she left, my friends continued to come into my room as they came into the unit from work. Even my fellow co-workers had come to check in on me. As I started to feel better, the subject was changed, and we all did like we normally did, laugh and encouraged each other. It was hard being in prison, but it was really hard when you were faced with the truth that you had no choices and that was what had happened to me this day. Yes, I had a lot of pain, but that was not what hurt me the most. It was being treated like I did not matter. God brought me back around with the love of others. That is what fellowship is all about. God reminded me that I did matter. It was not about how I was treated that day, but what I meant to God.

The next day, when I was able to think clearer, I started to study about Spiritual Warfare, and that was when I realized that was what I was in; our struggle is not against flesh and blood, but against the rulers, against the powers, against the world forces of the darkness. In reading Ephesians 6:12 it became clear what was going on, I was under attack; a spiritual attack from our enemy the devil.

1 Peter 5:8 *Be of sober spirit, be on the alert. Your adversary, the devil, prowls around like a roaring lion, seeking someone to devour. (NASB)*

I had read all this before, but I had not slowed down long enough to really look at what was going on. I believe we all do this when we are under attack. Even the food poisoning, it was so brutal, and it all came to a halt when Trevor prayed and demanded for the devil to leave. I was so weak at the time; I did not put much thought to what was really happening. God was using our gatherings to help a lot of women to grow in Him and to come to Him. The devil did not like this; he was trying to stop me. We are to take up the armor of God everyday, and many of us get lazy and don't take the time to do this; I, too, am guilty of this.

Ephesians 6:10-17 *Finally, be strong in the Lord and in the strength of His might. 11) Put on the full armor of God, so that you will be able to stand firm against the schemes of the devil. 12) For our struggle is not against flesh and blood, but against the rulers, against the powers, against the world forces of the darkness, against the spiritual forces of wickedness in the heavenly places. 13) Therefore, take up the full armor of God, so that you will be able to resist in the evil day, and having done everything, to stand firm. 14) Stand firm therefore, having girded your loins with truth, and having put on the breastplate of righteousness, 15) and having shod your feet with the preparation of the gospel of peace; 16) in addition to all, taking up the shield of faith with which you will be able to extinguish all the flaming arrows of the evil one. 17) And take the helmet of Salvation, and the sword of the Spirit, which is the Word of God. (NASB)*

I was studying the Word everyday, but I did not always start my day with prayer. I have never been a morning person. Getting up and going to work as early as I had to, was not easy for me. I would get up and get dressed and out the door with a cup of coffee in hand. What I needed to do was wake up a little earlier every morning so I could start my day with a devotional and a prayer, putting on the armor of God as you may say. The danger on the battlefield is that we do not take the enemy seriously and therefore fail to put on all of the armor. By faith, you put on the armor of God through prayer, which must be done at the beginning of everyday. Never underestimate the strategy and strength of the devil. God gives us everything we need for the battle we will face everyday, therefore, take up your armor and join many others and "STAND FIRM."

This doesn't mean that you will not face any battles; it only means that you will be better prepared for them. As I went to our fellowship group that night, I shared with all the women in the group what I had learned that day, about all the problems I had been having, and that it was not a battle of the flesh, but attacks of the enemy, the devil. Once I put this out, many of the other women also shared how they had also been under attack. We spent several weeks studying how to be better prepared when the enemy attacks. I was better prepared, and the women in the group were also. This was a blessing to me as a new attack was launched on me.

I started my day as I normally did with prayer and a devotional. I got dressed and made myself a cup of coffee, and off I went to meet the truck to be picked up with the rest of my crew by Mr. Chris. As Mr. Chris picked up our crew, we went about our early morning duties, checking everything that needed to be checked. Then Mr. Chris informed us that a few of us would be installing a water softener in the power house. Mr. Chris already had it all laid out and how it was to be installed. We would be doing all the piping ourselves and this meant soldering. Normally Mr. Red's crew, the plumbers, would do all the piping, but they were busy, and Mr. Chris wanted to get it done, because the equipment in the cooling tower worked better when a water softener was filtering the water that was running through them. Mr. Red gave Mr. Chris some dos and don'ts, and we began. Mr. Red was always a call away on the radio.

We had hardly gotten started on the piping, and I had to go to the restroom. I ran to the restroom with diarrhea. My stomach was cramping badly. I finished going to the restroom and went back out to help Mr. Chris with the piping. I was not back at work even a minute when I had to run back to the restroom. This went on for about an hour. Mr. Chris had already asked me was I okay and I had answered him, not sure yet. I did not feel sick, like the flu, and it did not feel like food poisoning ether. I was confused and so were my co-workers. After about six trips to the restroom, I started to feel weak. I knew I needed to go to medical. Once I got back out to the area where Mr. Chris and the rest of the crew were working on the water softener, I told Mr. Chris I needed to go to medical. He looked at me and said, "I agree." Mr. Chris told medical that he was sending a worker over that did not look too good, and that I needed to be seen right away.

Once we arrived at medical, I could hardly walk. The women who were working in medical told me to have a seat, and they would be right with me. One of the

A Journey Behind Prison Walls

women in the waiting room knew me and asked me what was wrong. I explained to her what was going on and to please to pray for me. I started to shake; it was so bad that when they called my name to come back, I could not walk without being held. My hands started to constrict, and I could not hold them open. I prayed even harder as they took me to a room in the back. Once I was placed into a room, the doctor assistant came in to check on me. I knew her to be a nice woman, one who cared about inmates. Her name was Miss B. She was always good to us all and she always did her best whenever she was on duty to help us. I was so happy to see her.

Once she was in the room, I told her about my hands and how I could not stop shaking. She asked me to calm down and let her try to examine me to see what was going on. She started to ask me what I had eaten and how many times I had the diarrhea. I answered all the questions the best that I could, but it was getting harder for me to even talk. Miss. B was standing over me and looking at an EKG and kept saying, "that can't be right. Do it again." I looked up at Miss B and told her "Miss B, don't let me die in here." She answered me saying "no one is going to die on my shift. Relax and let me do my job" As she looked at me and tried to figure out what was going on with the EKG, I kept shaking. I then closed my eyes and began to pray and asked God to help me, I demanded, in the name of Jesus, for the devil to back off of me and leave my presence.

All of a sudden, my hands returned to normal and I stopped shaking. Miss B looked at me and said, "What happened?" I responded, "I prayed." She smiled and said, "Okay then, is this over?" She looked me over again and repeated the EKG and her response was then, "that is more like it." I asked her what did she mean by that, and she said, "You were all over the place a minute ago, but now you are in sinus rhythm, where you need to be." She told me that she wanted me to stay in from work for a few days and get some rest and drink plenty of fluid. As I put my feet on the floor, I was able to walk without a problem. I walked out into the waiting room, and there sitting in the waiting room were many of my friends, all praying for me. I looked at them and asked, "Are you all here for medical also?" They all responded at the same time, "no, we are all here to pray for you." I was in shock. How did they know? I asked them, "How did you know?" They responded, the woman sitting in the waiting room when I first came in, had gone and told everyone that I needed them all to pray, and they came. The one woman, who was sitting in the waiting room when I arrived earlier, had gone and gathered everyone she could find to pray for me. She had remembered the study we had done on spiritual warfare, and how I had been attacked by the devil recently. She saw what was happening to me was spiritual warfare.

As I walked back to my room, I was overwhelmed with how all these women had come into medical to pray for me. In prison, you are not allowed to go anywhere without having an appointment, but these women came to medical and sat in the waiting room praying for me without having an appointment. All of them could have been written up for being out of bounds. Being out of bounds meant not being where you are supposed to be. Every one of these women had taken a chance in being out of bounds to pray for me. When they all saw me walk out of medical without any one holding me, all the women in the waiting room started to praise God, thanking Jesus for hearing their prayers. I shared with them all what had happened only a few minutes prior in the back, that, all of a sudden, my body stopped shaking and my hands returned to normal. I looked at them all and said, "I know now why; because of your prayers." Yes, I was praying, but there is power in numbers, and every woman in that medical waiting room took a chance to be there, and God heard them. They all had responded to a need, and came and prayed and did not think about themselves for a moment. This is rare in prison. I was overwhelmed with everything that God was allowing me to witness. God was moving in each of these ladies, and I, again, was being allowed to have a front row seat. God works in mysterious ways. So often, we miss it all because we are not paying attention. I was so happy that I did not miss this one.

Chapter 19

Holidays in Prison

Coleman did a lot of things for the inmates during the holidays, but it really doesn't matter to you in the first year what anyone does for you. All you can think about is being back at home with your family. We would have special visitation hours, so family could come and visit with us on the holidays. We even had a special menu that consisted of all the holiday foods most of us were used to.

The camp even allowed inmates to volunteer to help out with all the extra cooking. But my first Christmas was really hard for me. I could not find any joy in the day at all. I wanted to be with my family so badly that it consumed me. My friends around me encouraged me the best they could. We prayed and cried together as we all missed our loved ones.

We all ate together in the cafeteria, and then we all went back to the unit to make phone calls home. I was dreading making a call home. I knew once I made the call home, reality would hit me hard that I was not home with my family, but I needed to call, not for me, but for my family.

I knew this was not going to be easy for them. We had never been separated during Christmas, and I had always prepared the Christmas dinner, and then the whole family would come over, and we would all celebrate the birth of Jesus together. This year, they would have to prepare the dinner on their own.

I had been communicating with my daughters the week prior to Christmas, giving them all the recipes for all the items I usually cooked. I had already instructed them how to cook the turkey, ham, cornbread stuffing and collard greens, yams and snap beans. But the one thing that my family always looked forward to me cooking was my sweet potato pies. I had been using the same recipe since 1980. My mother-in-law had given it to me one year, and I had been using it since. I had it written on a piece of paper in the cookie jar, and I had already told the girls where it was, and to follow it to the letter and their pies would turn out great.

Every Christmas Eve, I would read the Christmas story to my grandchildren. They would all gather around me in my living room, and I would have a book that was age appropriate for that year. Then I would read the story of how Jesus was born and remind them of the real reason for Christmas. This was all done before they would be off to bed. My family also had a tradition that on Christmas Eve, you would always be allowed to open one present. This present would always be the same thing, pajamas.

These would be the pajamas you would wear on Christmas Eve to bed. The grandchildren had already opened their pajamas and had them on as they would gather around for the story. At this time, I had four grandchildren, two were six years old and one was four, and the other was only about one. Once the story was read and all the questions were answered, we would all pray and then off to bed they would all go. This was going to be the first year that I would not get to do this either. Someone else would have to do this also.

I knew the reason for the season was the birth of Jesus Christ. I understood that I could celebrate anywhere I was, but my emotions were getting the best of me. I could not find my joy in what was my favorite time of the year - Christmas. My heart was so broken that I could not be with my family, it was consuming me. I was crying out to God to help me and forgive me. I kept saying to God "I am trying God, but I am failing. I need your help." And now, it was time for the phone call home. As I walked to the front of the unit where the phones were located, I found a long line of other women also waiting to call home. I asked who was last, and motioned to the one who answered, that I am after you. I had about ten women in front of me.

I was going to have to wait for about thirty minutes. We had five phones in our unit and a limit of fifteen minutes per phone call. As I stood and waited, I continued to talk to God. I asked God to help my family and me that this phone call would not be of tears, but joy. I asked God to help me shine for Him and, even in this, we can find joy if we seek you and trust you Lord. As I finished my prayer, one of the women behind me called out my name to inform me that it was my turn on the next phone.

I picked up the phone and dialed my house. I had been told that they would all be at my house cooking together. Once my daughter, Faleasha, answered the phone, I took a deep breath and told her "Merry Christmas." Her response was surprising to me; she was laughing. She was laughing so hard that she could hardly talk. I started to laugh hearing her laugh, and I did not even know what we were laughing about. I kept asking her, "What are you laughing so hard about?"

But she kept laughing. Finally she caught her breath and attempted to tell me what not only she was laughing about, but the whole household was. Faleasha continued, "Mom, you know your sweet potato pie recipe?"

I answered "yes." "We have cooked everything, and everything has turned out real good. We then moved to cooking the pies." She continued to tell me the process of the pies. "Mom, we took your recipe, and followed to the letter, but we did make one change. We knew you always fixed eight pies, so we took your recipe and times it times eight." I busted into laughter that very moment. I had tears running down my face from laughing so hard, and my daughter on the other end of the phone was also laughing along with the rest of the family in the background.

My sweet potato pie recipe was for eight pies. When she said she times it times eight, they had made enough pie batter for 64 pies! I had a hard time getting myself together. My daughter continued to explain to me the rest of the story. She told me, "Mom, we could not figure out what was going on, why we had so much; so we called Grandma Ruth." Now, Grandma Ruth was the mother-in-law that had given me the recipe years ago.

My daughter explained to me when they called her; she explained to them that the recipe was for eight pies. Faleasha then shared how they had times the recipe by eight. Their whole household busted into laughter also. Their Grandma Ruth was laughing so hard that their grandfather had to get on the phone and have Faleasha explain what was going on because Grandma Ruth could not talk, she was laughing so hard.

As I stood and listened to my daughter laugh and tell the story that they had been living since the night before, joy filled my soul. God had answered my prayer in a way I could not have imagined. God was not only blessing me, God had given us all a gift on this Christmas day – laughter!

Luke 6:21 *"Blessed are you who hunger now, for you shall be filled. Blessed are you who weep now, for you will laugh." (NKJV)*

God's Word is so true. God had heard my cry, heard myself and my family weep; but now we had laughter. As my son-in-law June came to the phone, he continued to tell me how he kept telling the girls at the store that the cart looked too full with sweet potatoes. He told them, "I don't remember your mom ever having this many sweet potatoes." June continued to tell me, "they did not listen and bought them all anyway." He also described how the kitchen and my daughters looked. They were both covered with flour and yams.

The kitchen was a mess; all from the sweet potato pie batter. They had enough mixture to freeze and have plenty to share with others. I only had fifteen minutes to talk on the phone, but the entire time I was laughing and hearing my family laugh; the best Christmas gift any of us could have received. It was time to say goodbye, but we were not crying. We said our goodbyes, and I told them I would call them later that night. I reminded them that Jesus was with us, and they all agreed.

As I hung up the phone, I had many women asking me what was so funny. God gave me an opportunity to share the story of the 64 sweet potato pies; and they, too, laughed. The gift that God gave me and my family, kept on giving throughout the whole day and night; God's gifts keep on giving, if we will only let them.

I had to decide once I was off the phone that I would share what God had done for me and my family, which was the only way it would bless others. My family and I made it through the first Christmas that I was behind prison walls, but it was only because we trusted and called on our Lord Jesus Christ. I watched many others that did not weather the holidays well. I tried to give them the gift of Christ, but many rejected.

They were not rejecting me, but Jesus. My heart would break for them because I knew that the only answer to their pain was Jesus Christ. I would continue to pray for them as I prayed for myself and my family. Prayer is not about a prayer life, but a life of prayer. The enemy wants to keep us from our Father in heaven, and this is done by keeping us from praying. I encourage you to focus on your attitude of prayer; don't let it be the last thing you do; let it be the first.

Many holidays came and went while I was in prison. Each one brought its own hardship. My family and I had to focus on Jesus in everyone of them; we could not let our guard down. The enemy is waiting for us to let our relationship weaken with our Lord. This is when he will punch.

1 Peter 5:8 *Be of sober spirit, be on the alert. Your adversary, the devil, prowls around like a roaring lion, seeking someone to devour. (NASB)*

We don't have to allow the roaring lion to devour us; we have the power in us through Jesus Christ to stop this. It all lies in our relationship with God, so we will not be deceived by the enemy's lies. Our emotions can get the best of us. God gave us our emotions and, if we will only allow God to help us control them, they can be used for God's glory and not a tool of the devil's to make us stumble.

Proverbs: 3:25-26 *Do not be afraid of sudden terror, Nor of trouble from the wicked when it comes, 26) For the Lord will be your confidence, And will keep your foot from being caught (NKJV)*

On my Journey behind prison walls, God kept showing me that we will have tribulations, but the outcome of them in our lives depends on how we see them and weather them. The enemy was not going to give up on distracting me from my Lord. It was up to me to stay focused on my God and keep my relationship intact. This is something we have to work at; you have to have a mind-set of God every day, all day. This time, it was the emotions that the holidays brought, but tomorrow, it would be something else. God was teaching me that I had to be alert. The enemy wanted to have a beachhead in me; it was up to me to allow God to help me to not let the enemy gain any territory in my life.

STAND FIRM.

Time Alone with God

Fiona and I had been watching for a window room to come open for the both of us to move into together, and one directly across from us was going to be open. But we would not be able to move both at the same time. We both loved being roommates. We were both Christians and our lifestyles were similar. Living together was easy and we encouraged each other and prayed together daily. The room across from us was going to be empty soon. Both women in the room were going home, but only one woman at a time was leaving.

One of the women was going to be leaving within a few weeks, and then the other one would leave within sixty days. We would both have to put in our requests, and pray that we were both approved when the time came for us to submit. You were not allowed to request the room until it was empty. Window rooms were given out by seniority, and we both had been at Coleman about two years now; it was 2006. We were both taking a chance. Fiona could move, and I may not be approved.

We then would be separated, and we could end up with roommates that could be difficult to live with. We prayed about moving. We were willing to stay in the room we had, but in praying about it, we both agreed that God was showing us to make the move. The window rooms were nice to have. You could see outside, and you could even open a small part of the window to get fresh air.

I would have to stay in our current room for sixty days, waiting for the other woman to go home, and then make a request to move into the room with Fiona; if she had been approved to move. We both had agreed she would move first. If she was turned down, I would not even attempt the move without her. Fiona made her request, and she was approved. I helped her pack up and move.

In the sixty days we had to wait for the other woman to go home, during the sixty day wait I never received a new Bunkie. This was strange in itself. You would normally not go longer than a few weeks without a new

Bunkie. Fiona was directly across the hall from me, so we visited everyday and still prayed together. I was also enjoying the time alone. I had not had a room alone since I had been in prison. I was able to spend a lot of quality time with God. I enjoyed a lot of peace and learned a lot during this time alone.

I had many in my life from my past that I had not forgiven. I had not even realized it prior to coming into prison. I thought, in my mind, that I had done all that was necessary to forgive all of the ones in my past that had hurt me so badly; and there were many.

During this time in being alone with no roommate, God was able to bless me and teach me about forgiveness. It changed my life, and I gained more peace than I thought was available. While I was in prison God had taught me how to dig deep in the Word by doing word studies. I took the word forgiveness and started to study what the Word of God had to say about it, but I started by looking up the word forgiveness and what the definition was.

(Forgiveness): the act of pardoning somebody for a mistake or wrongdoing; to stop feeling anger or resentment against; to absolve from payment of.

I want to take some of the words within the definition forgiveness and look deeper into what the definition of each of these words mean. This was how God was able to minister to me in what I had not yet done in reference to all that I still needed to forgive. Looking into the meaning of each word, in reference to forgiveness, gave me a clearer understanding in how God forgives us. As

A Journey Behind Prison Walls

we look into each word my prayer is that God will speak to you as He did me.

1. (Pardoning): to officially release from any, or any further, punishment somebody who has committed a crime or wrongdoing
Punishment: a penalty that is imposed on somebody for wrongdoing

2. (Anger): a strong feeling of grievance and displeasure
   Grievance: bitterness or anger at having received unfair treatment
   Displeasure: a feeling of annoyance or dissatisfaction

3. (Resentment): aggrieved feelings caused by a sense of having been badly treated
Aggrieved: to cause somebody pain, trouble, or distress, to inflict injury on somebody

4. (Absolve): to state publicly or officially that somebody is not guilty and not to be held responsible; to release somebody from an obligation or requirement.
Obligation: something that somebody owes in return for something given, e.g. assistance or a favor.
Requirement: to have something as a necessary precondition

Ephesians 4:31-32 *Let all bitterness, wrath, anger, clamor, and evil speaking be put away from you, with all malice. (32) and be kind to one another, tenderhearted, <u>forgiving</u> one another, just as God in Christ forgave you. (NKJV)*

When you first read this definition of forgiveness, it can be overwhelming. I remember my first thought when I read the definition of forgiveness. I went to God and said, "God, can I do this? I don't know how." I realized quickly that I had not forgiven everyone in my past in the way I was supposed to, but I needed to. God's Word is clear that we need to forgive others as He forgives us.

__Colossians 3: 12-13__ Therefore, as the elect of God, holy and beloved, put on tender mercies, kindness, humility, meekness, longsuffering; (13) bearing with one another, and forgiving one another, if anyone has a complaint against another; even as Christ forgave you, so you also must do.(NKJV)

The first step for me to be free, from all the ones that I had not forgiven, was for me to first realize that I had not forgiven them. Saying you forgive someone, and doing it, is two different things. I had thought up until this point that I had forgiven everyone from my past and what they had done to me, but the people of my past still had a hold on me. God showed me that I was withholding forgiveness, and because I was, there were many from my past that still held me bound. When we don't forgive the ones that have wronged us, it slows us down. It is like they have a string attached to us, and we are dragging them everywhere we go, or try to go. Some of us have so many people that we are dragging around, it is hard for us to do anything because of the dead weight. God wanted me to be free, and He was taking this time that I was alone in my room to show me how this was affecting my life and my walk with Him. It was not going to be easy to relive the things of my past and forgive all that I needed to forgive, but this was necessary in order for me to be free of all the dead weight that I was carrying around.

As I read the definition of forgiveness, it became clear that I had not forgiven the way the definition stated. Pardoning someone was releasing them and not feeling anger or resentment against them. I had many that I still harbored anger toward. I was saying to God, "I forgive them Lord, and I give them to you," but I still felt anger toward them for what they had done to me. I did not know that feeling anger toward them was a true sign that I had not forgiven them. I did have some people in my past that I did not feel anger toward, but as we go on in the definition of forgiveness, I had other areas that also did not line up in reference to true forgiveness, resentment. We see this is being aggrieved, meaning that we still want somebody to feel pain or trouble or distress. We do not want well for them. I was not praying for anyone to have bad times, but if they did fall into hard times, I did not feel bad for them either, so where was my heart truly in regarding them? For the first time in years, I was facing my true thought toward many that had hurt me in my past, and it was clear that I had some work to do.

When we require something from the one who wronged us, we have not absolved them. We say we forgive them, but we want them to remember that we forgave them, and, when the time comes, they better remember they owe us. This is not how we are to forgive. As I searched my heart, this was something I held against my Mom. My Mom could never repay me for the forgiveness I thought I had given her, because she was already dead. This was an area that held me bound the most. I needed to release my Mom and truly forgive her. The forgiveness was not for her, but for me. The devil did not want me to do this. My Mom was gone, and she could never do anything to help me move on from the past that she and I shared. God could, and it started with me forgiving my Mom. As I sat in my room all alone, I began to pray. I asked God to help me forgive and release my Mom. I told God, I want to forgive my Mom with no strings; I told God I wanted to forgive my Mom completely and let it be finished. After I finished with forgiving my Mom, I asked God to help me to release all the others in my life that I had not forgiven. One by one, I lifted them to God and let it go. When I was finished praying with tears running down my face, I felt at peace.

The devil had been tricking me, and I was listening to his lies. When I precondition or made requirement to those I was giving the forgiveness to, it was not true forgiveness. The sad part about this was that, most of the time, the one giving the so called forgiveness is the only one that knows of the precondition. When we forgive in this way, we are blinded. We can't see clearly that this is not how God wants us to forgive. But, when we sit down and see what God's Word says about forgiveness, and we gain a true understanding of what true forgiveness is, we should want to take action quickly. This was my situation, and I took immediate action and went to the Lord in prayer to help me to forgive His way. I had to make a choice and act on the knowledge that God had given me. Now it may be your turn. The Word helped me a lot in the importance of this. Yes, the divination helped me understand what I was not doing. Reading God's Word was what helped me do what I needed to do.

A Journey Behind Prison Walls

Mark 11:25, *And whenever you stand praying, If you have anything against anyone, forgive him, that your Father in heaven may also forgive you and your trespasses. (NKJV)*

God has forgiven us of so much, and when we look at how much God has forgiven us, and then we, of all people, should find it not that difficult to forgive others. So often when we approach God in our prayers, the forgiveness we should have given to others gets in the way of God being able to bless us. As I was blind to so many thing that God wanted to show me and give me, I needed to forgive and release so many, and, once I did, I was free to, not only see, but, receive. God has a plan for all of us, but too often we are unable to take the journey that God has for us because we are too weighted down. It is time to let the weight go. Stop dragging all the things of your past around with you. Forgive, and move on. In the definition of forgiveness, remember this is what God has done for you through your faith and acceptance of His son Jesus Christ. Now look to Him. Through His love and grace, you will not only learn how to forgive, but to love. In this process, God will show you how to love yourself and others. As you start to forgive others, you will find it easier to forgive yourself.

As the days went by, and I waited for the window room to come available so I could move in with Fiona, the more I stayed by myself the more God was teaching me. One night when I had gone to bed with my uniforms still hanging on the bed to make a fake closet, I had now been in for almost two years, and, yes, I was still hanging my uniforms up on the bed above me. This night, when the officers came around to do count time, I felt someone in my room. When I opened my eyes and looked up, a woman officer was standing in my room that I knew well. She had taken my uniforms down and laid them on my locker. She leaned down and whispered to me, "Lanette, you know you are not supposed to do this, and we are being forced to enforce all the rules with our new boss." I smiled at her and said, "thank you, I understand." She then walked away, and I sat up in my bed. I started to pray and asked God to help me with my uniforms being removed. He said to me, "you don't need them anymore, trust Me."

As I lay back down in my bed, without the uniforms hanging, I realized I did not feel any anxiety at all. I pulled the covers up over myself and closed my eyes and I fell fast asleep. The next morning, I got up feeling refreshed and full of energy. God spoke to me in my prayer time and said, "All you have to do is trust me. Many things that used to be in you are now gone. You are free."

All the areas that God had been helping me with, and freeing me from, were things that had held me bound for years, like the closet. I realized that the true Lanette was beginning to come to the surface, and I liked her. It was clear that I had not been me for a long time. I was beginning to get to know the real me for the first time in my life. As Fiona and I had prayed to be moved into the window room, it became clear to me that it was not about us getting the window room at all.

It was all about God providing me with some special alone time, so I could work on some things within me that would need my undivided attention. Now I was free and I could move in with Fiona again, but if I did not, that, too, was okay.

God Was Not Finished with Me Yet.

As soon as the other woman living in the room with Fiona went home, I then went to the office and put in a request to move into the window room with Fiona. It was approved. Fiona along with some of my other friends helped me move in. We were happy to be back together. As soon as I moved out of our old room, the next day someone moved into it. All I could do was laugh and say, "thank you, Lord, for the special time we had."

Fiona and I got all settled in, and it was a relief that we were both back in the same room. We had heard God correctly, and we now were blessed with a window room. I still had a little more than a year left to do, and I felt an urgency to see what else I could do while I was at Coleman. I was still involved with the church on the campus, and I even sang in the choir. The chaplain still gave out my name and room number to all newcomers that came to Coleman in case they needed someone to talk to. I often prayed with many women of different faiths, but one night I was asked to do something for the Muslim women in my unit that shocked me.

I had been communicating with a lot of Muslim women in what the differences were in our faiths. Many of the women I talked to were of the understanding that we all served the same God. The only difference to them was that we called him by a different name. I assured them that this was not the truth; we usually parted agreeing to disagree. One day, I heard a woman on the phone cry out. The cry sent chills down my spine. Often in the unit, we would all hear a woman on the phone cry out. Normally she would be hearing bad news from home. As soon as I heard it, I ran to the front to see if it was one of my friends. It was one of the Muslim women.

I did not interfere; we all respected each other's boundaries. I returned to my room and prayed for the woman that I heard scream. Within a few minutes a woman came to my room. She was also a Muslim. She asked me if I would come and pray for her friend. She told me that she had received news that her baby boy of about two years old had been in a car accident and was in ICU, and he was not expected to make it through the night.

I answered her, "sure, I would be happy to, but you know I am a Christian and I will be praying in Jesus name." She said they were all aware of that, but they had noticed that when I prayed things happened. I was in awe. God you are so good in how you arrange things. I gathered up my Bible and followed the woman to the cell. Once I arrived at the cell, I found about 20 women within the cell or on the wall; all were Muslims or close friends. I opened my Bible and read out loud Psalm 119. After I read the Word, I positioned myself on my knees in front of the mother of the child in ICU and put my hands on her knees. I looked in her eyes and asked her if it was okay for me to touch her and pray for her and her baby. She answered, "Please do." I prayed out loud for her and her son and all her family. Once I was done and stood up, I could see that all in the room were crying. I gave the woman I prayed for a hug and told her if she needed me again no matter the time of day to come and get me. She thanked me and I went back to my room.

Once back in my room and on my bed, I continued to pray for all of the women that I had left in the room. I asked God to plant a seed of His Word in each of them. I asked God to help them see the truth of the true living God and see that they needed Jesus for their Savior. As I finished praying, I felt a peace come over me. I thanked

God for His presence and for using me. I found it difficult to sleep that night. I kept going over the events of the night in my head and how God planned it all. I was realizing more and more that God will use us just like He used me that night. We only need to listen. We have allowed so many barriers to come between us and others, and, because of this, we limit ourselves to whom God can use us to minister to. God was teaching me how to listen to Him, but God was also helping me to see the barriers that needed to be torn down. I was learning that barriers came in all kinds of ways, cliques, and different classes and, of course, the most common ones, race, sex and religion. In prison, we experienced many others also. The unit you lived in was one, but even how much time you had in prison separated many. But it doesn't matter if you are in prison or free, we all have barriers in our lives that we ourselves have allowed to form. We all need to make a decision to not allow the things of this world to come in and separate the body of Christ and the work that God has for us all.

Getting Settled In

It was hard being in prison. God was using me, and I had become close with many women. I enjoyed watching them all grow with Jesus, but I was still away from my family. Visitation was something I looked forward to, but it was hard to watch them go back home. I was involved in a lot, but I decided to get even more involved. It was now about 2005 around October give or take a month or so. A notice was put out if anyone wanted to join Toast Masters to come to the next meeting and sign up. I had not been involved with Toast Masters on the outside, but it was something that I was interested in. Toast Masters helps you learn how to be a better speaker; more effective. When I went to the meeting, I signed up immediately. We had meetings every week, and we all would take turns doing speeches. Once we paid our dues, we would receive a package in the mail, and each of us would have ten speeches that we would have to complete, and be graded, on before we could move to the next level. I enjoyed being a part of this group, and it helped me fine-tune my speaking abilities. So often in prison, we lose some of our skills due to not using them or perfecting them while inside of prison. Then once you go back into the professional world, you are at a disadvantage. I was happy that I was going to be able to fine-tune my skills and not lose them.

One day, all of us in the Toast Masters team got to leave the camp to participate in a speech competition. We first had a competition at the camp, and our top two speakers would get to compete in the competition. I did not get to compete, but I did get to go along and support our teammates. It was a lot of fun being out of the camp, but at the same time it was difficult. We all had to wear our green uniforms, so everyone knew who we were and where we came from. Everyone we came in contact with was friendly and did not treat us any differently than anybody else at the competition. When you are in prison, it is easier to be behind prison walls if you don't think about being free. All of us were excited to have a chance to leave the camp, but on the other hand, it was also difficult at the same time. Being out was good, but we still had to go back. For a day, we were being allowed to feel what it would be like to be free again, and this would cause an inundation of emotions. We had several women on the team that would not go for this reason; they could not handle the emotion of it all.

It was hard for me also to leave the camp in army-greens, dressed as a prisoner, but I prayed through it, and God blessed me. On our way back to the camp after the competition, we were all allowed to stop at a restaurant to eat. Each of us women was allowed to remove twenty dollars from our commissary accounts at the camp before we left for the competition. This, in itself, was out of the norm. Inmates were not allowed to have money on them at any time. An exception was being made for us. We were instructed that we could not take any money back with us to the camp, not even to put back in our accounts. We would have to spend it all at the restaurant. It was strange having a waitress coming around the table to each of us to collect our orders. Each of us had to have our own ticket and pay our ticket, with our twenty dollars. The waitress did not know who we were or where we were on our way to. Our green uniforms were old army-green uniforms and many thought we were in the Army. It felt good to be treated like everyone else. The officers with us made an extra effort to make us women feel comfortable and not to draw attention to us. They went so far as to tell us that it was not necessary for us to share with anyone that we were prisoners, for us to enjoy ourselves and behave, and they would do the same.

As we finished our food and paid our bills, we all went back to the bus for the hour drive back to the camp. We were not allowed to take any leftovers back with us, but the taste of the food would stay with us for many days. We laughed and went over all the events of the day as we traveled back to the camp. Once back at the camp, we had to be searched and signed in before we could go back to our rooms.

Once in our rooms, we quickly got into bed in order to go to work the next day. As I lay back on my bunk, this was when the emotions of the day really hit me hard, tears rolled down my face due to me wishing I could be home with my family. I was not sorry I had gone, but I did understand why some did not go. I only had a year and a half left to do. Most of the women had five or more years to go. It would not be easy for them to see outside and come back with that kind of time still left to do.

Laying there in my bunk, I called out to Jesus to help me with all the emotions I was feeling. I asked God to please help me to enjoy the day that I had been blessed to have and not think about going home. God heard my prayer, and I was able to focus on the recent events of the day, the fun and laugher and not on home.

The next day, everyone wanted to know what we did, and how it all went, and did we win; we were the talk of the camp. We didn't win, but that was okay. We all enjoyed being out and in the competition. We encouraged everyone to join Toast Masters and get involved if they had not gotten involved in something. Being involved was helping me a lot, so I decided to look around and see if I could get into anything else. I had already taken every fitness class you could take, computer classes, also. This was when I saw a notice on the bulletin board asking for volunteers to teach additional classes. You could even make a suggestion to what you wanted to teach. I decided to go to the meeting and see what it was all about. Maybe I could teach a class or two. I was excited just thinking about it.

I asked a few women around the camp if they knew anything about the notice on the bulletin board asking for volunteer teachers. I found that many had heard about it, and they, too, were excited. As I arrived at the meeting, the room was full of women from the camp. I was hoping that there would be enough positions for us all. As the meeting came to order, we all found out that it was not positions that were available, but if we were willing to teach, there would be room for us all.

All we had to do was submit what we would like to teach, and, if it was an approved subject, we would be given a room and a day with a designated time to teach. Each class would be posted, and all women in the camp would be allowed to sign up for the classes they would like to attend. Everyone at the camp was excited. We all had to attend classes to show our unit team that we were involved, but, after a while, you did not have much to pick from. Now, everyone was going to have a much larger variety of classes to pick from.

I submitted both areas that I would like to teach, Credit Awareness and Team Building. I was familiar with both of these areas, since I had taught them in the business world. I was aware that many women inside of prison had been victims of identity theft. Some women had been in so long that they had no idea in how to protect themselves from being a victim. Most had not checked their credit score for over five years, and some had not even had a bank account. I wanted to teach them the basics to help them to get started and help them to protect themselves from being scammed. Team Building was needed for anyone inside of prison. While in prison, you are encouraged to not give your input on anything. You are to be seen, not heard, unless spoken to. This concept was also taught on whatever job you held while in prison. I wanted to teach everyone, who attended my class, how to be productive on any team that they may join once free from prison.

It was not long before I noticed the listing, of all the classes that would be offered, posted on the bulletin board. Now I had to wait a few weeks to be notified to how many would sign up for the classes that I was offering. I was informed I could teach both subjects, but I needed to combine them into one class. I provided all the material and content of my class, so this was not difficult for me. I was excited that I was being allowed to teach. In prison, nothing happens fast. Now I had to wait to receive my list of names and when I was allowed to teach. I did not mind the wait. I looked around in what else I needed to be doing while I waited.

Chapter 20

God Used Grandma Billy to Reach Many and She Could Not Even Read.

God was not done using Grandma Billy, but this time it included others and not only me. As I would sit with Grandma Billy, I learned to how much she loved God, but she was unable to read His Word. She loved the Old Testament, but she was not able to even go to church, because it was too difficult to sit in the pews. Grandma Billy missed hearing the Word of God. This was when I asked her if she would like me to come to her every night and read the Bible to her for about an hour before lights out. She was so happy and full of joy with this suggestion. It was settled. We would start that very night.

I went to Grandma Billy's room, and we began to read from Genesis 1:1. Her face glowed with enthusiasm to hear God's Word. When I saw what it meant to her to hear God's Word, it gave me a greater joy to read it for her. I went to her room every night, as I promised. I found her always ready and willing to listen. After about a week of this, I noticed something had changed. As I sat in the chair next to Grandma Billy's, bed I looked up and around; we had an audience. Women from other rooms were on their top bunks, propped up on pillows, listening to me read Grandma Billy the Word of God. I did not want to draw attention to them and make them uncomfortable, so I did not say anything. I looked at Grandma Billy, and she motioned to me that she had also noticed the same thing.

As I finished and we closed in prayer, I was then able to lean over and whisper to Grandma Billy to what we both had noticed. This is when Grandma Billy amazed me again. She shared with me this, "oh, Lanette, they were there after the first night. I guess I am not the only one that can't read" I could only laugh. I encouraged Grandma Billy that her not being able to read was being used by God for others to hear the Word of God. These women may not have been reading God's Word on their own, even if they could read. I told Grandma Billy that God was providing for all of the other women around her room to hear God's Word by using something in her life that was embarrassing. She smiled at me, and I could tell this made her feel good. Grandma Billy was always humiliated that she could not read. God was showing her in this, that He can and will use everything for His purpose; even the things in our lives that may be embarrassing to us.

So often when we have a testimony of something that could be about a time in our life that was difficult, maybe even embarrassing, we are ashamed to share it. God was showing me, by using this area of Grandma Billy's life that she was embarrassed about, there is nothing in us that God can't use, if we would only let Him.

As we continued to meet every night to read the Word of God together, God did an amazing thing. We did not only have women listening from their beds, we also had women come right into the cell and ask could they join us. Before Grandma Billy and I knew it, the room was full. Women were sitting on the floor and on Grandma Billy's bed. This started to turn into a small Bible study without us even knowing it. We were not only reading, questions were being asked about what was going on, or even why they did that and so on. I started to prepare for questions every night, like I would if I was doing a lesson. This is where the Friday night fellowship group was born. We were growing in numbers and we could not all fit in Grandma Billy's room any longer. God brought so many that wanted to study His Word. Now Grandma Billy did not want to go anywhere else, so I would still read to her one on one, but God birthed a small group out of this very cell.

God was now showing me it was time to teach an organized Bible study. Remember, when I first came to Coleman, I attempted to gather a group of women together to study the Word of God, and God showed me it was not time; now it was time. I presented it to all the women that were gathering in Grandmas Billy's room to read the Word, would they like to meet weekly and study the Word together. The response was unanimous. All would love to participate. We all decided on the time and the day of the week we would like to meet. We would meet every Friday night at 7:00 PM. The group was called Friday night Fellowship. I again went to the chaplain to ask for a room to meet in. This time I would be asking chaplain B. She had been our chaplain for some time now. She told me I did not need a room, and she did not have one to give me anyway, but not to let that discourage me. Chaplain B told me that I was free to meet anywhere on the compound that I wished.

On the camp compound, there was an area of tables that a lot of women would gather nightly and play cards. We, as a group, prayed about where to meet and God showed us to meet in this area. Some were concerned with the noise and the women who would be around us, not interested in the Word of God. But I could see the wisdom of God in this. These women would not come to us, so we were going to them. What better place to meet than in the middle of everyone that was not entertaining the Word of God, for all to hear. The first night we all met, we had so many show up that some had to go back to their rooms and get chairs in order for us all to have a seat. We started with the book of Ruth. As I began to teach, I looked around our surroundings and noticed many women listening to the teaching that were not sitting with us that had come together to study. Women sitting at the other tables were listening as they played cards. I thanked God in my spirit and asked Him to soften their hearts and help them hear His Word.

Over the next month our group doubled in size. Women joined our group from around the camp that we would have never thought would have joined us. We had trouble on occasion when the weather was bad, we could not meet. I prayed about what we were to do. Were we to move? And God showed me that it was time to move. One of women in the group suggested that we ask to use the visitation room. Many others used it.

We should be allowed also. I went to the chaplain and she said she would look and see if it was available. I informed chaplain B that we only needed one of the small rooms off the visitation room not the visitation room itself, if it was not available. To my surprise, the visitation room was free on the day we needed it, Friday night. Chaplain B did tell me if the visitation room was needed for a program, we would not be able to use it. Friday night was a common night that we would have ministries from the outside come and minister to us women at the camp. We did not mind this condition, because we would not meet on any night that we would have visitors come

A Journey Behind Prison Walls

to the camp. Most of us did not want to miss whoever God brought in to minister to us all.

As our group met every week, I was blessed to watch many women come to the Lord and accept Jesus as their Savior. I was also blessed to see many women freed from the many things that had been holding them prisoners for years. We grew in numbers in our Friday night Fellowship group. Many came and many went home from our group, but God blessed us all who participated. There was a small part of the group that I was closest with. They were my dear friends and we did many things outside of the group that was between us. This small group consisted of Beth, Donna and Lynn. These women were my closest friends. We spent many nights praying for one another and encouraging each other. God used them in my life in a mighty way, as God used me to teach them. In turn, each of them taught me more than I could have ever taught them. They all had such a deep love for God.

They respected what God was doing through me and in me and encouraged me to keep seeking after God and not to give up. There were many days and nights that I don't know what I would have done without them. God used them all to bless me beyond measure. We all need to have close friends that we can depend on, people of God. God uses them in our times of need when we may not be able to see something on our own. This group of friends has to be a group that God puts together, ones you can trust and see that their lives reflect the things of God. God gave me a group like this while I was in prison, and God has also given me one now that I am home.

The only way God can do this is if we look for it, and ask God to show us who these people in our life should be. A good friend will tell you what you need to hear, not what you want to hear. These three ladies were just that for me as I walked my journey behind prison walls. How about you? Do you have a close group of Christians in your life that will keep you accountable? If you don't, I would like to encourage you to ask God to show you who these people should be in your life. The devil will deceive you at times, and you may not even notice it or catch it, but close Christians friends can help you see his lies when you may be missing them. When you are part of a group of Christian believers, you are also their accountability partner. It is not always easy sharing with a friend what they need to hear, instead of what they want to hear. We have to do this in love, and with prayer that God will guide us and give us the words to say. I found, when I did this, God always went before me and prepared the heart to hear what I was given by Him to say. Now I did not always get to see the change come forth, but the words were received and then it was up to them to make the changes. I had to do the same thing when one of my close friends would come to me and share something with me that I needed to address. It was up to me to not only receive what they said, but take action and make a change.

Proverbs 1:5 *A wise man will hear and increase in learning, And a man of understanding will attain wise counsel. (NKJV)*
Proverbs 11:14 *Where there is no counsel, the people fall, but in the multitude of counselors there is safety. (NKJV)*

I want victory in my life, and I am sure you do, also, and the Word of God shows us how to acquire it. If we are not careful, we will be drawn into the world's ways of doing things. We must be careful and be on guard at all times. Be careful who you call friend. Are they really? I was one that wanted to be liked by everyone. I cared what others thought about me, and I wanted them to like me.

This is not a bad thing within reason. Some people, we are better off in keeping them at a distance, not allowing them to have an impact on us, influencing us or enticing us with the things of this world. God showed this to me in this way. We need to function in two modes; fellowship mode and ministry mode. Fellowship mode, you are open to give and receive from those around you. In ministry mode, you are focused on ministering to and not receiving. God will teach us something in everything, but in ministry mode, I am only receiving directly from God, and those around me are not influencing me. I was a people pleaser. I did not realize that I cared more about what people thought about me than God. I had to realize that I was not going to make everyone happy.

God had to remind me that many rejected His son Jesus, why would they not reject me. Once I realized that I could not make everybody happy with me, I was freed from being a people pleaser. I focused on God and what He wanted of me, and I lived by what His Word said, not others. In doing this I found that many did not like me or care for what I believed in. I was judged at times, and even accused that I thought I was better than everybody else. But I also found that many were drawn to me, not because of me, but because of the Jesus in me. I realized, as I allowed God to prune and polish me, I was more useful to God and for His glory.

This was what I wanted, and it gave me great joy. My will was finally aligning with God's will for me. My prayers changed and I was receiving more yeses from God than no's. Throughout the whole time that I was in prison, I was learning something every day. As soon as I thought I had got it all, here came other lesson for me to learn. In each lesson that God taught me, I was freer than the day before. I was amazed in how much joy and peace was available to me, right inside of prison. We all have to decide that God knows best and listen, even when it is something that we may not want to hear. God used my circle of good friends to teach me. He will do the same for you if you will let Him.

So much was going on, I was teaching the fellowship group on Friday nights, and God was blessing us all. Then I received a list of all students that would be in my first class of Credit Awareness. I had a full class, and there was also a waiting list for my class. I was overwhelmed with joy. I looked at the names on the list, and I knew some of them, but not all. I was going to now be exposed to many other women at the camp that I did not know and had not been able to reach up until now. God can truly use anything to reach His children. Yes, I was teaching about credit awareness and team building, but everything I did was rooted in the Word of God, and the message of God was at the center of everything.

I had already asked my daughter to mail me all my material from home. This way I could make copies of everything I would need to hand out to my students. In preparing for my first class, I was so excited. I found myself able to sleep better at night. I was now so busy that I did not spend too much time thinking about going home. My focus was on the women at the camp and teaching them all I could before I left. At times, I even thought to myself, "Lord, I don't have enough time to teach everyone that has signed up for my class before I leave. I don't have enough time left here." One of the staff members had shared with me that my class was the most sought after class to take; my waiting list was the longest and still more were signing up.

I was given a room to teach in, and my day of the week was every Thursday night at 7:00 PM. From the first night that I started teaching, it was like I was not even in prison any more. I was so busy preparing the material and teaching that I did not think about being inside prison walls any more. Once in a while, the devil would try to distract me, but I would tell him to back off of me in Jesus name and he was gone. My small group of close friends was used by God in helping me stay on track and not fall to the devil's tricks. Due to all the things that God had helped me with up until now, I was amazed more everyday in how free I was. I was able to focus so much more on God and what He wanted me to do. This was what God meant in His Word in James 1:2, when He tells us to count it all joy when we encounter various trials. God was perfecting me, and I could see the results. I was weathering the storm with Jesus as my captain, and I was learning the things that God had for me to learn.

Mr. Chris Comes to Know Jesus as His Savior

A lot was going on in the last year of my Journey behind Prison Walls. I was teaching the fellowship group and the credit awareness classes. I was still involved in Toast Masters and the Choir. I was called to the chaplain's office on many occasions to pray for the chaplain and to help with the new believers' classes.

Who could have thought that you could be so busy in prison! I was now in a place that I had to be careful to not allow myself to be too busy; to only say yes to the things that God wanted me involved in and not everything that everybody else wanted me involved in. The devil will use our time against us if we are not careful.

This was an area that I was weak in before I came into prison. I hated to tell people no, and saying yes to everything is not the will of God. I found myself overwhelmed often and no time left for me or God. This is what a, people pleasers will do. They will overextend themselves because they want everyone to be happy with them. I was not going to allow myself to fall into that trap again.

I now had learned how to say no, and I had to often. I still needed to leave time for my private time with God. If we are not careful, we will do so many things in the name of serving God that we end up entirely too busy to spend any time with God.

This had happened to me to many times. I was on guard now that it would not happen to me again. When we don't spend time with God, Him and us all alone, we grow weak and ineffective in doing the things of God. This is because we are doing them by our might and not God's.

It did come to a point, while I was in prison, that I had to come up with something that would let others know to not disturb me, and to come back later. I found myself with someone always in my room, and if I was not in my room, women would approach me everywhere I went. It was not a bad thing, it was good, but I had to also give myself time alone to spend with God, so I would not grow weak. Remember in prison we have no privacy, and at Coleman we had no doors.

The freedom was good, but it also had a down side. I spread the word if anyone came to my room, and I had my back to the door, they could come back in an hour or so. Once I did this, I felt the power of God throughout me. When I first did it, I had not realized that I was growing weak. Again, God used one of my close friends to help me realize this was happening to me.

One day Beth had come to see me, but I was with someone, so she decided to come back later. This went on for hours. When she finally caught me with no one in my room, she asked if I was free. I answered her that I had been trying to spend some quiet time with God, but I had been unsuccessful. She looked at me and asked, why? I shared with her that every time I attempted, someone would come to my door and need me to help them with something or pray with them.

Beth looked at me with love and said, "Lanette, don't you think your quiet time with God is important?"

I answered her, "well yes, but I hate to turn anyone away in need."

Beth said something to me that changed my attitude toward my time with God, "There will always be people in need, but you can't help them if you don't spend the time you need first with God. You need to let people know that you are not to be disturbed during that time." She was correct, and I thanked God for using her to show me this.

Everyone respected my time with God after that, and I knew with all my heart that everyone would have sooner, if I had demanded it. Everyone was consuming my time only because I was allowing it. Once I communicated my need, everyone was more than willing to comply. I was only interrupted on a few occasions, and it was due to emergencies; news of a death or sickness. Making sure we have our special time with God is something we all have to work at, and, when we do, God will be able to use us even more to help others. I was blessed to be able to watch many women that were being used by God, because of how their relationship with God had grown.

I watched them grow from having no interest in God to living for Him. This was one of my biggest joys to watch while on my Journey behind Prison walls. So many women living for Christ! All over the compound, I would see women praying for one another, holding small studies in their rooms or mentoring new believers. God was changing so many at Coleman, and it was not only going to affect those at Coleman, but these women would leave prison and take the message home to their families and friends. God is so amazing, and I was truly blessed to watch it all.

One morning, I went out to the meeting place to be picked up for work by Mr. Chris, as I had always done. Mr. Chris pulled up, and once we were all in the truck, we were all off to work. I continued a conversation that I had been having with one of the women on the crew while we had been waiting for Mr. Chris to pick us up. I was sitting in the back seat, and Mr. Chris was driving. I made a comment in reference to my Jesus, and, from the front seat of the truck, Mr. Chris responded by saying He is my Jesus also. I stopped immediately in what I was saying and asked Mr. Chris if he would explain. He responded, "Yes, I will, but later." I was full of joy. Mr. Chris was saved. He had accepted Jesus as his Savior! I wanted to scream with joy. As we dropped everyone off at their respective powerhouses they worked at, we then went to the main powerhouse that myself and a few other women worked at along with Mr. Chris. As soon as we all got inside and settled into our duties, Mr. Chris asked me to come into the office.

As I walked into the office, Mr. Chris was full of joy. He had a smile on his face and a presence about him that I had never seen before in him. I thought to myself, "Yes, he did accept you, Jesus. Thank you, Lord." Mr. Chris asked me to be seated, and, as I sat, I asked if he was going to explain his comment in the truck. He looked at me and smiled and said yes. Mr. Chris said to me, "Miss Black, from the day you started on this crew, I knew there was something different about you. I have been in the prison system for many years. I have seen jail house religion come and go. Some come into prison with it, some gain it while they are in prison, but I watch them all still keep coming back into prison. They would all speak a good game, but I never saw them walk the talk, until you came to my crew. I could not understand why you were here.

We are told not to look up inmates cases. We need to stay impartial as officers. But in your case, I needed to know why you were here. I looked up your case, and you are innocent, in my opinion. I know you don't deserve to be here. But you have never complained, or even cried out how you don't deserve to be here. You are my hardest worker.

I know with all my heart that you came into prison for me. I watched you on my crew, how you were always full of joy and peace. You treated everyone with kindness and love even when they were mean to you. Remember when Cathy was on this crew and she was so awful to you?" I responded, "Yes." "I watched you in how you handled that situation, and how you handled the situation showed me a lot in how you lived for your God that you believed in. For the first time in my life, Miss Black, I met the man Jesus Christ in you. You lived the life in what the Bible teaches. You did not only preach it; you lived it and I had a front row seat to watch you. I know with all my heart that you came to Coleman for me. I would not have heard the voice of Jesus any other way."

"My mom and sister have been trying to get me to go to church for years. I would not go. Every holiday that I would go to a family dinner, as soon as they would start on me about Jesus, I would leave. I was not going to church. I was not going to watch it on TV, and you know what kind of music I listen to. Lanette, I was not going to let Jesus in my life willingly. Then God put you on my crew where I could not run from Him. This weekend, for the first time, I went to a church because of you. I wanted to hear more, and I accepted Jesus as my Savior. I want to thank you for all that you have done. I am one that has been blessed by your walk with Jesus. Lanette, I am now not afraid to die, and it is all because you came to my crew and brought Jesus with you."

Tears ran down my face with joy. I told Mr. Chris that he had made my day, and if I did come to prison for him, it was worth it. We continued to talk, and Mr. Chris asked me many more questions about the Bible that he did not understand. I answered as many as I could without having my Bible with me. This was when Mr. Chris asked me a great question. He said, "Lanette, would you mind to bring your Bible and study reference material to work and teach me how to study the Bible?" I smiled at him and said, "I would love to." From that day on I ate my lunch at the powerhouse in order for Mr. Chris and I to study the Bible together. Other women from the crew

A Journey Behind Prison Walls

also joined us. Mr. Chris had only been saved for a few days, but his hunger for the Word of God amazed me.

Mr. Chris's life changed drastically every day, the music he listened to, his language and how he treated others. Before Mr. Chris was saved he would get angry easily. Now I was able to watch him as he had more patience with others and did not lose his temper easily. As I worked next to Mr. Chris, I was blessed to watch how he grew more dependent on Jesus every day. I thanked God for using me to reach Mr. Chris. God reminded me that I never know who is watching; that I needed to be mindful of God at all times, that he can use every situation for His Glory if I would allow Him too.

Chapter 21

News of Daughters cancer

Fiona and I were doing great. She was busy and so was I. Fiona was going to be going home soon, and I was going to be left behind with about eight months to go until I would go home also. I was already praying for my new roommate, and, whomever she would be, that God would use me to reach her for Him, if she did not know Jesus as her Savior. Here I was with a little more than a year to do, and I had found my peace. It was still hard at night, but, for the most part, I had settled in that I would not be going home until January of 2007.

God had already blessed me by removing the lump from my breast. I had also come into prison with a diagnosis of heart disease; that, too, had been removed from me. God was working not only in me and bringing me to a fuller life with Him, but he was touching my health also, but there was a new storm on the horizon that, again, I did not see coming. God had promised me in the beginning of my Journey behind prison walls, if I took care of His, He would take care of mine, my family. God had done this on many occasions up to this point, giving them peace when they needed it so much. My family had many hardships due to money while I was in prison, because my income had been removed, and my husband had moved out of the house within the first six months of me being in prison, leaving our oldest daughter, Keasha, and her family to pay all the bills of the house on their own. My daughters had many testimonies in how money would show up in the mail at the exact time needed. The bills were paid, but no money was left for food, God took care of all their needs, as He promised he would. God was again going to bless me, and keep His promise to me in taking care of my family. This time it hit me hard and I only made it through because I trusted Him and the promise God had given me.

In the later part of 2006, I called home one night to talk to my oldest daughter, Keasha. She had been pregnant and found it to be within her tube and had to have surgery to have it removed before it could kill her. My daughter had not had a check up in a while and was well over due for one. In her follow up appointment with the doctor, she was given a full work up. This night I was calling her to see how she felt and check on all her test results. The doctor already had some concerns because he had found some cancer cells in a regular pap smear. Now we were getting the results of his further testing due to his original findings. Once Keasha was on the phone, I could tell that something was not right. She was not herself. I asked her if she was okay and how she felt. She responded, "Okay, mom, but I have some good news and bad news." My stomach dropped to my feet. I knew we were waiting on test results. I said a quick prayer before I answered her. I answered her by saying, "okay, dear, give me the bad news first."

My daughter proceeded to tell me, that she had gone to see the doctor to receive the test results and this was what the doctor said, "Mommy, the doctor told me I have stage four cervical cancer, and most women in my situation, he would be telling them they only had six months to a year to live." I interrupted and said, "Honey, you need to tell me the good news quickly." At that moment, I felt my knees buckling up under me. I did not know how much longer I was going to be able to stand.

That was when she gave me the good news. She proceeded to tell me, "Mom, the doctor said he thinks the cancer is all contained, and he believes he can remove it all. I will more than likely have to have a hysterectomy and then radiation and chemo. The doctor is scheduling the procedure, and, when he goes in, he will be able to tell how much he will have to take out and what our course of action from there will be." Tears started to roll down my face, and I could hear my daughter, on the other end of the phone, was also crying. I asked God to help me be strong; "my daughter needs me and you, Lord, right now." As I started to talk, the tears stopped. I encouraged her that God had promised me that He would take care of her, and God has not brought us this far to leave us now. I told her, "we have to trust God in this, and we all must pray everyday for you to be healed." My daughter answered that she understood, but she was frightened. Keasha was a full-time student, close to getting her bachelors degree to become a teacher. She was also teaching full time as a substitute in the school system. Keasha already had two girls and a husband to take care of, and the worry and pain she dealt with daily with me not being home with her; and now she was going through a cancer scare. This was a lot for her, and she needed a praying mother more than ever.

As the time came close for us to get off the phone, I kept reassuring her that God was with us and that we all had to pull together as a family. I reminded her that she could send me as many emails as she wanted, if she needed to vent some things out, and not to worry about worrying me. "That is what moms are for and I am here for you even though I am not home." We had been blessed with a pilot program at Coleman that we were able to use emails to communicate with our close family and friends. The cost was lower than talking on the phone. It was five cents a minute, but it gave family members a way to communicate with a loved one in prison, and they did not have to wait for them to call them, or write a letter that would take days. This only took a few hours and inmates were allowed to check their email as often as they wanted. Both my daughters were grateful when the email system came to Coleman. They were always used to picking up the phone and calling me whenever they needed to talk. When I went into prison, it was hard for my daughters to not have that link to me, but now they could write me at any time of the day and I would receive it quickly. It gave them that link back to me that they were longing for and missing.

As I got off the phone, I was numb. I walked back to my room and sat on my bed and began to pray for my daughter to be healed. I reminded God of His promise to me that He would take care of mine if I took care of His, and now mine needed Him and His healing hand. I pulled out all the Scriptures that I had already looked up before, when I prayed for my healing of the lump in my breast. I started reading them and praying for my daughter to be healed. That night I sent my daughter a copy in the mail of all the Scriptures that I wanted her to read and pray over for her healing. I also made a few copies and handed them out to a few of my close friends to join me in prayer for Keasha to be healed. They, in turn copied the Scriptures I gave them, and they gave them to friends of theirs to join us in prayer. Before I knew it, there were women all over the camp praying for my daughter. I also mailed many prayer requests to those on the outside to pray for Keasha also. She was added to prayer lists all over Florida and out of Florida from what I was told. As women approached me and told me that they were praying for my daughter, it would bring tears of joy to my eyes. I would thank them and let them know as soon as I knew anything I would put the word out in how she was doing once out of surgery. They all assured me to not worry about getting to them. They would find me.

It was hard being so far from my daughter. As a mom, I wanted to hug her and touch her. But I could not do that, and because of her health, she had not been able to come and see me for months. I was missing her so much. I was at a place in my faith that I had to trust God completely with my daughter. It was out of my control. God had given me a promise and I now had to trust Him at His Word. It was not easy. I had to stay in prayer and God's Word. Everyday the devil tried to get me to believe in his lies that my daughter was going to die. Whenever the devil tried to fool me, I would pray and ask God to help me; and He did. In the book of James, it tells us to submit to God, resist the devil, and he will flee from you; and this was what was taking place for me. I submitted to God and the devil had no choice but to flee. Many of us try to battle the devil on our own. We are not to fight the devil; that is to be left for God. When we encounter the devil on his grounds we will lose, but God will not. That was what happened to Eve. She should have never had a conversation with the devil. She would not have eaten the apple. Too much of the time we are entertaining a conversation with the enemy, the devil, when we are to only submit to the Lord and the devil will flee.

James 4:7-10 *Therefore submit to God. Resist the devil and he will flee from you. 8) Draw near to God and He will draw near to you. Cleanse your hands, you sinners; and purify your hearts, you* *double-minded. 9) Be miserable and mourn and weep, Let your laughter be turned to mourning and your joy to gloom. 10) Humble yourselves in the presence of the Lord, and He will exalt you. (NASB)*

As the day grew closer for my daughter to have surgery, many were coming to my room and praying for me to be strong for Keasha. I was so thankful for all the women that God had brought into my life while I was in prison. I had so many women of God that were in agreement with me for my daughter. I was truly blessed. Many women had even started to write my daughter and send her encouraging cards. I did not know this was being done until my daughter would tell me when I called her, or she would let me know in an email when she received a card. I did not have enough breath in me to thank everyone. Some women I did not know. God was blessing my family and me more than we could even measure.

All of us at the camp started praying for the doctors and nurses around Keasha also, that this situation would minister to them, and if any of the doctors did not know Jesus as their Savior, that this situation would lead them to accepting Jesus as the Christ, and a relationship with Jesus as their personal Savior. As morning came and went, I was so excited to hear from my daughter what had happened in surgery. As soon as I came in from work, I went directly to the phone and got in line to wait my turn to call home. As soon as the women in line saw it was me, everyone asked me to come to the front of the line. They all knew I was trying to find out how the surgery had gone with my daughter, and they did not want me to have to wait any longer.

When a phone came free, I dialed my youngest daughter's number, Faleasha. I knew she would be able to answer my question. Keasha may not be awake yet or she could be resting. I did not want to have to call back later. As Faleasha answered the phone, she did not hesitate to update me once she was on the line. In prison, when you make a phone call, there is a recording that you have to listen to first and then answer yes, accepting the call before the phone call is connected. Once we were free to talk, she proceeded to tell me the events of the day. She said, "Mom, you won't believe it," and then she said, "oh yes, you would. When the doctors took Keasha into surgery today, they did not find stage four cervical cancer. The only thing that the doctor saw that needed to be done was scraping some cells from her to do a biopsy. Keasha did not need a hysterectomy, and she will not need any chemo or radiation treatments either. Mom, the doctors came out and told us they could not explain it. What their test results had revealed before was not there." She then said, "Mom, you know what we told them? We shared with them how we all had been praying for God to heal Keasha, and God did. They did not understand what we were telling them, Mom, they could not refute it." I could not help myself. I screamed, "Praise the Lord, thank you Jesus." Everyone in the unit looking at me was quiet and waiting for me to explain to them why I had screamed. I looked at them and said, "She did not have cancer. It was gone when the doctors went in to remove it." The whole unit started yelling and thanking God. Women from the back of the unit started to come up front where we were to see what all the commotion was about; and they, too, rejoiced. My daughter asked what all the commotion was. I told her, "Everyone is rejoicing in

Keasha's healing. They all have been praying for her." Faleasha told me to tell them all "thank you." I responded, "I will, but our true thanks goes to the Lord Jesus Christ." She agreed.

As I ended my phone call with my daughter, I was rushed by everyone that had been standing around me waiting for me to get off the phone. Everyone started hugging me and crying out with joy in how our Lord had answered our prayers. There were a few in our unit that did not believe as we did, but they rejoiced in the good news with us. My daughter was well. Even other faiths could not rebuff what had happened. They did not give Jesus any credit openly, but the evidence could not be refuted. It was count time and we all had to go to our rooms for count, but after count, the compound would be opened for dinner, and I could not wait to get out and tell all who had been praying how God had answered our prayers. My daughter, Faleasha, was making all the calls to all who had been praying on the outside, so they would not have to wait for me to mail them a letter. Once count was clear and we were called to dinner, I started to spread the good news to all. It did not take long before the whole camp knew and were rejoicing with my family and me. There was even staff that had been praying and waiting along with us for this good news. The camp was bursting at the seams with gladness and joy. It was such a good feeling for all.

I was not able to talk to Keasha until the next day, but when I did, she sounded good and full of joy in what God had done for her. She updated me on more of the details and on all of the doctors' recommendations. She was to be tested every six months, and she needed to wait a year before getting pregnant. Other than that she was in great health and cancer free. My daughter and I had a lot more to go through before I would be able to go home, but our trust in God had grown in a big way. When my daughter found out that she had a tubal pregnancy and had to go through surgery to have it taken care of, we all looked at it to be a terrible thing. We all thought, here we go again, one more bad thing happening to our family. But in reality it was the very thing that saved my daughter's life. Keasha had already had one miscarriage, even before this tubal pregnancy, and she had still not gone for her yearly work-up that was so much over due. When the tubal pregnancy happened, she had no choice but to do the work up because the doctor took some samples while she was in surgery. God used the tubal pregnancy, something that looked bad to all of us, as a tool to save my daughter's life. Again this reminded me that we have no idea to what God may be up to in all situations. We have to keep an open mind and allow God to reveal His plan in every situation in our life. We have to be patient and exercise our faith at all times.

Keasha was not to get pregnant for at least a year, but that was not what happened. Within three months, Keasha was pregnant with my fifth grandchild, her third child. She had not completely healed from her surgery, and the doctors were concerned for her and the baby she was carrying. Keasha had to be on bed rest, and, even in the hospital, for a good part of her pregnancy. The doctors kept telling us that we were going to have to abort the baby because Keasha was not producing enough fluid for the baby to live. But we all stood strong in what God could do and told the doctors no. We all, at the camp, started back up the same prayer chain that had been in place, when Keasha had been given the report that she had cancer. Keasha was not supposed to ever be able to have any more children if the cancer had taken the path that the doctors said it would. But God had other plans, and we all were going to wait and see what God was going to do in this situation as we had done with the cancer.

Keasha was able to carry the baby until full term, and she had a healthy baby girl. Keasha was being taken care of by the same doctors who had taken care of her with the cancer. Our family again told all the doctors and nurses that God can do anything; all we have to do is pray and have faith. God blessed us with a baby girl named Breah. She is a blessing to us all to this day. Breah has a great love for Jesus, even as a small child, that has amazed us all. We all can't wait to see what God will do with this miracle that only He provided a way to come into this world and bless us all.

Less than a year, time to go home

The time was drawing near for Fiona to go home. I was going to miss her a lot, but the good news was she had completed her journey behind prison walls, and now it was time for her to go home to be with her family and daughter. I had been blessed to watch Fiona grow in the Lord during the time that she and I were roommates. Fiona knew the Lord when she came in to prison, but now, she did not only know God, but her bond was strong and unshakable. As the day grew closer, we both were experiencing joy and sadness at the same time. Inmates are not allowed to communicate with each other, once they leave prison, until they have completed their probation period. We both had three years of probation once we left prison. This meant we would not be able to communicate with one other once she walked out the prison doors, and, if we did, it would be years. We had been told how many women, once they left prison, did not follow the rules. Many women, who had left, would continue to communicate with women that were still inside of prison by emails, letters and some even used the phones. Fiona and I had always tried to go by the rules while we were inside of prison, and we were not going to start breaking them once out. Our goodbye would be goodbye, unless God brought us across each other's paths again. As Fiona packed and gave things away, reality hit the both of us that we were going to have to say goodbye soon. Fiona did not take much home with her, not many inmates do when they go home. Normally, most inmates leave most of their belongings behind for friends or other inmates that are unable to buy much off of commissary.

The night before Fiona was going to leave, it was hard to sleep for the both of us, her being eager to go home; and, for me, I was going to miss her. I started praying for my new Bunkie. I knew, being in a window room, I would not be in my room for long by myself. I prayed for God to use me in whatever way my new Bunkie needed. I did not pray for a Christian Bunkie. I prayed for God to bring to me whoever He chose, and to give me all the wisdom I would need to help her. Fiona left that morning, and we received a new shipment of ladies the next day. My new Bunkie was Terry Lynn. Normally window rooms have women within the unit waiting for a window room. Once the window room is empty, they submit a request to move into the window room. This did not happen this time with the vacant bed in my room, and that was strange. In all the time that I had been in prison, I had never seen a window room come open and someone not have their eye on it, to move into it. When I came in from work the following day after Fiona had left, I was surprised that I did not have a new Bunkie from within the unit. As we waited for the new women to come into the unit and see what rooms they had been assigned, I was surprised to find that one of them had been given my room. Even the officers, who worked in the front office processing new inmates, normally keep window rooms free for others within the unit to transfer into them, but not this time.

As Terry Lynn came into my room, I helped her settle in and tried to reassure her it would be okay. We hit it off right away. She was a new Christian, and she had been praying for a Christian Bunkie from the day of her sentencing, when she was told that she was going to prison. She and I talked for hours. God used me a lot that first night I spent with Terry Lynn. Terry Lynn was hungry for the Word of God and to gain understanding in what God wanted of her. She really wanted to live for God. Terry Lynn could not get over how God had answered her prayer. She believed that God gave me to her as her new Bunkie to help her grow with God. I shared with her how I had prayed for God to send me a Bunkie that He chose, and to give me the wisdom needed to help her. We both agreed that God had answered both of our prayers. Terry Lynn had a lot of things to work through. We stayed up most of our nights, for hours after lights out, praying and reading the Word together. I was blessed again to watch a baby in Christ grow and have an overwhelming hunger to get to know Jesus. Terry Lynn made a lot of mistakes. She would get mad at me, and then come back to me within an hour and apologize. My peace with Terry Lynn amazed me. She could not make me angry, no matter what she did. With all the things that Terry Lynn would do, I never lost my temper. It was not hard for me either. Nothing she did fazed me; I was always able to maintain my joy. This was evidence to me that I had truly changed. What others did to me did not affect me like it used to in the past either, and, best of all, my response to them was not dictated by what they did, but how God wanted me to respond. Being a people pleaser in my past, I would lose my joy quickly over what someone thought of me, or if someone was mad at me or did not like me. I would have, in my past, done something to make them change their mind or I would not have any peace until they did. What others thought of me did not have control over me anymore. I was free and it felt good.

God was using me to help Terry Lynn, but God was also using Terry Lynn to show me the finished work that God had done in me. God wanted me to have confidence in what He had done in me over the last three years, so I could walk boldly. I was not the same women of God that had come into prison three years ago. I was now looking at myself differently. I believe this was the first time that I had realized how much I had changed. Now it was time for me to prepare to go home. I had stopped thinking about going home over a year ago, and now I had to change my focus and look at going home, and what I would do once I was home. I already knew that I was not going to have a husband. Anthony was waiting for me to come home to file the divorce papers. A marriage of twenty one years was over. "What do I do now, Lord?" I asked God. All kinds of things went through my head. Where would I work? How would I make it on my own without a husband? Who was going to hire me now with a prison record; a felony? I have to admit that the thought of it all at first frightened me, but I quickly went to the Lord in prayer, and asked Him to help me. God does not give us a spirit of fear. I knew my fear was not of God, and, all I had to do was ask God to help me with it, and He would; and He did.

Chapter 22

Furlough Home

I had not been home for three years. The day of sentencing, I had gone to the courtroom with the understanding that I would be allowed to go home and prepare for whatever the sentence the judge gave me, but that did not happen. My oldest daughter and her family were now living in my home, taking care of it until I was allowed to come home. I was now being allowed to go home on a furlough for seven days to help me adjust to going home.

To qualify for this privilege, you had to have less than six months left in prison and to have never been on a disciplinary action. I met all qualifications. Once all the paperwork was done, my daughters would mail in some clothing for me to wear home. I had lost twenty pounds since I had been in prison.

My daughters had to buy me something new to wear. I remember when the box arrived and I was allowed to go to R&D to try on everything to make sure it fit; I was in shock to how much weight I had lost. It felt good to look in the mirror and see myself in what we called freedom clothing. I took the clothing off and put it all back in the box and R&D would hold it until the day I would go on my furlough.

I was actually getting to go home. It was hard to believe three years had gone by; not that it was easy. I had learned to appreciate the little things in life, my family and friends. Being able to go to the church that you choose, getting up and going to a job that you have a future with no matter how small that may be. I had been living in a place for three years that I did not have any say over what I did every day. I worked hard, but it was not a job that had a future. I took on the attitude that I was working for Jesus. My promotions lay with Him, and this gave me peace. This was a concept that I was taking home with me. My thinking had changed in so many ways. I knew that all of us have what I like to call "stinking thinking" that needs to be changed. We learn so much over the years of being on this earth that is not God's way of thinking. We all must submit to God and allow Him to change our "stinking thinking".

I had done this, but I also understood that I needed to be on my toes. My thinking needed to be put on the altar daily in order for it to not be polluted by the world's ways of doing things. I had missed many foods while I was in prison, but I do have to admit that where I was at Coleman I had it better than most that were in prison. The food was not that bad, but it was not the same as being home. I kept a few things in my locker to appease some of my cravings from home. I love tomato soup.

We did not have tomato soup in prison, so I would order V8 juice off of commissary, and heat it up in the microwave, with a little salt, pepper and some powdered milk to make my own version of tomato soup. It did not taste the same, but it was close enough, and I was appreciative to have it. We were also allowed to buy peanut butter and jelly off of commissary.

This was a treat for me to have a peanut butter and jelly sandwich, reason being, we were not allowed to bring bread back to our rooms. But on occasion, we would be given a bag lunch with bread in it, and I was able to make a peanut butter and jelly sandwich. We could bring the peanut butter and jelly to the dining hall, but it was not the same as sitting in your room and enjoying it without all the distractions of the dining hall.

I enjoyed eating in my room when I could. It was quiet. Like I said, I learned to appreciate the little things of life, and eating in quiet was one of them. I learned to cook many things in the microwave while I was in prison. Many times, my friends and I would get together and make our own dinner and eat together as a family without all the distraction of the dining hall. These were precious times. As I prepared to go home, I prayed that God would help me keep my appreciation for the little things in life, and that I would never forget what I had learned while I was at Coleman.

The night before I was going to go on my furlough home, one of my friends gave me a manicure and a pedicure. It felt great, and I had not had either done since I had been in. Many women did things in trade for item off of commissary as a form of payment. I had to be careful with the amount of money I had for commissary, and I did not have any room for extras like pedicures or manicures. My friend did it for me at no cost. The time we spent together was precious, and I was thankful to know her and call her friend. She had been in a lot longer than me and had five years still left at Coleman.

We talked about how I felt going home and what were some of the things that I wanted to do when I first got home. I was going home on my birthday. I was excited to be able to go home on my birthday and not have to spend it in prison. Any holiday in prison is hard; this one I was going to be home. As Stephanie finished up and I thanked her for all she had done, I gave her a hug and she said she would be praying for me to have a great time with my family. She reminded me that I had been gone from home for a while and I had to understand that I was not the only one that had changed, that my family had changed also, and we all needed to be patient with one another. I thanked her again and agreed with her wisdom.

Once Stephanie was done with me, the rest of my friends told me that they needed me to not go to dinner in the dining hall that night, but to join them in the multiple purpose room. This was the room that most would get together in and eat or play games, etc.

Earlier in the week, my friends and I were talking about birthday parties and I had shared with them all that I had not had a birthday party in over 20 years; they were all in shock. Donna, my best friend, came to my room and told me to follow her. We walked down a long hall to the multiple purpose room, and, when Donna opened the door, all my friends were sitting around several large tables yelling surprise.

Tears of joy began to run down my face. Everyone at the table stood up one by one and gave me a hug and expressed how much they were going to miss me. I was going to miss all of them also. We knew that I was only going to be gone for seven days, but that was not what we were all talking about.

We all knew I would be going home soon for good, and I would not be able to see them or talk to them again until I was done with probation. This was hard for all of us to think about. Most of us had become as close as sisters, family. And we knew, when any of us would go home, we were not allowed to communicate with one another. But the furlough I was going on, I would be able to return and tell them everything my family and I did.

Many foods had been made by many of the women sitting at the table. We had pizza and even chocolate cake made out of Oreo cookies. It was amazing how good the food was. All the food was made with a microwave and all the food was bought off of the commissary. Many ladies had made me gifts that I could use once I was home. One of the most memorable gifts was a scrap book that was made from magazines, with ideas to what kind of clothing I should buy once I was home. My friends knew that I did not have any clothing at home that would fit me due to all the weight that I had lost, so they fixed a scrap book to help me on the shopping spree my daughters were going to take me on while I was at home on furlough. We went through it page by page with them all giving me instructions to what to buy and not to buy.

We laughed and enjoyed each other immensely. As the night came to an end, we all cleaned up and gave each other a hug. I would not see most of them in the morning before I would leave. As I walked back to my room, I felt a strange sadness, "Lord I am leaving so many good friends here and it hurts me that I can't stay in touch with them. Lord, help me with this pain and sadness."

As I sat on my bed, Terry Lynn came in my room and asked what was wrong, "did you not enjoy the party?"

I responded, "oh yes, it was great. I am only sad that I will be leaving you all and not able to see you again; I have come to love you all."

Terry Lynn then leaned over and gave me a hug and told me that I, too, was loved and "we all are going to miss you, also. But it is time for you to move on to the next mission field. You have done a good job in teaching us. It is time for us to let you go and you let us go. If it is meant for us to see each other again, God will make sure we do."

I looked up at Terry Lynn and recognized that God was using her to answer my prayer. I smiled at her and agreed that she had grown with God a lot in the short time we had been together. It was time for me to go home, and I needed to trust God in leaving all my friends behind. He had been taking care of them up to this point, and He would continue to do so. I thanked Terry Lynn, and I started to pack in preparation to go on furlough the next day. Anything that I took home with me, I would not be allowed to bring back. I was taking home everything that I would not need for the next six months.

This would make it a lot easier when it came time to go home for good. I would not have as much to pack then. I had also made a lot of things for my family. I had crocheted a blanket for each daughter and dolls for my granddaughters. I made hats for the boys and I crocheted a football for my grandson. It was hard to believe, once I had everything packed, that all of it had come out of my locker. It sure looked like a lot packed in boxes.

Throughout my journey behind prison walls, God spoke to me in how He was going to use me once I was home. This journey behind prison walls was God's boot camp in preparing me for a journey that was still ahead. God wanted me to share what I had learned on my journey with as many that would listen. God did not want me to be sidetracked by what it looked like in my flesh.

I needed to look at what was ahead of me with my spiritual eyes. We can do all things through Christ who strengthens us. My last year in prison brought new lessons, things that needed to be learned before I could go home. Most of the situations that occurred, before I went home, only confirmed to me that I was ready to go home. Things did not bother or control me like they used too.

I was all packed, and now it was time to get some sleep so I could wake up early in the morning and be ready to meet my daughters at 9:00 o'clock. This was not easy. I was so excited to be able to go home and spend some time with my family. I was also going to be able to go to my home church. I could not wait. I prayed for a long time, and asked God to help me sleep, but I did not sleep much. Once the officers had come by and finished the five o'clock count, I jumped out of my bed and started to prepare for the call for me to go to R&D to be released on my furlough. My daughters were picking me up at 9:00 AM. This meant they would have left home by 5:00 AM in order for them to be at the prison to pick me up on time. It was going to be a long day for them also.

I had spoken to my daughters the night before, and they, too, were so excited they did not know if they would be able to get any sleep. I was praying that God would protect us and keep us while we were driving home and to get us all home safely.

I had taken my shower, and one of my friends helped me to put on my makeup and do my hair, and then I waited to hear my name called over the loudspeaker to go to R&D. When my name was called over the loudspeaker to go to R&D, I almost jumped out of my skin. I was almost crying with excitement; I was really going home.

Once in R&D, the officer gave me my clothes that my daughter had mailed to me to wear home. As I got dressed, the officer searched all my things that I was taking home. I had all the medications that I was taking in some envelopes. I could not bring the medication bottles because I could not bring anything back in. I was told at this time, that I could not take my medication home in envelopes. Medical was supposed to give me a one-week supply of all my medication that I could use while I was home on furlough.

Now I was nervous; I had no idea to how long this could take. I was not allowed to leave without my medication. Now I had to wait and I was not allowed to go outside and explain to my daughters why I was late. It did not take long, and my medication was brought to me. I was praying the entire time I was waiting that the medication would come quickly, and that my daughters would not be worried. God answered my prayers-"thank you Lord". Once I had my medication, I was free to go. I had a cart with all my boxes, and as soon as I stepped out the door, my daughters approached me and we all hugged. I was in tears. We loaded the boxes in the car, and I then returned the cart, and the officer told me to enjoy my family. I gave her a grin, and said, "thank you I will."

As my daughter began to drive out to the parking lot, we could see a large group of women over by the side of the prison waving at us. It was all of my friends. We all laughed and waved back and we were off for home. It was my birthday and my favorite perfume at the time was White Diamond.

My daughters gave me a brand new bottle once I was in the car, and I sprayed it on myself as soon as they gave it to me. It was a great feeling being free and wearing my own clothing and now I smelled good! It had been a long time since I had been allowed to wear perfume. It had been a long morning, and they wanted to stop and eat some breakfast, and I was in agreement with that. I remember walking into the restaurant with my daughters and feeling real strange.

My daughters and I had been seated in a booth, and I looked around the restaurant soaking in everything. When the waitress walked over to me and greeted me with a smile and asked me if she could get me some coffee, I realized she did not know who I was and where I had been for the last three years. I was not an inmate anymore, at least for seven days. I responded with a yes and when I looked around the table at my daughters, they were looking at me with a strange smile and asked, "How do you feel Mom?" With tears in my eyes, I responded, "it is hard to explain, but great." We enjoyed our food. I was not able to eat much being so excited to get home, but it was good to be sitting in a restaurant and enjoying my two daughters like we had done so often before I had gone to prison.

My two daughters and I used to have girls-night-out often. I always enjoyed them. We would go out to eat and then a movie and catch up with each other in what was going on in all our lives. It was special memories that I had with the both of them, and I was happy that we had started our seven days together with just the three of us. We had a three and a half hour drive ahead of us. I had already spoken to many people that were waiting for my call once I had gotten into the car; I could not wait to get home.

The drive did not seem long to me because we all talked all the way home. Once we were close, my stomach started to get butterflies. Once we pulled up in my neighborhood, tears started to come to my eyes. As we pulled into my driveway, I was a bundle of nerves. I had not seen my house since that day I left to go to the courthouse for sentencing.

As I walked up the steps to the front door, I felt overwhelmed. My daughters asked me if I was okay, and I responded, "Yes, I am only happy." When I opened the door emotions of all kinds overwhelmed me. I was home, but I was different from the last time I stood in my house. I looked at the walls and the color they were painted and asked my girls, "who painted these walls?" They responded, "You did, Mom." I looked at them and said, "They are ugly and too dark." I did not realize until I walked into my house how much I had changed. The way I looked at things was different, even the colors on the walls were foreign to me. I don't think my girls understood what was going on at the time, but I did. I would help them understand later.

As my oldest daughter, Keasha, took me upstairs to my bedroom, which she and her husband had been staying in after Anthony, my husband, had moved out, she informed me that she and her husband would be staying in the room downstairs, so I could sleep in my room while I was home. This made me feel good, because I was not sure where I was going to stay once I was home, and I really did not care. I was so glad to be home.

As I looked around my room, I could see that a lot of things had not been moved since the day I had left, even the items on my vanity were still there from that day that I had prepared to go to court for sentencing. I turned and asked my daughter why she had not put my things away and given herself more room for her things. She responded, "I could not bring myself to move your things, Mom. Leaving your things there made it easier to bear that you were not here."

I walked over to her and gave her a hug and told her I was sorry for all the pain she had been through. She looked at me and told me, "It was not your fault, Mom. We have all had to help each other get through this and we have. It is almost over and you are home now and I am glad. We all love you and miss you." Both of my daughters had told me that, after I had gone into prison, they used to sleep in my jogging suits to feel close to me, and they still had them. This was something they had not told me before. They did not want to worry me in how hard it was for them when the bailiff took me away in the courtroom. I was learning now for the first time what all my daughters had to do to bear the pain of me being gone.

Both my daughters left me alone in my bedroom so I could get settled. I think they knew I needed some time to cry and absorb everything. My daughters worked hard in keeping many things from me while I was in prison. They did not want me to worry about them. They knew I could not do anything to change our situation, and they did not want to make it any harder for me than it already was. I was thankful for my girls, and I was proud of them both. I knew, before I came home, that I was going to have to face a lot of things that I had not known over the last three years.

God had prepared me for it all, but it was still hurtful, and I had to work through the emotion, but God had taught me how. As I looked around my room, I noticed, one by one, my things that had not been moved. I then started to feel the pain that my daughter had felt over the last three years living in my house. I fell to my knees and prayed for myself to be able to work through what I was feeling, but I also prayed for my daughters to heal from all the pain that they both had experienced over the last three years. I knew we all had a lot to get past, and now that I was coming home, I had to realize that my family was not the same either. We all needed to get to know each other all over again, and, most of all, we would all have to be patient with one another.

As I put some things away, and found some things I may need while I was home, I then cleaned up my face and went back downstairs to join my girls. We would all be going out to eat for dinner together for my birthday. I would be seeing my grandchildren soon. As we all came together and prepared to go to dinner, I was overwhelmed with joy. "Lord, I am truly blessed."

I thought I would be sad while I was home knowing I had to go back, but I did not even think about going back to prison while I was home. I embraced every minute with my family. I had a great time at the restaurant. We went to a steak house to eat, and I had the biggest steak I could order. My son-in-law said, "You take home whatever you don't eat. I want you to enjoy your day to the fullest." When the waiter came over to sing happy birthday to me, the whole restaurant sang. I was in amazement; again, no one knew who I was or where I had been. It felt good to be free.

The next day, my daughters and I had to go and do some shopping for some new clothing for me. I had lost about twenty pounds, and I needed some new clothes to wear once I would be released from prison. I was going to be released from prison in January of 2007 to a halfway-house. I would not be allowed to stop and shop for anything on that day. The furlough in the prison's perspective was a time to also prepare for when you would be released. It was one of the reasons they granted the furlough to begin with.

Obviously, I had not been shopping in a long time, so my daughters told me that they would pick out some clothing for me to try on. My daughters and I went around the store picking out some different items to try on. Many of the things that I thought would be nice, they disagreed and I put them back. We had a lot of fun picking out items for me and trying them on. I tried on many outfits while my daughters stood by and said yes or no. After we were done with one store, we would go to the next; shopping took up most of the day. Once we were done, we went out to eat and continued to share and spend quality time together.

Both of my daughters were going to school, while they still held down jobs and took care of their families; not to forget coming to see me every other weekend. My girls had full plates and I was proud of them both. My youngest daughter, Faleasha, was doing a class project that consisted of decorating a garage and making it like a shopping store for girls in distress.

The women in this program were young women who had become pregnant and had nowhere to go. In this area, where this garage was, were several homes that these women lived in and had their babies. The store garage was a place that they could come and get items for themselves and their babies at no charge. My daughter invited me to attend; I was excited, but nervous at the same time. I was going to meet her fellow students for the first time. What was I going to say? Most people, in the attempt to make conversation upon meeting someone for the first time, ask what you do for a living.

I was not sure how I was going to answer this question. I prayed for God to give me wisdom in this. I did not want to embarrass my daughter. My daughter had also told me that the news media would be there. My other daughter, Keasha, would also be going. I had to sign a paper in leaving the prison when I started my furlough that I would not be on any news or have my picture taken by any media while I was home. I had to be careful that I did not get in a picture without knowing it.

I did not share all my concerns with my daughter, because I did not want to worry her on her exciting day that she had worked so hard for. I was used to living everyday being an inmate; my girls were not, and I did not want them to have to start looking at all the things that I had to. When we arrived at the garage that her classmates and she had decorated to make it look like a department store, I was amazed. They all had done such a good job. I was full of pride for my daughter and her classmates. I was introduced to all of my daughter's classmates.

They all shared how it was working with her and all her ways. It was going great and then the TV news crew started taking pictures of the students and their families. I ducked into the dressing room until they were gone. When my daughter caught up with me, she asked where did I go and why did I not get in the picture with her and Keasha? I then shared with her why. She smiled and said that was close; we both laughed it off and the day finished great. I was asked by a few, what organization I was with, and I responded that I was there to support my daughter and her class-mates in a job well done. This worked great. It took the attention off of me and back on my daughter and her classmates where it belonged.

The seven days went by fast. We had accomplished everything that we needed to do. I was even able to get a new prescription for contact lenses. My daughter would then be able to order them before I came home so I would have them when I went to the half-way house. I had been able to spend time with my family and some of my friends. I was even able to attend my church. It was great to see everyone. My family and I were encouraged to stay strong, that we were close to the end of this storm. We were reassured by them all that they were still praying for us all and they would continue to do so.

But it was now time to prepare to go back to Coleman prison. I was surprised that I was not sad. I knew I would not be gone long, only six months. I encouraged my daughters that we had all done three years, and the next six months would go by fast. They agreed. As I packed my things away that we had bought for me to have once I came back home, I smiled. "This storm is passing, Lord; it is almost over." I was coming to the end of this journey; one that I did not think on many occasions I would make it through. But God had been faithful to me and my family. We still had a lot of healing to do, but God was with us and we could do anything as long as we stayed focused on Him.

The morning that we had to go back to Coleman prison, we all had to get up early. We all got dressed, and I had some well-needed coffee, and off we went to Coleman Fl. The trip was going to take three and a half hours. We had also planned a stop, prior to reaching the prison, to have one last meal together before I had to turn myself in. From what I remember, I needed to be back by 3:00 PM. This was before count time.

During the trip back to Coleman a lot of things were going through my mind. Being home made me face how much I was out of the stream of things. I was going to have to start all over. I did not have a job. I was not sure how I was going to gain employment with a felony on my record. I was still nervous about this. Being in prison, I had come to get used to my surroundings. I had a job, ministry and women inside that I called family. I did not have to be concerned in how I would pay the water bill or utilities, etc. I had gotten comfortable, and I now needed to change my mind-set, and this was going to take some concentration on my behalf and a lot of help from God.

As we got closer to Coleman prison, I was surprised in how comfortable I was in returning. It was like I was going home. As eager as I was to go home and be with my family and begin my new life, it was becoming more clear to me how much work I had ahead of me in preparing to go home; and I only had six months to do it.

As we pulled up to the front of the prison, our goodbyes were short. I could see in my daughters' eyes that it was not easy for them to say goodbye to me and leave me back at prison, but it was not as hard as we all thought it would have been. Both of my girls looked at me and said, "Mom, we all only have six months to go before we can come and pick you up for good. We can do this. Don't cry!" I smiled at them both and gave them a hug and turned to walk into the prison. As I walked into the prison, I was still surprised that I did not cry. I was checked in by one of the officers manning the front desk, and then I was allowed to walk out onto the compound.

Right away I spotted several of my friends walking across the compound, and, when they saw me, they came running to me. We all embraced, and they started with many questions in how my time was at home with my family. As we sat down, I spent hours going over all the different things that I had done, while I was home, and what I had learned. Everyone wanted to know what I had eaten and was it hard to come back. I shared with them that it was not hard to come back, because I knew that I had only six months left to do before I would be able to go home. But I also shared with them how I learned that I still had a lot of work to do in preparing to go home and six months was not that much time to do it all.

At first all my friends were confused when I shared this with them, until I explained. I explained to them that God had shown me that my way of thinking had been conformed to living at Coleman. I had gotten comfortable and had adapted myself to prison life. This was necessary to live in prison, but now I had to change my way of thinking and prepare myself for going home and starting my new life. I had not put any thought to this until I had gone home. As I went through, one by one, how I had gotten used to not paying my own bills, and not even thinking about what I would eat, my friends could then understand what I was trying to explain to them, because they, too, had the same way of thinking. I encouraged each of them to look at how much more time they had at Coleman prison and to start working on changing their way of thinking. I explained to them, in doing this, they would be better prepared to go home.

We all can learn from this in the respect of leaving any storm or tribulation in our lives. Often times, we do adapt ourselves to the situation in order to make it through, but what we have to learn is that we need to readapt ourselves in order to live outside the storm. Yes, we learn many things during the storm if we allow God to teach us. I was in a storm that took me away from my family and all that I knew. I had to adapt to my surroundings.

Now it was time for me to leave these surroundings behind and readapt to my life at home, bringing with me what I had learned during my storm. But I also needed to leave something behind. This was the hard part. Many of the things that I had gotten used to while I was at Coleman prison, God used to teach me many things, but I did not have to take them all home.

While I was at Coleman, I had to learn to have a protective guard up, and I could only allow a choice few into my inner circle. I was in a war zone, as you may say, but now I was going home, and I needed to be more open to my family and friends that I had left behind. I explained earlier, in the different modes we have to learn to operate in, ministry mode and fellowship mode. I had been functioning in ministry mode, for the most part, during the last three years. I was now going to be able to function more in fellowship mode than ministry mode. I had some adjustments to make, and God was showing this to me, and He was going to help me make the adjustments. But I was learning that this happens to us in everyday life. We have to be ready to change to the situation that God presents to us. Now I was going to put into practice what God had been teaching me for the last three years.

Chapter 23

Preparing To Go Home:

Isaiah 40:31 But those who wait on the Lord shall renew their strength; They shall mount up with wings like eagles, They shall run and not be weary, They shall walk and not faint. (NKJV)

As I sat in prison, with only about three month left before I could go home, I could not help myself from thinking about how much my life had changed since I had been in prison. Being in prison will change you in itself, but in what way it will change you is up to you. The first decision you must make, in entering prison, is will you let this Journey change you for the better or the worse? It is impossible to leave prison the same way you went in. You will leave either bitter, or better. God had changed me for the better, but I had to let Him; and then I had to make a decision that I would take action on all of the areas that God showed me that I needed to change in.

2 Corinthians 5:17
Therefore if anyone is in Christ, he is a new creature; old things have passed away; behold, all things have become new. (NKJV)

I remembered back to a day that I had made a decision to live for God and His ways and not my own. A day back in 1999, I dethroned myself and allowed Jesus to be on the throne of my life, not only as my Savior. I went through a process that changed my life forever by dethroning self and letting Jesus be in charge of everything in my life. This process was not easy for me, but the day that I realized that I was not allowing God to be in control of all the areas of my life, I decided that day I would turn it all over to Jesus Christ. As I went through this process, I acquired a love and understanding for the Word of God that I had never had before. The Word came alive for me. The Word was so alive for me; it was like I was watching a movie. I could see it like a vision in my head as I read. I had never understood the Word of God like this before, and now it was having a life changing effect on me. In 1999, after about three months of surrendering to the Lord and allowing Him to have His perfect work in me as I read His Word, God called me into full-time ministry. My senior pastor, at the time, Dr. R.C confirmed my calling and my Journey began.

One day, back in 1999, shortly after God called me into ministry, I was driving into work, praying in my car as I always did, but this particular day my conversation with God was going to change my life forever in how I looked at God, my Father. It had only been about a month since I had answered the call to ministry. I was growing daily, and, this particular day, I was going to grow even more. I always prayed in my car on my way to work. I was alone and no one could interrupt me.

This day, I was praying and asking God to forgive me in how much time I had wasted in not serving Him. I continued to express to God I did not know how I would be able to stand before Him with my head held high on that day I would die and come to heaven due to me being so ashamed. This was when God spoke to me loud and clear; and this is what the Lord said to me: *"My child, if you would only look into the mirror and see what I see; you would only feel great joy."* Tears started to roll down my face so abundantly that I had to pull the car over and stop. For the first time in my life I was seeing my Lord as a loving Father, and not a judge. This was the day that my Lord in Heaven became my daddy and not only my Lord that looked down on us all. I called out to the Lord and thanked Him for showing me so much love. I then asked Him to help me love as He does, and to see His children as He did. God answered my prayer that day, and, as I sat in prison preparing to go home in the year 2006, I looking back over the years that I had spent in prison. It became clear to how much God had answered my prayer that I had prayed back in 1999.

***Jeremiah 18: 1-6** The word which came to Jeremiah from the Lord, saying **2)** Arise and go down to the potter's house, and there I will announce My words to you. **3)** Then I went down to the potter's house, and there he was making something on the wheel. **4)** But the vessel that he was making of clay was spoiled in the hand of the potter; so he remade it into another vessel, as it pleased the potter to make. **5)** Then the word of the Lord came to me saying **6)** "Can I not, O house of Israel, deal with you as the potter does?"declares the Lord. "Behold, like the clay in the potter's hand, so are you in My hand, O house of Israel. (NASB)*

God had given me a gift to see His children as He does. This was why I was able to minister to so many while I was on my Journey behind prison walls. God had taught me how to love unconditionally. This was the only reason why I was able to reach so many with the Gospel. It was making so much sense to me now as I remembered back to the day that I had asked God for the ability to see His children as He does. We get in the way of God more times than we would like to admit in reaching the multitude with God's Good News, the Gospel. If we would only move out of God's way, and do what God shows us to do, and let His Word speak for itself, many more would not be left behind. God had truly changed me like the clay in the potter's hand, but I had to be a willing soul and listen. The clay does not tell the potter what to do. The potter knows already what he will form out of the clay. We have to allow the will of the potter to finish the good work He has planned for each of us. God did this throughout my Journey Behind Prison Walls.

When I asked for God to show me His children as He sees them, I made my request from the bottom of my heart. It was genuine. God was now showing me, at the end of my Journey Behind Prison Walls, how He had answered this prayer that I had prayed back in 1999. God showed me first that my request was not selfish. I asked for something to help me reach and understand His children. I had no idea, at the time, how important the request was, but it was genuine and from my heart.

The more humble I was, the more God was able to mold me like the pot. I did not understand, at the time, that there was so much in me that needed to be removed in order to make more room for God. I had so much of my past, hurt, pain and forgiveness that had not been healed yet, and, because of all this, there was no room for more of God in me. As I healed and let God remove the things that were not of Him, He then replaced more of Him in me, because I asked.

The JOURNEY BEHIND PRISON WALLS was not easy, but it was what I needed. I am asked often, if I was given a wish by God, that I could change one thing in my life, would I ask God to remove the Journey behind Prison Walls. I have to answer honestly, no. My life was changed so much for the better. I am happy with the women of God that came out of prison. I know my God in a way now that I would not want to lose. I understand the love God has for me now. Knowing this, I understand also that if God could have taught me in any other way the lessons that I learned behind prison walls, He would have. God doesn't want pain for us. God loves us, and He wants well for us. But because He loves us so much, He will do what is necessary to bring us along side with Him.

1 Peter 5:6-7 Therefore humble yourselves under the mighty hand of God, that he may exalt you in due time, 7) casting all your care upon Him, for He cares for you. (NKJV)

Hebrews 10:36-37 For you have need of endurance, so that after you have done the will of God, you may receive the promise; (37) "For yet a little while, And He who is coming will come and will not tarry." (NKJV)

Think for a moment about some of the promises that God has given you. Remember we all who are saved in Jesus Christ have many promises throughout the Word of God, but you will not know what they are if you don't read God's Word. But most of us, as Abraham, have a more personal promise from God. Now, examine your own faith and discover why God has not been able to allow this to be fulfilled in your life yet. Sometimes we are the reason that God has not been able to fulfill all the things that He has promised for us or has for us.

Our lack of faith and obedience in God keeps us from so many things that God has for us. But be of good courage, the Word shows us how we can overcome our lack of faith, and, once your faith starts to grow, you will fall more into obedience with God because your love for God will also grow. Once you change your priority, and put God at the top of your list as number one, and the time you spend with God reflects in your schedule that He is a priority, you will find yourself being more obedient because of the love you have for God. You will not be obedient because you have to; you will want to. Your desires will change in what you want to do. God will become the center of your life. But this only happens if you spend time with God and read His Word. It is impossible to spend quality time with God and not change. Try it and see if you learn the same things as I did; you will not regret it.

Romans 10: 17 *So then faith comes by hearing, and hearing by the word of God. (NKJV)*

How much time do you spend with God? We learn in many different ways, self study or group study. All are important for our faith to grow. Examine you daily schedule. How do you spend your time? You may be surprised what actually consumes most of your time. The things, in our lives that we spend most of our time in, are what influence us the most. Now ask yourself, is it God? If not, what is it?

Hebrews 11:6 *But without faith it is impossible to please Him, for he who comes to God must believe that He is, and that He is a rewarder of those <u>who diligently seek Him.</u> (NKJV)*

Who Diligently Seek Him

When we diligently seek God, we are in relationship with Him. This is how God guides our will to line up with His will. When this happens, our prayers change and we are able to see God move in a mighty way. God wants to give us the desires of our heart, but they must line up with God's desires for us.

1 John 5:14-15 14) Now this is the confidence that we have in Him, that if we ask anything according to His will, He hears us. 15) And if we know that He hears us, whatever we ask, we know that we have the petitions that we have asked of Him. (NKJV)

When you are born of God, you are born to win. Your first birth made you a sinner, but your second birth makes you a conqueror. The world wants to entice you, and the devil wants to seduce you, but Christ will give you the victory you need if you trust Him. Everything is linked to your faith. Don't you think it is well worth your time to seek God in order for your faith to grow? He is waiting; all you have to do is call on Him.

Psalm: 34:4 I sought the Lord, and He heard me, and delivered me from all my fears. (NKJV)

> *Are you still waiting on a promise?*
> *God will do as He promised you.*
> *Trust God, take Him for His Word*
> *He will never let you down.*
> *I waited, and it was worth it.*

My Journey behind prison walls was linked to a promise that God had given to me and a desire within me to be closer to Him. God's Word promises to finish the good work in us all and that was what God was doing in me. How about you? Are you allowing the tricks of the enemy to keep you from God's promises? Remember God's ways are not our ways. We have to learn to trust God and take Him for His Word that He loves us, but to do that, we have to read God's Word. My prayer for you is that I have encouraged you as we walked my Journey Behind Prison Walls together, that your relationship with God has been increased. The best place to start is in the Word of God. My Journey Behind Prison Walls was now coming to an end. I could only pray that what I had learned on my journey would help me in the future storms that would come my way, and they would come and go. We are not promised to have an easy life. On the contrary, we are told in God's Word that we will have trials and tribulations. As I left Coleman Federal Prison and looked to what was ahead of me, I have to admit that I was a little frightened. But I knew that God was with me and would guide me, if I would only let Him in whatever I had ahead of me. I was not the same woman of God that went into prison. I had lightened my load. I left a lot of baggage behind that needed to be unloaded. As I walked out the doors of prison, I was not only free from being imprisoned, but my spirit was free of my past and the many things in my life that had held me captive.

I was now on a new journey, one that I was excited about. As I walked out the doors of Coleman Prison and saw my two daughters waiting for me, I felt great excitement in me grow. I was really free. I still had three months in a half-way house and then home, but the journey home had started. My life had changed in many ways. I had to focus on getting divorced from a twenty-one year marriage and gain employment for myself, but I was not alone. I was blessed to have so many that had stuck by my side, and I was thankful for that. I had learned, while I was in prison, not to ponder so much on what I did not have, but on what I did have; and I was blessed. I had changed and so had my family. We all now had to be patient with one another as we got reacquainted. The short time that we had spent with each other, while I was home on furlough, revealed to us all that we all had changed a lot, but that was to be expected. I did not do prison alone. My family was imprisoned as much as I was. I knew, with all my heart that it was much harder for our loved ones that we left behind outside of the prison walls, than those of us that were inside.

The purpose of this book was not to prove my innocence to anyone. I pray that you have not been distracted in anyway by me being innocent or guilty; that was not the message I was trying to proclaim. It did not matter why I was in prison. What did matter was what God had for me to learn. This is the real purpose of every storm in our lives. What the enemy may mean for bad, God means for our good and His glory. My prayer is that, by telling my story, A Journey Behind Prisons Walls, will encourage you and equip you to be better prepared when the storms in your life roll in. We cannot predict tomorrow, but we can prepare ourselves spiritually to face whatever comes our way with God as our Helper. Stand strong in God's Word and hold dear all His promises to you. The light that shines on your path will be the light of Jesus coming from within you. It will direct you when everything looks dark. In this walk called life, we will all find ourselves in dark places, but we all have a light within us called Jesus Christ, if you have accepted Him as your Savior. Trust in

Him. He will never leave you or forsake you. This, too, is a promise.

> *God didn't go halfway when He went to work on my behalf during my Journey Behind Prison Walls.*
> *He did it all.*
> *When I couldn't feel God or sense Him,*
> *God was working on my behalf.*
> *When I faced far worse than my worst imaginings,*
> *Something unexpected and wonderful happened.*
> *I realized that God was in control*
> *and God is good.*
> *Even when bad things happen in our lives.*
> *I didn't know what I might have to go through next, but I learned how to rest and accept it.*
> *Because now I knew when I let go,*
> *I would fall into the*
> *strong hands of my God*

On my Journey behind prison walls, God carried me, for the most part, in the beginning, but then I learned to walk with God, trusting in Jesus Christ and listening to His guidance. God knows what the storms in our lives will bring out of us, if we would only allow Him to do the good work in us. My prayer for you is that as we have finished this journey together that whatever you are facing in your life currently, or even in the days ahead, that you are more able to focus on where God is in your storm. Look into your storm, and see something good coming out of it, Jesus. As Jesus is approaching you, I pray you will allow Him into your boat and not be afraid and allow Jesus to calm your storm as He did mine.

As I sat in my daughter's car after being released from Coleman prison to go home, I found myself looking out the window watching the cars pass us by. This took me back to the beginning of my journey when I was sitting in a van and being transported to Miami FDC after sentencing. I was remembering it all like it was yesterday. Tears started to form up in my eyes just thinking about how I felt back in January of 2004 as I sat in that van. I was remembering how I felt that everyone in the cars passing me by had hopes and dreams to pursue, and I had nothing anymore. I felt my life was over then, but now, as I looked out the window of my daughter's car, it was clear to me that my hopes and dreams had never been removed from me at all. It was all in my perspective of the situation. The tears stopped. This reminded me that I had to be on my guard at all times for the devil's lies.

When I was sitting in that van back in 2004, I was not listening to God, but the devil. Nothing had been removed from me. God was with me and I still had hope and dreams. My life was not over by a long shot. I had allowed the devil to convince me to give them up, but they were still there all along. The enemy is always there, but we don't have to give him the time of day. If we would only trust God and stay close to Him, the enemy would not fool us.

I looked out the front window of my daughter's car and smiled. A new life had started and it was going to be what I let it be. I had a choice to follow God and listen to Him or do it my way. My choice, I was going to follow God, and I was excited in what the future held for me.

We all have a choice to make in who we will follow. I pray you choose today to follow God in everything you do. If you have already made this choice, I am excited for you as I am for myself. We all have a great adventure ahead of us, one with God.

> *The road may seem hard and full of rocks*
> *that may cause you to stumble.*
> *But if you would only take your eyes off the ground*
> *to where you walk and look up.*
> *You will see the horizon, and the glory of God.*
> *He will direct your path and give you peace.*
> *All you have to do is*
> *trust Him.*

Leave the past in the past. Embrace the present and leave the future to God. Live today to its fullest and receive all that God has for you in it. The storms will come and go in our lives, but they too shall pass. God is the same yesterday, today and forever. God is consistent and we can put our trust in Him. As we walk our everyday lives, all those who watch us should be able to see Jesus in us. Shine your light for all to see today and every day.

We have our dark days as Christians, but they are never as dark as the days for those who do not have Jesus Christ as their Savior. Will you shine for Jesus Christ today? Trust me; there will be someone in your path today that will need to see your light.

Do not withhold it from them. As God used me on my Journey Behind Prison Walls, He also wants to use you right where you are today. We don't always feel like shining for Jesus, but we don't have to. The light of Jesus in us is so strong and bright; it will shine even when we don't feel like it. All you have to do is take a step of faith and ask God to help you in your everyday walk with Him. Shine for Jesus today. There is someone waiting for you. Don't keep them waiting.

Copyright page

All scripture is quoted from the two listed references below

1. "Scripture taken from the NEW AMERICAN STANDARD BIBLE, Copy right 1960, 1962, 1963, 1968, 1971, 1972, 1973, 1975, 1977, 1995 by the Lockman Foundation, Used by permission."
2. Scripture taken from the NEW KING JAMES VERSION, Copyright 1970, 1980, 1982 by Thomas Nelson, Inc. Used by permission. All rights reserved.

About the Author

Lanette Escobar was a business woman for twenty years until the Lord called her as the founder of Financial Freedom Christian Counseling. She served in ministry for five years teaching financial stewardship and sharing the powerful testimony of her childhood in "Broken Child" when the Lord suddenly changed the course of her life.

Being in full time ministry and with a heart to grow ever closer to God and her knowledge of Him, Lanette prayed for the freedom to spend three years in seminary. This mother of three and grandmother of five unexpectedly found herself falsely accused and imprisoned for a crime she did not commit. With a sentence of fifty-four months, she realizes today that God answered her heart's desire for time to learn from Him as she grew more in prison than she thought was ever possible.

Lanette Escobar, motivational and spiritual speaker, and author of *A Journey Behind Prison Walls*, travels and teaches that life's trials and tribulations are not meant to break us, but make us if we would only allow them to. After enduring a hard childhood, rape, the loss of a child, physical and mental abuse, and falsely imprisoned Lanette learned how to forgive and heal. In doing this, she has been able to embrace life and live. Her passion is to teach others how to do the same. .

www.Godstrials.com

www.ingramcontent.com/pod-product-compliance
Lightning Source LLC
Chambersburg PA
CBHW032057090426
42743CB00007B/153